MONTEVERDI

Series edited by Stanley Sadie

The Master Musicians

Titles available in paperback

Berlioz *Hugh Macdonald*
Brahms *Malcolm MacDonald*
Britten *Michael Kennedy*
Bruckner *Derek Watson*
Chopin *Jim Samson*
Grieg *John Horton*
Handel *Donald Burrows*
Liszt *Derek Watson*
Mahler *Michael Kennedy*
Mendelssohn *Philip Radcliffe*
Monteverdi *Denis Arnold*
Purcell *J.A. Westrup*

Rachmaninoff *Geoffrey Norris*
Rossini *Richard Osborne*
Schoenberg *Malcolm MacDonald*
Schubert *John Reed*
Sibelius *Robert Layton*
Richard Strauss *Michael Kennedy*
Tchaikovsky *Edward Garden*
Vaughan Williams *James Day*
Verdi *Julian Budden*
Vivaldi *Michael Talbot*
Wagner *Barry Millington*

Titles available in hardback

Bach *Malcolm Boyd*
Beethoven *Barry Cooper*
Chopin *Jim Samson*
Elgar *Robert Anderson*
Handel *Donald Burrows*

Schubert *John Reed*
Schumann *Eric Frederick Jensen*
Schütz *Basil Smallman*
Richard Strauss *Michael Kennedy*
Stravinsky *Paul Griffiths*

In preparation

Bartók *Malcolm Gillies*
Dvořák *Jan Smaczny*

Musorgsky *David Brown*
Puccini *Julian Budden*

THE MASTER MUSICIANS

MONTEVERDI

Denis Arnold

OXFORD
UNIVERSITY PRESS

OXFORD
UNIVERSITY PRESS
Great Clarendon Street, Oxford OX2 6DP

Oxford University Press is a department of the University of Oxford.
It furthers the University's objective of excellence in research, scholarship,
and education by publishing worldwide in

Oxford New York

Athens Auckland Bangkok Bogotá Buenos Aires Calcutta
Cape Town Chennai Dar es Salaam Delhi Florence Hong Kong Istanbul
Karachi Kuala Lumpur Madrid Melbourne Mexico City Mumbai
Nairobi Paris São Paulo Singapore Taipei Tokyo Toronto Warsaw
and associated companies in Berlin Ibadan

Oxford is a registered trade mark of Oxford University Press
in the UK and in certain other countries

Published in the United States
by Oxford University Press Inc., New York

British Library Cataloguing in Publication Data
Data available

Library of Congress Cataloging in Publication Data
Arnold, Denis.
Monteverdi / Denis Arnold.—3rd ed. / rev. by Tim Carter.
p. cm.—(The master musicians)
Includes bibliographical references (p.) and index.
1. Monteverdi, Claudio, 1567–1643—Criticism and interpretation.
I. Title. II. Master musicians series.
ML410.M77 A8 2000 782′0092—dc21 00–040068
ISBN 0–19–816465–3

1 3 5 7 9 10 8 6 4 2

Printed in Great Britain
on acid-free paper by
Biddles Ltd.,
Guildford and King's Lynn

Preface

Two studies of Monteverdi's life and works, both based on recent research, are available in English. The preface for a third one must necessarily be an explanation for writing yet another. The main reason is simply that a series such as the Master Musicians can no longer neglect Monteverdi, whose greatness is now generally acknowledged; and the need for a book designed specifically for the English general reader is increased because the existing books were both intended for a somewhat different audience. Professor Schrade's *Monteverdi: Creator of Modern Music*, with its detailed analyses, is best read with the complete edition to hand; Professor Redlich's *Claudio Monteverdi: Life and Works* was written originally for the German reader with a knowledge of Heinrich Schütz and Samuel Scheidt rather than for the Englishman who knows Byrd and Wilbye.

I have therefore tried to write a study which will introduce Monteverdi and his background to readers with a limited knowledge of Italian music of the time. In the musical examples the filling in of the *continuo* part has been made as simple as possible, both to save space and to facilitate performance. It in no way represents my views on the method to be used in the performance of Monteverdi's work. The time-values of certain examples have been reduced to conform with modern notation. The bibliography is also a guide for the general reader rather than for the scholar.

Bearing this in mind, I have deliberately avoided marshalling all the arguments about such matters as the authenticity of *Il ritorno d'Ulisse* and the meaning of *canto alla francese*. But in one matter I have ventured to state my views at some length. Previous writers have all stressed the revolutionary nature of Monteverdi's music. After a fairly close examination of music by certain of his contemporaries, it seemed to me to be more accurate to consider him as a moderate and progressive rather than an experimental composer. Since the music of these other composers is not widely known, I have tried to give sufficient background material to justify this new approach, though not, I hope, at such great length that it distorts the broader picture which the general reader requires.

Extracts from Einstein, *Essays on Music*, and Strunk, *Source Readings in Music History*, are by kind permission of Faber & Faber Ltd (London) and W. W. Norton & Co. Inc. (New York).

Two engravings of Venetian scenes are reproduced by permission of the Trustees of the Victoria and Albert Museum. I have to thank my colleagues Professor Philip Cranmer, Mr Raymond Warren and Mr R. H. Semple for reading either the whole or part of this book in manuscript and making some most helpful suggestions; Dr G. B. Gaidoni for checking the translations from Italian; Mr Gordon Wheeler for reading the proofs with a splendidly keen eye and compiling the index; and my wife, who not only typed the book from an illegible manuscript, but encouraged me to finish it.

Belfast,   D.A.
September 1962

For this new printing I have taken the opportunity to add information concerning Monteverdi's family background included in Elia Santoro's *Claudio Monteverdi: Note biografiche con documenti inediti*, and to correct a number of minor errors.

October 1968.   D.A.

NOTE TO THE 1975 EDITION

Little of note has been discovered concerning Monteverdi's life since the last impression, and the biographical chapters therefore contain only very minor amendments. Nor do the chapters discussing the secular music seem to me to require alterations. On the other hand, my views about his religious music have changed in the decade since the book was first published. In 1963, performances of the church music were rare, with the exception of the 'Vespers' of 1610; and that work was then known largely in the rather Romantic versions of Redlich and Goehr. Since then, performances of much of the Venetian church music have become more frequent, and the style of these performances, as also those of the 'Vespers', has become more authentic and alive. In these circumstances, I have come to the conclusion that I underestimated this aspect of Monteverdi's art and am pleased to have the opportunity of redressing the balance. Similarly, a new conclusion to the final chapter has become inevitable.

University of Nottingham,   D.A.
September 1974

Note to the 1990 edition

Denis Arnold's untimely death in 1986 deprived English musicology of a pioneer in Monteverdi studies: his achievement inspired a generation and more of students and scholars — myself included — to explore the riches of music in late Renaissance and early Baroque Italy. Although his admirable *Monteverdi* for Dent's 'Master Musicians' series is well into its third decade, it still stands out as perhaps the most accessible English-language introduction to the composer and his works, combining clear social and historical perspectives with humane critical insight into the music. The aim of the present revision has been to retain as much as possible of Professor Arnold's rich prose, modifying and emending his remarks only when absolutely necessary in the light of recent scholarship: anything else would have missed the point, and for the worse.

The text and music examples remain in general as in the 1975 edition, with the exception of changes in styling, although I have slightly altered the discussion of the staging of *Orfeo* and of the composition of *La finta pazza Licori* and have refocussed some other minor points. Translations from Monteverdi's letters and other contemporary documents have been done anew: it was tempting to adopt Denis Stevens's exemplary translations of the letters, but their broad sweep proved unamenable for the excerpts needed here (none the less, Stevens's impressive grasp of early seventeenth-century idioms will be readily apparent in my own perhaps too literal versions). The footnotes are almost entirely new, directing the reader to more recent sources in somewhat greater detail (although I have followed Arnold in keeping them to a minimum to avoid encumbering the page). Here ASM(G) stands for Archivio di Stato, Mantua, Archivio Gonzaga, and ASV, Archivio di Stato, Venice; and citations use short-title forms when a given work is listed in the Bibliography. Appendix A (Calendar) is rewritten to take account of new biographical information; Appendix B (Catalogue of Works) is done afresh in the light of recent worklists; Appendix C (Personalia) is revised and slightly expanded; Appendix D (Bibliography) is updated; and the original Appendix E is omitted (the Venetian documents originally included here are now largely available elsewhere; where this is not the case, Arnold's transcriptions are given in the notes).

The final addition is a new Chapter 9, written much in the spirit of the 'Note to the 1975 Edition'. This survey, although necessarily brief and, for that matter, somewhat personal, gives an overview of developments in the study of Monteverdi's music since the 1967 quatercentenary. Thus the reader will find discussion of issues and debates – for example, the vexed question of *L'incoronazione di Poppea* – that Arnold was unable to include but which his own work did so much to stimulate. Here and elsewhere I owe a debt to Elsie Arnold and Nigel Fortune for generously sharing their ideas with me. For the rest, I lay no claim on this book, which in the end rightly belongs to Professor Arnold and indeed to Claudio Monteverdi.

Royal Holloway and Bedford New College,   Tim Carter
University of London
April 1990.

Contents

Illustrations

x

Cremona

'*Cremona* is built on the banks of the *Poe* . . . tis eight miles in circuit, environed with Walls Bastions, and Ditches, and hath one Cittadel on the Eastpart, the most stupendious, strong and formidable work in all *Italy* . . . The ordinary buildings are so great, that they may be termed Palaces, reared with great expense and excellent Architecture. It hath broad streets, with Orchards, Gardens, and Mills as well within as without the City, a Chanel for driving them being brought from the River thorow the City,'[1] In this way a seventeenth-century English writer describes Cremona, where Monteverdi was born. The town lies some fifty miles from Milan in the heart of the great plain of northern Italy. It is comparatively unvisited today, except by tourists who wish to look at the cathedral and the splendidly tall clock tower. Indeed it seems an almost isolated town, not even on a main road to the east or south.

Yet in the sixteenth century it was a good place for the musician or artist to be-born in. If in itself Cremona was too small and too provincial to be very important, it was near several centres of Renaissance society. Parma, whose ruling family, the Farnese, were deeply interested in music, provided a fitting setting for several great composers, including Cipriano de Rore and Claudio Merulo. Mantua, to the east, was ruled by the rich and cultured Gonzagas, who also liked good music and painting. A little farther away were Ferrara, the most progressive court, musically speaking, in Europe; Venice, the heart of music publishing and full of fine composers, players and painters; Florence; and the Transalpine courts of Bavaria, Innsbruck and Graz.

We are not sure of the exact day when Monteverdi was born. The first record to be found is of his baptism, which took place on 15 May 1567. He was the eldest child of Baldassare Monteverdi, a barber–surgeon who eventually became a fully qualified doctor. His mother, Maddalena, had married Baldassare in 1566, and gave Claudio a sister in 1571 and a brother, Giulio Cesare, two years

---

[1]Edmund Warcupp, *Italy, in its Original Glory, Ruine and Revival, being an exact survey of the whole geography and history of that famous country* (London, 1660), pp. 107–8.

later. She died prematurely, possibly in the plague epidemic of 1575–6 which swept northern Italy. Within a year Baldassare had married again, having three more children by his second wife; but Claudio's stepmother also was to die young, for Baldassare took yet a third wife sometime after 1583, just when Claudio was beginning to publish his first compositions. What this tragic sequence of events meant for the children we can only surmise. We know that Claudio was given a good musical education, perhaps as a choirboy in Cremona Cathedral (though the records are silent about this) or as a private pupil of the Cathedral's *maestro di cappella* Marc'Antonio Ingegneri.

Lacking the natural focussing point of patronage which a prince and his retinue provided for larger cities, the most important centre of music-making was undoubtedly the principal church of the town, usually the cathedral. This would normally have a small choir of about ten men and up to fifteen boys. Some of the men may also have played instruments, but the only professional player would be the organist. At the head of these was a director of music, or *maestro di cappella*. The Cathedral chapter tried to find a composer for this post, since he was expected to provide music for the more important festivals. He was also expected to conduct the choir, and to instruct both priests and boys in the art of music. The priests for the most part only learned to sing plainsong. The boys, on the other hand, received a complete education in music, as well as being given the elements of a literary education by a teacher called the *maestro di grammatica*.

Compared with court musicians, the servants of the church were not very well paid, but they were comfortably enough off and a modest social status was accorded to them. Further down the social ladder were the town musicians, or *piffari*. These were wind-players, and were employed by the municipality for various purposes. They entertained the populace in the town square, as Montaigne found at Piacenza (in the Duchy of Parma, not far from Cremona) and wrote in his journal: 'They sound the reveille morning and night for one hour on those instruments which we call oboes and on fifes.'[2] At other times they accompanied the mayor and town dignitaries in procession to church. In some towns they had to teach anyone who wanted to learn an instrument. For such duties they were paid very badly, though in the end they probably made enough money from casual engagements – playing at weddings and banquets, or in church when hired by the *maestro di cappella* for a festival. Socially

[2]Michel de Montaigne, *Journal de voyage en Italie [1580–1]*, in *id.*, *Oeuvres complètes*, ed. Albert Thibaudet and Maurice Rat (Bruges, 1962), p. 1332.

they were usually considered a cut below the more dignified musicians of church and court, but they were men of considerable skill. Some of them could play virtually any wind instrument and sing as well. Entry into their ranks was usually by apprenticeship, and in the manner of the guilds they were strict in the upkeep of their standards.

Finally, the musician could sometimes gain an education and a livelihood from the academies which were so important in the sixteenth century. These were not teaching institutions. They were associations of upper-class gentlemen who wished to discuss literary topics, learn a little music or otherwise follow the curriculum laid down by the courtesy books such as Baldassare Castiglione's *Il libro del cortegiano* (*The Book of the Courtier*, 1528). Some of these academies paid musicians quite well to instruct and entertain their members. Others employed them more casually. But whether employed full-time or not, these musicians were generally more intelligent and better educated than those of church or town. Their patrons often discussed the basic philosophy of music with them, and at least in some of them there was a very close relationship between musician and gentry.

Monteverdi must have learned his music from the church and its seminary. A boy from a doctor's family would never have been apprenticed to a town musician. And although we know that there was an academy in Cremona, Monteverdi was too accomplished a musician at a very early age to have picked up his knowledge amongst amateurs, for by 1582, at the age of fifteen, he was ready to publish a book of motets with the distinguished Venetian publishing firm of Gardano. The title-page tells us that they are sacred songs for three voices and that the composer is a pupil of Marc'Antonio Ingegneri. Ingegneri, whose pupil Monteverdi was proud to acknowledge himself, was *maestro di cappella* at Cremona Cathedral. He was exactly the kind of man we should expect to find there. Born and educated in Verona, he started as a singer at Cremona before being promoted to be director of music. He had published some madrigals and church music by the time Monteverdi produced the *Sacrae cantiunculae*, and these reveal him as a sound rather than brilliant composer, inclining to the older methods of contrapuntal music which we associate with the Franco–Flemish school. Nevertheless he was not completely old-fashioned. He knew something of the newer style of Cipriano de Rore, and he must have been a good teacher, for Monteverdi's pieces show every sign of proficiency.

It is not surprising that a choirboy should set Latin words rather than attempt the madrigal style straight away; nor that this book was for three voices, which are easier to manipulate than the five or six voices usual for motets at this time. What is a little surprising, perhaps, is that the book appeared under the imprint of the most famous Venetian publisher, especially since the dedication is to a cleric and not to a member of the nobility who might have provided a subsidy. The reason for Gardano's acceptance may well have been the easiness of the music for the performer, and the fact that it was suitable for domestic devotional singing as well as for churches with very small choirs. In any case we find Monteverdi continuing in this vein, for in the next year he produced a set of *madrigali spirituali* for four voices – again no mean achievement for a boy not yet sixteen. This time he had to rest content with a less distinguished publisher in Brescia, and since the dedication is to a Cremonese nobleman, this book almost certainly was subsidized. Continuing his career as a prodigy, Monteverdi in his eighteenth year saw yet another book in print. This time it was a book which broke away from the ecclesiastical traditions – a book of canzonets for three voices (1584). This was a popular genre at the time, and the book was likely to sell. Monteverdi tried yet another publisher in Venice, the house of Vincenti and Amadino, which accepted the work. Whether they made any money out of it we shall never know, but Amadino's shrewdness was continually to profit him, for he published most of Monteverdi's later music, including the very popular books of madrigals which went through many editions.

Then comes a gap of three years in our knowledge of Monteverdi's life and works. Some writers have surmised that he attended the University of Cremona, but there is no evidence for this – rather the reverse, in fact, for later in life he was to say that he never understood the antique signs and notations of the Greeks, something about which he would surely have been less modest if he had had a normal education in classical thought. Certainly there is little evidence that he was widely read, or that his knowledge of the classical philosophers was any more than he might have obtained in discussions with members of an academy. It is more probable that he continued his studies to be a professional musician; on the title-page of his next book, his first book of madrigals (1587), he still proclaims himself a pupil of Ingegneri. The dedication is to a Veronese Count, Marco Verità,[3] and so experienced does Monteverdi seem by this time that we are a little surprised to find in it a modest declaration: 'I must not expect for compositions so much the product of youth, such as are

---

[3]Marco Verità was later an interlocutor in Pietro Pontio's *Dialogo . . . ove si tratta della theorica e prattica di musica* (Parma, 1595). For his other activities as a patron, see Fabbri, *Monteverdi*, pp. 17–18.

these of mine, other praise than that which is usually given to the flowers of spring in comparison with that awarded to the fruits of summer and autumn.' Monteverdi was nineteen and had published four books in a little over four years. He was evidently an ambitious young man; we may note that in the secure surroundings of his later life he never published his work so eagerly.

His ambitions were certainly not to be fulfilled in his home town, and like other composers from Cremona he began to think of leaving it: the dedication of the first book of madrigals to a Veronese is revealing. Benedetto Pallavicino was now at the Mantuan court; so was Giovanni Giacomo Gastoldi, who had left nearby Caravaggio. Costanzo Porta had gone away to Padua, and Tiburtio Massaino to Salzburg and Prague. All had improved their position by leaving Cremona; and the style of Monteverdi's madrigal book shows that now he could learn little more from Ingegneri. An early attempt at finding a post away from home apparently was directed towards Milan. His father had had dealings with the Milanese health authorities as the representative of the Cremona Doctors' Association and no doubt had friends there. Claudio Monteverdi went up to the city in 1589 and tried to obtain the influence of Giacomo Ricardi, then President of His Catholic Majesty's most excellent Senate and Council in Milan. He was unsuccessful – luckily, since Milan, under the influence of the Spanish, was a backwater at this time and remained so during the seventeenth century. He seems to have made some friends who were to help him in his Mantuan years, but for the time being he had to return to Cremona.

Back there, he put his energies into the preparation of a second book of madrigals, which came out in the following year. This was dedicated to Ricardi, perhaps in the hope that something might still turn up in Milan. This madrigal book still acknowledges the teaching of Ingegneri on the title-page: its contents do not. On the contrary, the mature style of these madrigals reveals more clearly that Monteverdi was looking far beyond the confines of Cremona, and was studying the works of more famous and more modern masters than his old teacher.

The exact date, and even the year itself, when Monteverdi left Cremona was unknown to us. In one of his letters written in 1608 he writes of his nineteen years' service in Mantua, which, if true, means that he must have started his life there as early as 1589. Another of his letters, written in 1615, speaks of twenty-one years of service, and since he was deprived of his post there in 1612, this suggests that he went to his new post in 1591. Against this must be placed the fact that a list of musicians compiled by the treasurer at the Mantuan court in this later year does not contain the name of Monteverdi.[4] Perhaps the most reasonable explanation is that he went to Mantua in the two or three earlier years to take occasional and part-time engagements, of which there were plenty to be had, and then was given a permanent place in the latter part of 1591. Of one thing we can be certain. By the time he was ready to publish yet another madrigal book in 1592 he was *suonatore di vivuola* to Vincenzo I, Duke of Mantua, and in his first permanent post.

[4]ASM(G) Busta 395. The letters in which Monteverdi refers to his years of service in Mantua are: to Annibale Chieppio, Cremona, 2 December 1608, in Monteverdi, *Lettere, dediche e prefazioni*, ed. de' Paoli, pp. 33–9 (Stevens, *The Letters of Claudio Monteverdi*, pp. 55–61); to Annibale Iberti, Venice, 6 November 1615, in Monteverdi, *op. cit.*, pp. 76–8 (Stevens, *op. cit.*, pp. 103–5).

2

Mantua

The visitor to Mantua may find it hard to believe how great was Monteverdi's success. The town today seems rather forlorn, its huge palace a museum, its present *raison d'être* a market for the rich countryside by which it is surrounded. In the later years of the sixteenth century it was very different. Although never destined to be one of the greatest cities of Europe, Mantua was no mere provincial centre. The house of Gonzaga had brought the city to a fine prosperity, and encouraged by a succession of dukes who loved all the outward signs of richness, artists and musicians, actors and poets were glad to accept the bountiful patronage they were offered. Rubens, Tasso and Guarini are only three among many famous names in letters and painting that we find associated with the Mantuan court; and to these can be added a group of musicians just as distinguished.

By a singular act of good fortune, the prosperity of Mantua was assured by the sagacity of a duke who was both cultured and thoroughly educated. Duke Guglielmo, who succeeded Duke Francesco I in 1550 (although his effective rule dates from 1558), had a flair for organization and was progressive in his methods of government. Tasso could write of him that he was 'a prince of high talent and culture and most just and liberal'.[1] Under him Mantua achieved a rare stability, and music was perhaps his greatest love. Not content with being a patron of musicians, he was a composer himself and sent his compositions to Palestrina for comment and correction. It was not his fault that Mantua's music was not directed by Palestrina or Marenzio; both were too comfortable elsewhere. As it was, Giaches de Wert was Guglielmo's *maestro di cappella*, and he built up a group of musicians among the most famous of the age. Alessandro Striggio, Gastoldi, Pallavicino and Francesco Soriano were all well-known composers; Gastoldi and Wert indeed were world famous. Rome or Venice apart, Mantua's musicians could not be surpassed.

[1]See the comments in Fenlon, *Music and Patronage in Sixteenth-Century Mantua*, I.

If Guglielmo was something near to the ideal of a Renaissance monarch, his son, who became Duke Vincenzo I in 1587, was nearer the norm. Fond of women and gambling, he was in his youth at best an inconsiderate and inconsistent ruler, at the worst a brute and a murderer. He had no compunction about divorcing his first wife, accusing her publicly of physical deformity; and when the counter-charge of his impotence was made by her family, proposed a trial of his virility on a virgin girl in Venice. Yet he could be genuinely repent-ant, giving vast sums to churches and monasteries, or planning a pil-grimage to the holy places in Palestine (although this was prevented by his death). He also supported artists of all kinds. The ducal palace was further embellished in his lifetime. Music was encouraged, and drama was almost a passion with him. Was it a proposed production of *Il pastor fido* by Giovanni Battista Guarini in 1591–2 which pro-vided Monteverdi with one of his first engagements in Mantua? The music for this play was composed at least in part by Giaches de Wert, and the production was planned on a most sumptuous scale, to be given in the courtyard of the Palazzo del Tè.[2] The customary inter-polation of *intermedi* was planned with vast scenic designs and continuous music. There were to be four, representing *Musica della terra, del mare, dell' aria* and *Musica celeste*. Typical for Vincenzo was the fact that all this vast trouble and expense was to please one of his mistresses, the Spanish beauty Agnese Argotta, Marchesa di Grana. The play was put in rehearsal and arrangements were made for a brilliant illumination of the courtyard by a thousand torches and for vast tapestries to cover the walls. Alas, the performance never came off. The official reason given was the death of Cardinal Gianvincenzo Gonzaga in Rome; more malicious tongues whispered that the true one was the disapproval of the duchess. We know that musicians were to have been brought from as far as Venice and Verona and Ferrara, and they must have spent some time in Mantua rehearsing. May not Monteverdi have been among them?

This interest in drama was enough to make Vincenzo keep an adequate musical establishment, since plays always involved music, quite apart from the *intermedi* which were given between the acts with great machines, splendid scenery, and singing and dancing. Vincenzo seems also to have been fond of music itself. Admittedly he seems to have had less perception than his father. The really famous composers of the court – Monteverdi excepted – were those left over

[2]For *Il pastor fido* and Mantua, see Iain Fenlon, 'Music and Spectacle at the Gonzaga Court, *c*. 1580–1600', *Proceedings of the Royal Musical Association*, ciii (1976–7), 90–105.

from previous years. His performers, on the other hand, were excellent. The singers, especially, were the most famous of their age – and from all accounts such women as Adriana Basile and Caterina Martinelli were superb. This was the beginning of the age of virtuosity, an age where the prestige of the princely court was felt to be more at stake in the quality of the performers than in that of the composers.

Concerts took place every Friday in the great Hall of Mirrors of the Gonzaga Palace – so one of Monteverdi's letters tells us;[3] and although we have no descriptions of them, we can imagine what happened from a description of a concert at the nearby court of the Este at Ferrara. The two courts were very similar, and their composers often visited each other. The performers were more jealously guarded, and there was a great deal of rivalry between the two cities. Mantua could hardly compete with the grand vocal and instrumental ensembles of Ferrara, but the Gonzagas did everything to keep up with the standards of virtuosity set by several of the Ferrara singers. So we may take the letter of the Florentine ambassador at Ferrara, Orazio Urbani, as giving a lively account of the sort of evening which was so popular at Mantua also:

> Immediately after dining, a game of *primiera* [a game of cards] was begun in which the Duke, the Duchess, Donna Marfisa, the wife of Signor Cornelio, and myself took part . . . At the same time music was begun, so that it was necessary for me simultaneously to play cards, to listen, to admire, and to praise the *passaggi*, the *cadenze*, the *tirate*, and such things – all of which matters I understand little and enjoy less! This party did not last one minute less than four hours, since, after some other ladies had sung, Signora Peverara (the Mantuan about whom I have written in the past) finally appeared and, under the pretext of having me hear first one thing and then another, [she sang] both by herself and together with other singers, both with one and with several instruments, thus stretching out the affair as much as possible.[4]

To come from provincial Cremona into this atmosphere of courtly service, to mix with these great singers and players, to work under a fine composer such as Wert, must have changed Monteverdi's life considerably. Certainly it changed and matured his music, for he published his third book of madrigals in 1592, and this was no work of a provincial composer. The music of the other Mantuan

[3]Monteverdi to Cardinal Ferdinando Gonzaga, Mantua, 22 June 1611, in Monteverdi, *Lettere, dediche e prefazioni*, ed. de' Paoli, pp. 57–9 (Stevens, *The Letters of Claudio Monteverdi*, pp. 83–6).

[4]Orazio Urbani, dispatch of 14 August 1581, trans. in Newcomb, *The Madrigal at Ferrara, 1579–97*, I, p. 25.

composers had clearly had its effect – and this more up-to-date style made Monteverdi's music more popular. The book must have paid his publisher Amadino, since it was reprinted within two years. In the dedication Monteverdi naturally offers the book to his master, Duke Vincenzo. For the most part it is written in that conventional and flowery language we meet in all dedicatory letters of the time; but there is a hint that Monteverdi regarded 'his most noble practice of playing the *viola*', as he called it, more as a gateway into the world of the court music than as an end in itself. He was clearly hoping for the better things that befitted a composer. He was not disappointed, for the next news we have of him is that he has raised his status from player to singer; and by this time he was senior enough for his patron to take him on an expedition. Duke Vincenzo was called upon by the Emperor Rudolf to aid him in a war against the Turks. The Turks were now in possession of a great deal of south-east Europe, and were menacing Austria from Hungary. At first Vincenzo sent troops to be directly under the command of the Emperor. Shortly afterwards he decided to go himself, to be at the head of his own army. Following the custom of the day, he took a formidable retinue with him, and among them were some of his musicians.

Monteverdi was at the head of a little group of five musicians. The journey was no doubt exhausting but also beautiful: across the Alps to Innsbruck, then Prague and Vienna, before the plains of Hungary. The warlike activities were brief enough, and not particularly successful. After the assault of one fortress the duke returned home, having been six months away. Such an expedition would in the normal way be hardly worth mentioning; it can scarcely have added much to Monteverdi's musical experience. But it seems to have affected him deeply. He remembered it vividly nearly forty years later, and warlike scenes became one of his principal interests as an artist. It is no coincidence that his last book of madrigals contains 'madrigali guerrieri' ('warlike madrigals'), nor that he chose to set the battle scenes from Tasso's *Gerusalemme liberata*.

He arrived home richer in experience but poorer in pocket. As he said in a later letter: 'if [my fortune] did me the favour of being honoured by the Most Serene Lord Duke to be able to serve him in Hungary, it also did me the disfavour of making me have additional expenses from that journey which our poor household feels almost to the present day'.[5] To make matters worse he seems to have been

---

[5]Monteverdi to Annibale Chieppio, Cremona, 2 December 1608, in Monteverdi, *Lettere, dediche e prefazioni*, ed. de' Paoli, pp. 33–9 (Stevens, *The Letters of Claudio Monteverdi*, pp. 55–61).

disappointed when, on the death of Giaches de Wert in 1596, Benedetto Pallavicino was promoted to be *maestro di cappella* to the duke. Certain biographers of Monteverdi have sought explanations for the appointment of this mediocrity, as they have called him, over the head of a genius. The truth is simple. In 1596 Monteverdi was still not thirty, and although admittedly a composer of merit had shown no signs of that overwhelming popularity which was to appear ten years later. Pallavicino was older, had published a great deal of music and in any case at that time was not considered a mediocrity. Two contemporary writers – Giovanni Maria Artusi and Adriano Banchieri – both had good words to say of his music,[6] and some of it even today seems remarkably fine. So we have no need to assume any intrigues. Regarded in this light, it was merely a matter of seniority; and now Monteverdi headed the salary list of the singers at court and was next in line for promotion.

We hear nothing more of Monteverdi until 1599. Then he married a court singer, Claudia Cattaneo. It was a marriage in a modern tradition, for she presumably kept on working, as her salary was continued until her death, although she had had children. The pair were married on 20 May, but they had little time to enjoy themselves. Monteverdi again had to accompany his patron on a journey. In June 1599 Vincenzo set out for Flanders, to spend a month at the bathing resort of Spa before visiting Liège and Antwerp, where he bought paintings and antiques, and finally Brussels. This must have been a more interesting journey to a musician. On such travels the court was not content merely to listen to its own performers. Local singers and players performed before the duke and were well rewarded for their pains. It must have been from these that Monteverdi learned 'the French style of singing' which his brother mentioned some years later in his preface to the *Scherzi musicali* (1607). Again he returned home richer in experience and poorer in pocket:

> if [my fortune] had me called into the service of His Most Serene Highness in Flanders, it went against me even on this occasion by making Signora Claudia, remaining in Cremona, bear the expenses of our household, with maid and servant, yet she then had from His Most Serene Highness no more than 47 lire a month, besides the money which my father gave me beforehand.[7]

[6]Artusi includes Pallavicino in a list of 'excellent' and 'worthy' musicians in his *L'Artusi, overo Delle imperfettioni della moderna musica* (Venice, 1600), p. 3. For Banchieri's comments (in the *Conclusioni nel suono dell'organo* (Bologna, 1609), pp. 58–60), see Fabbri, *Monteverdi*, p. 153.

[7]Monteverdi to Chieppio, 2 December 1608 (see n. 5).

If Monteverdi was not happy, at least his fame was becoming more widely spread. In 1600 a theorist, Giovanni Maria Artusi, who lived in Bologna, produced a book, *L'Artusi, overo Delle imperfettioni della moderna musica*. The attack, as the title suggests, is on modern music, and although Monteverdi is nowhere mentioned by name, his works come in for the brunt of the assault. There are a number of quotations from some of his madrigals (not as yet published), all of them to show 'irregularities' of harmony or counterpoint. No one attacks mediocrities. There is no point in writing a book to criticize the work of someone completely unknown, and from the setting of the book, the private house of one of the Ferrarese gentry, we may gather that Monteverdi was a leading light of a circle of composers which included some of the most progressive of the day. For the moment this is more important news than the attack itself, for we have had no works from Monteverdi's pen published for eight years, and Artusi's evidence shows the way his mind was working and his standing in his middle thirties.

It is not very surprising, therefore, to find that when Pallavicino died in the following year Monteverdi applied to Duke Vincenzo for the post of *maestro di cappella*. The tone of his letter is interesting:

and finally, the world, having seen me persevering in the service of Your Most Serene Highness to my great desire and with your good favour after the death of the famous Signor Striggio, and after that of the excellent Signor Giaches [de Wert], and again a third time after that of the excellent Signor Franceschino [Rovigo], and finally now at this [the death] of the competent Messer Benedetto Pallavicino, could with reason rumour my negligence abroad if I did not seek, not through the merit of my skill but through the merit of the loyal and singular devotion which I have always held towards the service of Your Most Serene Highness, the position now vacant in this quarter of the church, and did not in all respects request with great eagerness and humility the aforementioned title.[8]

This letter, the first we possess, is typical of Monteverdi's writing, especially when he feels strongly about something. The almost complete lack of punctuation and the piling of clause upon clause gives us a vivid picture of the temper of the man. It requires little imagination to see him, now after about ten years at Mantua, rather jealous of others, conscious of every imagined slight on his worth

[8]Monteverdi to Duke Vincenzo Gonzaga, Mantua, 28 November 1601, in Monteverdi, *Lettere, dediche e prefazioni*, ed. de' Paoli, pp. 15–19 (Stevens, *The Letters of Claudio Monteverdi*, pp. 33–8).

and well aware that gossip could undermine his position. Mantua, with its enclosed atmosphere, had left its mark on Monteverdi's character. Who can wonder if he became considered a difficult man in this small community? On this occasion, however, he had no cause to complain. He was made *maestro di cappella* with full control of both court and church music. The addition to his income must have been welcome, since he was now the father of Francesco, born in 1601. The elevation in his status, one would imagine, must have contented him for a time, for his new post was equal to any in Italy, except some in Rome or Venice. And now the tide began to turn, at least as far as his fame was concerned. In 1603 he published his fourth book of madrigals with his old publisher Amadino. The contents were the work of several years, as he suggests in the preface (Artusi's attack of 1600 helps in dating some of them), and his dedication is not to anyone in Mantua but to the members of the Accademia degli Intrepidi at Ferrara, whose musicians were probably more his friends than those nearer home. The book was an immediate success and went through a number of editions quite quickly. Artusi followed up with another attack, this time naming the culprit who perpetrated his crimes against the traditions of music.[9]

Either the success of this volume, or the desire for an opportunity to reply to Artusi, made Monteverdi publish yet another collection of madrigals soon after this in 1605. Again the contents were the work of some years, and this time he wrote a preface to his 'Studious Readers' in addition to the usual dedication:

> Do not wonder that I should give these madrigals to the press without first replying to the attacks which Artusi made against certain short passages in them, since being in the service of His Most Serene Highness of Mantua I have not the time which would be required to do so. I have nevertheless written a reply to make known that I do not make my pieces haphazardly, and as soon as it is rewritten it will be published bearing the title *Second Practice, or On the Perfection of Modern Music*, which will perhaps surprise those who do not believe that there is any other practice save that taught by Zarlino. But let them be assured that, with regard to the consonances and dissonances, there is yet another consideration different from that usually held, which with satisfaction to reason and to

[9]Artusi, *Seconda parte dell'Artusi overo Delle imperfettioni della moderna musica* (Venice, 1603). Antonio Braccino da Todi (?=Artusi) issued a response (now lost) to the preface to Monteverdi's fifth book, and a *Discorso secondo musicale di Antonio Braccino da Todi per la dichiaratione della lettera posta ne' Scherzi musicali del sig. Claudio Monteverdi* (Venice, 1608).

the sense defends the modern method of composition, and this I have wished to say so that this expression 'second practice' may not be used by others, and moreover that the ingenious may reflect upon other secondary matters concerning harmony and believe that the modern composer builds upon the foundations of truth. Live happily.

The book to which he refers occupied his thoughts until his last years (see page 43), but it was never published. The reason was probably that he was conscious of his limitations as a writer and as a scholar. The apparatus of Greek philosophy which was expected of the writer on music was beyond him; and the fact that most of his contemporaries were equally in the dark but went on writing all the same did not encourage him.

Treatise or no treatise, this fifth volume of madrigals made Monteverdi's reputation quite secure. Not only was it reprinted within a year; publishers found it financially expedient to reprint his earlier books as well. But his position at Mantua was no happier than before. The irregularity in the payment of his salary was, to say the least, very trying. In a letter written in October 1604 we learn of his plight:

For my latest salary payment, it is necessary for me to have recourse to the infinite generosity of Your Most Serene Highness, for it is that in the end which directs your will concerning the payments granted me by your favour. I therefore come to your feet with as much humility as I can to beg you to turn your gaze not upon my boldness, perhaps, in writing this letter, but rather at the great need which causes me to write; and not upon the Lord President, who very many times has given the order 'yes' in so very friendly and polite a manner, but rather upon Bel'intento, who has never wished to carry it out except when it pleased him. And now that it has come down to this, I am required to accustom myself as it were to be obliged to him and not to the infinite generosity of Your Most Serene Highness . . . This letter of mine comes to your feet for no other end than to entreat Your Most Serene Highness to deign to direct that I should have my pay, which comes to the sum of five months, in which situation Signora Claudia also finds herself, and my father-in-law, and this sum still increases since we do not see any hope of receiving other future payments without the express commission of Your Most Serene Highness, without which support all my work will remain failing and ruinous, since day by day misfortunes are overwhelming me and I have not the wherewithal to remedy them . . . [10]

[10]Monteverdi to Duke Vincenzo Gonzaga, Mantua, 27 October 1604, in Monteverdi, *Lettere, dediche e prefazioni*, ed. de' Paoli, pp. 20–3 (Stevens, *The Letters of Claudio Monteverdi*, pp. 39–43). 'Bel'intento' was the court treasurer, Ottavio Benintendi: Monteverdi may have been intending a pun ('benintendi', 'hears well'; 'bel intento', 'good intention').

In other words the treasurer, with whom Monteverdi has quarrelled, was holding up his pay;[11] and Monteverdi's debts were mounting, in part because Claudia was again staying in Cremona with her father-in-law, having had her third child, a son, who was born in May and called Massimiliano.[12] Monteverdi himself went to Cremona, probably to be there at his wife's confinement, and a letter written to Mantua in December tells us something of the work he was engaged on.

Significantly enough it was stage music. Monteverdi must have had some experience in this genre as a performer, for Guarini's *Il pastor fido* had not only been put into rehearsal in 1591–2; it was finally given a full performance in November 1598. But this is the first knowledge we have of his composing for the stage, and at once we see his interest in the practical details. His commission was to write dances for what appears to have been either a pastoral play in the fashionable style of Tasso and Guarini or an *intermedio*. One dance is an *entrata* for the stars, another is for shepherds, and Monteverdi says in his letter that he cannot proceed until he knows the number of dancers involved, for he would like to plan the dance with a number of *pas de deux* intermingled with a refrain for the whole *corps de ballet*. So he has already written to the dancing master and when he has the information, he will immediately set to work.

This letter is interesting, for it shows Monteverdi already fully aware of the necessity to plan the staging and music together; and thus fascinated by the possibilities of dramatic music, he must have welcomed the opportunity to write an opera. This came when the festivities for the Carnival season of 1607 were planned. Few details of the conception and the performance of the new opera are known to us.[13] The idea of producing an opera must have been in Vincenzo

[11]This letter and later ones seem to suggest that it was mainly the treasurer who refused Monteverdi's pay and that the dukes of Mantua were generous enough. However, there are a number of documents in the Gonzaga archives which show the continual reluctance of the dukes to pay up. Perhaps the most pathetic is a plea from the town musicians of Mantua (ASM(G) Busta 402): 'A reminder to Your Highness from the players who served you at the baptism at which there were seven festivals and seven days during which they had been in the service of Your Highness of Gonzaga, begging Your Highness to give them satisfaction for they are poor men.'

[12]For details of the birth of Monteverdi's children, see Gallico, 'Newly Discovered Documents Concerning Monteverdi'. Only two of the three seem to have survived beyond early childhood.

[13]The best account is Fenlon, 'Monteverdi's Mantuan *Orfeo*', while issues of staging, which may have a bearing on the two endings of the opera, are also discussed in Pirrotta, 'Theatre, Sets, and Music in Monteverdi's Operas'.

Gonzaga's mind for some time, since he had seen the Peri-Caccini opera *Euridice* (libretto by Ottavio Rinuccini) in Florence during the wedding festivities of Maria de' Medici and Henri IV of France in 1600. Vincenzo's sons Ferdinando and Francesco were also interested in such activities, and as no doubt they were the mainstays of the Accademia degli Invaghiti, it was only a matter of time before this body decided to become a rival of the Florentine academies where opera had been born.

Monteverdi's opera was on the same subject as the Florentine opera of 1600 – the story of Orpheus and Eurydice; but the work was a local production. The Mantuan court chancellor Alessandro Striggio, son of the composer whom we have already mentioned, wrote the libretto. The Mantuan virtuosos were probably given the principal parts, although we know that at least one singer, Giovanni Gualberto Magli, was brought from Florence. The first performance took place before the members of the academy (on 24 February, probably in the Palazzo Ducale); and then the opera was given at least one more performance in front of the court with its guests. The libretto was published for the occasion, and the score of the opera two years later. No description of the production exists, but we can assume that, if it resembled other such entertainments for Carnival, it was a sumptuous one. In any case it was a great success, so much so that the Mantuan court must have looked forward to another opportunity for opera in the following year.

Professionally, *Orfeo* was a triumph, yet Monteverdi had little chance to enjoy it. His wife had been ill since at least November 1606, which was worrying enough in itself, and worrying because, as Claudia herself wrote: 'The serious illness which I have had has been the cause of making me spend that which I could not.'[14] In July of the following year we find Monteverdi in Cremona, where Claudia could be looked after by his father. Work still followed him there and the duke was wanting more music from him. Monteverdi could only reply that he was doing his best but he was tired and unwell. In August some of his music was performed before the Cremonese Accademia degli Animosi, and the academy made him an honorary member. Later in the month he went to Milan to show one of his oldest friends, Cherubino Ferrari, the score of *Orfeo*. At about the same time his *Scherzi musicali* were published in Venice with a new reply to Artusi, this time (and understandably in the circumstances) written by Monteverdi's brother.

[14]Claudia Cattaneo to Annibale Chieppio, Mantua, 14 November 1606, in Claudio Gallico, 'Monteverdi e i dazi di Viadana', p. 242 n. 4.

In spite of all these successes, the honour in his home town, the popularity of the new book, the praise of his Milanese friend, and the publication of yet another book of madrigals (old ones turned into *madriguli spirituali* by another friend living in Milan, Aquilino Coppini), personal tragedy was overwhelming. Claudia Monteverdi died on 10 September and was buried at Cremona. Monteverdi was at this time forty years of age, and he had been married for eight of them. His surviving children were aged six and three. It is no wonder he was in despair. Ironically, now was the least convenient time to give way to it. Francesco Gonzaga, Duke Vincenzo's eldest son and heir to the throne, was to marry Margherita of Savoy. The celebrations were to include as many magnificent entertainments as possible, including a new opera by Monteverdi.

He had the desire neither to resume work nor to return to Mantua. Why should he return to where the envy of colleagues and the lack of appreciation of his talents had made his life a misery, and everything about him must remind him of Claudia? Only a letter from his friend Federico Follino, court chronicler, could make him consent to leave his father's house at Cremona:

> Signor Claudio,
>   I do not know how to dissemble nor am I a flatterer, so please believe me that I have seen in the eyes of the prince and I have heard from his voice such things in praise of your genius that I have good, even excellent hopes for you; I believe that in the past you have known me to be affectionate, even most affectionate to my friends, and in particular to you yourself in such matters; so accept my advice, which is to forget now all these troubles, to return here and quickly, since this is the time to acquire the greatest fame which a man may have on earth and all the gratitude of the Most Serene Prince.[15]

Monteverdi returned to Mantua to try to submerge his sorrows in work.

There was plenty of this. The entry of Francesco and his bride into Mantua after their wedding in Turin was to mark the beginning of a week of dramatic entertainment which for splendour and expense even in its own day was exceptional. Royal weddings had to be accompanied by such costly rejoicing, for these were the occasions when the succession was assured (or at least so it was hoped). Elegant and prosperous festivity was reassuring to all parties, quite apart

---

[15]Federico Follino to Monteverdi, Mantua, 24 September 1607, in Davari, *Notizie biografiche del distinto maestro di musica Claudio Monteverdi*, p. 12.

from providing the occasion for hero-worship on the part of the lower orders. Given this custom and the newness of Mantua's discovery of opera, we can understand how the celebrations of 1608 took shape. There was to be the usual play – Guarini's *L'idropica* – with *intermedi*, a triumph or masque by the bridegroom himself, two ballets – one of them in the opulent French style – and of course the new opera. No expense was to be spared. Naturally some singers would have to come from elsewhere – from Florence. When it became evident that Monteverdi and the other Mantuans could hardly be expected to compose everything, another Florentine, Marco da Gagliano, was commissioned to write one of the ballets and an *intermedio* for *L'idropica*. Yet one more Florentine was involved, the poet Rinuccini, who had supplied the texts for the earlier operas produced in Florence and who was now to write the libretti for the new opera and one of the ballets.

Monteverdi's share of the work was enormous. The new opera *Arianna* was his; so was the music for the prologue to *L'idropica* and for one of the ballets. This was a staggering task, the more so since the wedding seemed likely to take place early in the new year and the music had to be composed and rehearsed by the Carnival season.[16] Monteverdi arrived back in Mantua early in October. On 9 October he had no libretto and obviously felt the pressure of time, since Prince Francesco wrote to his father:

> Yesterday evening Monteverdi came to speak with me, and showing his desire to serve Your Highness well in these wedding festivities and especially in the pastoral play which is to be set to music, he insisted that I should write to you that it would be necessary for him to have the words in the next seven or eight days so that he could begin to work, since otherwise it will not be enough for his spirit to do good work in the short time there is between now and Carnival . . .[17]

We know from other letters that Monteverdi was not a quick composer, and to have under four months to produce a complete opera, a genre in which he had had little practice, was nearly impossible. In November Ferdinando, Francesco's brother, was taking precautions to see that there would be an opera during Carnival, even if it was not Monteverdi's, and had written to

---

[16]The preparations for the 1608 Mantuan festivities are fully documented in Reiner, 'La vag' Angioletta (and others)', with additional information in Carter, 'A Florentine Wedding of 1608'.

[17]Prince Francesco Gonzaga to Duke Vincenzo Gonzaga, Mantua, 10 October 1607, in Fabbri, *Monteverdi*, p. 126.

Florence for Gagliano, who came to Mantua with the score of his *Dafne* (already composed though not as yet produced). This was put into rehearsal and performed probably in early to mid February Nevertheless, Monteverdi had not failed his master. By the beginning of February *Arianna* was almost finished.

At this point there was a new disaster. The prima donna who was to sing the title-role fell ill with smallpox. This was a severe blow for Monteverdi. It came so suddenly (the singer had taken part in *Dafne* a week or two earlier) that it completely disrupted the production of *Arianna*. More than that, Caterina Martinelli was one of Monteverdi's closest friends. She had been brought to Mantua from Rome in 1603, aged thirteen. The possessor of a particularly fine voice, she was the pride of the court and had lodged with Monteverdi since her arrival. Although, as it happened, she did not 'create' the role of Arianna, it was certainly created for her, and her illness was the worst thing which could have happened at this time. At first it looked hopeless, then she improved; finally she died, after being ill for over a month.

By this time Carnival was over, but fortunately all was not lost. The ceremonial entry into Mantua had been put back into the spring, and the best thing to do was to postpone the performance of *Arianna* until the main marriage celebrations at the end of May. The first idea for a new singer was a daughter of Giulio Caccini, but she was singing another part and this would have meant two changes in the cast. Monteverdi then suggested a singer from Bergamo, who, however, would not come. Then someone had the brilliant idea of asking one of the actresses from the cast of *L'idropica*. She turned out to be suitable and rehearsals went ahead. In the meantime, Monteverdi had still to write the music for the prologue and compose a long ballet, the *Ballo delle ingrate*.

The prince and his new wife arrived from Turin on 24 May with a train of guests from all over Italy. Four days later *Arianna* was given. There were some four thousand people – only a few of them from Mantua – packing the court theatre, and their enthusiasm is described by Follino in rapturous terms:

This work was very beautiful in itself both because of the characters who took part, dressed in clothes no less appropriate than splendid, and for the scenery, which represented a wild rocky place in the midst of the waves, which in the furthest part of the prospect could be seen always in motion, giving a charming effect. But since to this was joined the force of the music by Signor Claudio Monteverdi, *maestro di cappella* to the duke, a man whose worth is known to all the world, and

who in this work proved to excel himself, combining with the union of
the voices the harmony of the instruments disposed behind the scene
which always accompanied the voices, and as the mood of the music
changed, so was the sound of the instruments varied; and seeing that it
was acted both by men and by women who were all excellent in the art
of singing, every part succeeded more than wondrously, [and] in the
lament which Ariadne sings on the rock when she has been abandoned
by Theseus, which was acted with so much emotion and in so piteous a
way that no one hearing it was left unmoved, there was not one lady
who did not shed some little tears at her beautiful plaint.[18]

As we have seen, Follino was a close friend of the composer, and
anyway, as court chronicler his account of *Arianna* would have had
to record a great success. But there are many ways in which we can
confirm his judgment. Time after time there are passages in
Monteverdi's letters which refer to the power of the opera. The
theorist Giovanni Battista Doni knew the score of at least the lament
about 1640, a long time for any music to be remembered in the
seventeenth century; nor must we forget that the opera was revived
at least twice in the next thirty years,[19] again unusual for a work
which was written specially and hurriedly for a great occasion. As for
the lament which Follino praised so lavishly, imitation certainly
proved the sincerest form of flattery, for laments became the
stock-in-trade of composers for half a century. They appeared not
only in operas but also in the song-books and madrigal-books,
written by bad, mediocre and good composers.[20] Monteverdi
himself was able to make money from his lament and published
arrangements of it. In fact, the *Lamento d'Arianna* was the first great
popular operatic *scena*.

[18]Federico Follino, *Compendio delle sontuose feste fatte l'anno MDCVIII
nella città di Mantova* (Mantua, 1608), in Fabbri, *Monteverdi*, p. 133.

[19]The planned revival of *Arianna* for the birthday celebrations of Caterina de'
Medici, Duchess of Mantua, on 2 May 1620, never came to fruition, see Fabbri,
Monteverdi, pp. 235–7. *Arianna* was, however, revived at the Teatro S. Moisè,
Venice, in Carnival 1640. For other possible performances of the opera, see
Fabbri, *Monteverdi*, p. 383 n. 41.

[20]On other 'Arianna' laments, see Guglielmo Barblan, 'Un ignoto "Lamento
d'Arianna" mantovano', *Rivista Italiana di Musicologia*, ii (1967), pp. 217–28;
Lelia Galleni Luisi, 'Il *Lamento d'Arianna* di Severo Bonini (1613)', in
Monterosso (ed.), *Claudio Monteverdi e il suo tempo*, pp. 573–82; and the
preface to Claudio Pari, *Il lamento d'Arianna: quarto libro dei madrigali a 5
voci*, ed. Paolo Emilio Carapezza, 'Musiche Rinascimentali Siciliane', i (Rome,
1970). Some useful remarks are also made in Nigel Fortune, 'Sigismondo
d'India: An Introduction to his Life and Works', *Proceedings of the Royal
Musical Association*, lxxxi (1954–5), 29–47, at pp. 41–4.

After *Arianna* the music for the prologue for *L'idropica*, and even the *Ballo delle ingrate*, must have seemed less important. The prologue was as ephemeral as most of these productions, and the music has disappeared. The ballet has survived, for later in life Monteverdi included it in his eighth book of madrigals.[21] It is an important work, and clearly in its staging made a great effect, yet the music shows signs of the haste with which Monteverdi wrote it, and it remains little to console us for the loss of *Arianna*, the score of which has not yet been discovered.

'The greatest fame which a man may have on earth and all the gratitude of the Most Serene Prince' – these were Follino's inducements to return to Mantua. Both were Monteverdi's in June 1608. Neither could alleviate his misery. He returned to Cremona in a state of complete collapse. In November his father was desperate enough to write to the Duchess of Mantua to ask if Claudio could be released from his duties:

> If he returns to Mantua under those heavy duties and the [unhealthy] air, his life will soon leave him, and those poor children will rest on my shoulders, which are most weak because of age and expense, having a wife, children, maids and servants [to support], and for having spent on the aforesaid Claudio on several occasions 500 ducats and more when he served His Most Serene Highness in Hungary [and] in Flanders, when he came to Cremona with his wife, maid, servants, carriage and children . . .[22]

If his father was worried by the prospect of his return to the court, Monteverdi himself was furious, and when a letter came on the last day of November, bidding him return, he replied at great length and with considerable heat. What has he ever gained from Mantua except hard work and debts, he asks. What has he gained from his splendid success at the recent wedding festivities? All that has happened is that his wife's salary has been stopped, and even the pension of a hundred scudi which the duke had promised him has turned out to be only seventy. No other Mantuan musician has had such bad treatment and certainly no foreigner. Bitterly he asks the court chancellor:

---

[21]The version of the *Ballo delle ingrate* included in the *Madrigali guerrieri, et amorosi* (1638) was, so Denis Stevens discovered, as revised for performance in Vienna, 1628; see the discussion in Tomlinson, *Monteverdi and the End of the Renaissance*, pp. 206–7.

[22]Baldassare Monteverdi to Eleonora de' Medici, Duchess of Mantua, Cremona, 27 November 1608, in Fabbri, *Monteverdi*, pp. 148–9.

What clearer proof does Your Most Illustrious Lordship want! To give 200 scudi to Messer Marco da Gagliano, whom one could say did nothing, and to me who did all that I did, nothing! For the rest, knowing how ill and unfortunate I am in Mantua, I beseech the Most Illustrious Signor Chieppio that for the love of God you help me have an honourable discharge from His Most Serene Highness, for I know that from this will come all my well-being. Signor Don Federico Follino promised me by way of a letter summoning me from Cremona to Mantua last year for work on the marriage celebrations, he promised me, I say, that which Your Most Illustrious Lordship can see in this letter of his which I am sending, and then in the end nothing has come of it, or if I have had anything, I have had 1500 verses to set to music.[23]

Monteverdi was not accorded permission to leave. Instead his pay was raised to three hundred scudi a year, and his annual pension, 'for himself, his heir, and successors of any kind . . . of a hundred scudi each worth six lire of our Mantuan money',[24] was formally granted to him.

When he actually returned to the court is unknown. His two surviving letters of 1609 were written from Cremona, but as they date from 24 August and 10 September it is possible that he had gone back to his father for the summer, after working again during the Carnival season. These letters and others in the next two years show us that the worst of his depression had passed by now. In mid 1610 he was putting the finishing touches to a collection of music for Mass and Vespers, and was working on a book of madrigals, including an arrangement for five voices of the *Lamento d'Arianna* and another lament in commemoration of Caterina Martinelli.[25] Later in the same year he went to Rome to present his *Missa . . . ac vespere* (published in September) personally to the Pope and also to try to obtain a scholarship to the Roman Seminary for his son Francesco. He could count on the influence of Ferdinando Gonzaga, now a cardinal, to whom Vincenzo's heir, Francesco, wrote in advance on behalf of the composer. Nothing came of either venture.

Was Monteverdi seeking a new post at this time? It seems quite likely. For a man not much given to travelling about, his Roman journey was unusual. Even less usual was his new interest in church

[23]Monteverdi to Chieppio, 2 December 1608 (see n. 5).

[24]Duke Vincenzo Gonzaga's decree of 19 January 1609 is in Fabbri, *Monteverdi*, p. 151.

[25]The *sestina* 'Incenerite spoglie, avara tomba' (subtitled 'Tears of a lover at the tomb of his beloved'), see Strainchamps, 'The Life and Death of Caterina Martinelli'.

music. We do not possess a note of his Mantuan church music before 1610. Then we find him writing a Mass in the Roman *a cappella* style, a Mass which cost him a great deal of study and hard work. We also have a letter which tells us that Monteverdi presented Prince Francesco Gonzaga with a setting of 'Dixit Dominus' for eight voices and also a 'little' motet for two voices to be sung at the Elevation and another for five voices in honour of the Blessed Virgin, in March 1611.[26] It is possible that the death of Gastoldi – the official *maestro di cappella* of the ducal chapel of S. Barbara – had caused this new activity, and Monteverdi's own tragic experiences of recent years were doubtless enough to invoke a new turn to religion on his part. But it can scarcely be a coincidence that the principal posts in Venice and Rome demanded a knowledge of church music.

For Monteverdi was now at a difficult stage. He was so distinguished that, if he wished to move, posts which would be suitable for him were rare. As a court musician his chances were meagre. The Este court was now much reduced, following the secession of Ferrara and its province to the papal dominions on the death of Duke Alfonso II. Parma, Turin and Milan were far less interested in music. Florence had its own composers. To accept an ordinary post as *maestro di cappella* at a cathedral was to retreat in social and financial status. Only St Mark's in Venice and the larger churches in Rome were of the right dignity for such a distinguished composer. The matter became more urgent in 1612. Vincenzo Gonzaga died on 18 February, and his son Francesco ascended the throne. Monteverdi might well have been pleased about this, for Francesco had been especially keen on operatic entertainments. But in late July he suddenly dismissed both Monteverdi and his brother Giulio Cesare, along with other servants of the court.[27] No reason is given in the documents. Perhaps it was something to do with the usual festival which was mounted on these occasions. There was certainly a public

[26]Monteverdi to Prince Francesco Gonzaga, Mantua, 26 March 1611, in Monteverdi, *Lettere, dediche e prefazioni*, ed. de' Paoli, pp. 54–6 (Stevens, *The Letters of Claudio Monteverdi*, pp. 79–82). Stevens (*op. cit.*, p. 80) speculates that the setting of 'Dixit Dominus' is one of those included in the *Selva morale e spirituale* (1640–1) or the *Messa . . . et salmi* (1650); that the two-voice motet is either 'O bone Jesu, o piissime Jesu' (in Donfrid's *Promptuarii musici* of 1622) or 'Venite sitientes ad aquas Domini' (in Calvi's *Seconda raccolta de sacri canti* of 1624); and that the five-voice motet is 'Exultent caeli et gaudeant angeli' (in Calvi's *Quarta raccolta de sacri canti* of 1629).

[27]See the account in Venice, Biblioteca Nazionale Marciana, MS It. VII.1818 (9436), fol. 201v. Francesco was anxious to reduce court expenditure in an (unsuccessful) attempt to counter the deleterious effects of his father's apparent profligacy.

festival on 25 July to celebrate the election of a relative of Francesco Gonzaga as Holy Roman Emperor. The duke himself wrote a *torneo*, depicting the Rape of the Sabines; there were fireworks, and on the following Sunday some splendid music in S. Barbara.[28] Was Monteverdi ordered to write the music for church or *torneo*? If so, it would have had to be done at short notice, something which he always detested. He may well have refused to fall in with the duke's plans. In any case he left Mantua for good with just twenty-five scudi in his pocket as his savings after over twenty years in service there.

He returned to Cremona, and having nothing to do, went to Milan in September, probably to visit his many friends there. Malicious tongues said that he was intriguing for the post of *maestro di cappella* of Milan Cathedral over the head of the incumbent, who was pleasing the authorities there well enough. This story was not true, as the Mantuan ambassador in Milan reported after making inquiries. After this we have no news of the composer for nearly a year. Then his luck changed. The *maestro di cappella* at St Mark's in Venice, Giulio Cesare Martinengo, died in July 1613. The procurators of St Mark's, instead of merely advertising the post in Venice and its subject cities on the mainland, decided to make a wider search for a suitably distinguished musician, and wrote to the ambassadors and residents in Rome, Padua, Vicenza, Brescia, Bergamo, Milan and Mantua. The letter to Milan (for Cremona was in its province) shows clearly that they already had Monteverdi in mind:

> Since the Reverend *maestro di cappella* of our church of St Mark has died, there have been several people proposed, among whom is Signor Claudio Monteverdi, *maestro di cappella* to His Highness. We should therefore be happy to receive information on his worth and competence, and give us a report, and if you think of any other person we should be in your debt in having detailed notice of their status.[29]

This letter left Venice on 16 July. The procurators must have received a favourable reply, for by 19 August Monteverdi was in Venice rehearsing some church music with the players and singers of St Mark's. The rehearsal took place in the church of S. Giorgio, after which the music was given in the basilica itself. It was a sumptuous work which needed twenty players and two portable organs in addition to the thirty or so salaried musicians; and it pleased the

[28]See the report in ASV Dispacci, Senato III (Secreto), Mantova, Filza 1b, fol. 29.

[29]The request, dated 16 July 1613, is in ASV Procuratia de Supra, Reg. 193bis, fol. 64, given in Fabbri, *Monteverdi*, p. 177.

procurators. They appointed Monteverdi on the spot and gave him fifty ducats to show him how they did business.[30] Monteverdi went back home to Cremona to make arrangements for removing to Venice. On his way to take up his new appointment he had his last disaster. He was robbed by highwaymen and lost all his money. Then he crossed the lagoon to the city which was to be his final resting-place. Thereafter, in so far as he was capable of happiness, he was a happy man. Fame, prosperity and the better health which contentment often gives were to be his in the Most Serene Republic.

[30]For payments, etc., dealing with Monteverdi's audition and appointment (in ASV Procuratia de Supra, Reg. 140, 19 August 1613; Procuratia· de Supra, Cassier Chiesa, Reg. 10, 22 August 1613), see Fabbri, *Monteverdi*, pp. 177–8.

3

Venice

The procurators of St Mark's had made their choice with great speed. Usually they took their time in choosing a new *maestro di cappella*, with an interregnum of six months or more. They must have had unusual confidence in Monteverdi's reputation and demeanour. He was old enough, had experience in administration and was a famous composer. Someone of this stature was very necessary, since Monteverdi's predecessor had been a failure. Giulio Cesare Martinengo had come to St Mark's from Udine Cathedral. He left no mark on history as a composer, and worse still, he seems to have had unsatisfactory dealings with the procurators. The account books of the basilica show that he was constantly in debt almost from the moment he set foot in Venice. To pay his creditors he was continually asking for advances on his pay, and eventually died owing the treasurer several months' salary. To hasten the decline of Venetian music still further, the last of the great older school of composers, Giovanni Gabrieli, had died the year before Monteverdi's arrival. Given these circumstances, we can understand their welcome of an acknowledged master.

Monteverdi's new post was an onerous one. The musical establishment of St Mark's was large, perhaps the largest in Italy. There were about thirty singers, some of them *castrati*, and six players in regular employment, besides the boys of the choir school. In addition, on festival days it was usual to hire about fifteen extra instrumentalists and to pay them *per diem*. There were two excellent organists, often composers of merit themselves, and a vice-*maestro*, usually a promoted singer, who helped to maintain discipline and took on his shoulders the burden of teaching the boys and the younger priests the arts of plainsong and counterpoint. The minutes of the procurators' meetings show how much administration was involved in keeping the *cappella* routine in order. New singers to be tested and engaged, music to be composed and copied, the players to be hired — all these and many other duties must have kept Monteverdi busy.

For a *maestro* like Monteverdi, appointed mainly on his reputation as a composer, the frequency of the Venetian festivals must have presented many problems. There were about forty festivals, all of them celebrated with the greatest pomp and involving music. These were days which we can relive today only at coronations, royal weddings, jubilees and the like. A great procession would form in the Doge's Palace – the clergy in their robes, the ambassadors and papal nuncio in their most brilliant regalia, the Doge and Senate in their brightly coloured gowns – and then would go round the great square to enter St Mark's by its west door. There Mass and vespers were sung and played, and the procession would retreat in all its glory. The whole populace would also be there, staring from the porticoes in the square, leaning out of their windows, even climbing on the roofs of the Procuratia if they could find a way up. On Ascension Day the ceremonies were made even more picturesque by the use of the *Bucintoro*, the Doge's ceremonial galley, which took the Doge and the Senate to a place near the Lido, where the Doge threw a ring into the sea to 'wed' Venice to its mistress, the cause of its prosperity and glory.

This was all very well for the splendour-loving Venetian, but for the composer it meant a hardworking life from which there was no escape. For one thing, the liturgy used in St Mark's was unique, and therefore some texts were set only by Venetian composers. For another, the magnificence of the music required meant that the Masses and vesper psalms of composers outside Venice were rarely on a large enough scale. Sometimes works by recently deceased Venetians such as Giovanni Croce and the Gabrielis were used, but new music was always needed. For Monteverdi it can scarcely have been easy, since there was no other composer in St Mark's in his first few years, nor had his duties in Mantua really prepared him for the rapid composition of church music. So his letters to Alessandro Striggio at Mantua often have to apologize for a delay due to lack of time. In February 1615 Monteverdi is reluctant to leave Venice to fulfil a commission from the duke because of his duties in St Mark's, 'given the approach of Holy Week, at which time take place many functions attended by The Most Serene Signory [i.e. the Senate], which in that week comes to church'.[1] Four years later he was delaying work on the *ballo, Apollo*, 'on account of the affairs of Holy Week that will occupy me at St Mark's, and also the feasts, which are by no means few for the *maestro di cappella* at these times'.[2]

[1]Monteverdi to Alessandro Striggio, Venice, 11 February 1615, in Monteverdi, *Lettere, dediche e prefazioni*, ed. de' Paoli, pp. 70–2 (Stevens, *The Letters of Claudio Monteverdi*, pp. 97–9).

[2]Monteverdi to Alessandro Striggio, Venice, 7 March 1619, in Monteverdi, *Lettere, dediche e prefazioni*, ed. de' Paoli, pp. 112–13 (Stevens, *The Letters of Claudio Monteverdi*, p. 145).

Yet it would be a mistake to interpret these as complaints, or even as meaning that he felt he was wasting time when he could have been writing opera. Certainly there was a great change in Monteverdi himself. From the tired, depressed, ageing man he seemed in the later years at Mantua he became a renewed, invigorated and thoroughly alive composer and *maestro*: clearly his new working conditions, and doubtless Venice's political organization and even climate, suited him well. The amount of work he did in his first few years at Venice was enormous. The Acts of the Procurators show that he thoroughly reorganized the *cappella*. He gradually brought the choir up to strength, hired more virtuoso *castrati*, and made them all work harder. Whereas in former years singers were needed only for the greater festivals (indeed this fact was used to attract good foreigners). Monteverdi insisted on sung Masses on the ferial days. He found that there was little music available for the choir, and persuaded the procurators to buy some part-books from the Gardano press to build up a repertory of *a cappella* music by Palestrina, Soriano, Lambardi and others. He also regularized the position of the instrumentalists. Instead of paying the majority on a daily basis as they were required, he arranged to have them placed on the salary roll of the treasurer, so that they were paid bi-monthly, as were the rest of the staff of St Mark's.[3]

In spite of this he found enough time to compose and publish secular music. The contents of his sixth book of madrigals were certainly written at Mantua, but he saw the book through the press only in 1614, putting his proud new title on the front page. Then there were commissions from Mantua (now rapidly going downhill as a musical centre and having no composer of distinction any longer), including a ballet *Tirsi e Clori*, which was composed in 1615, and what amounts to an opera commissioned in the following year. The latter, a *favola marittima* by Scipione Agnelli called *Le nozze de Tetide*, caused him a good deal of trouble before he finally abandoned it in January 1617. He seems to have spent over a month trying to make the libretto into something suitable and perhaps had even composed parts of it by the time he gave it up. He also seems to have fitted into the literary circles of Venice quite happily. He sent a copy of his sixth book of madrigals to a minor poet, the Abbot Angelo Grillo, whom he had known a little in his Mantuan days. Grillo wrote back thanking him and referring to some manuscript works,

in which you prove yourself such a great master, though you are given

3 ASV Procuratia de Supra, Chiesa Actorum 135, fol. 9.

less support by the text; but even a mule looks like Bucephalus under a heroic rider. You have bestowed too much honour on my poems by your praise and by your music. Where my lines sound worst, there is the sweetest harmony in your composition.[4]

The procurators appreciated his hard work, and after three years we find a tangible expression of their approval in their minutes:

> The Most Illustrious Lord Procurators, recognizing the worth and competence of the aforesaid Claudio Monteverdi, *maestro di cappella* of St Mark's, and wishing to retain him and to give him the incentive to attend with greatest spirit to the service of the church for the honour of God, and so that he might have the opportunity to resolve to live and die in this service, have voted and having voted agreed that he be retained for ten years, with a salary of 400 ducats per year with the usual and accustomed perquisites.[5]

By this time he had settled the main problems in restoring the music of St Mark's, and had managed to tempt a most promising composer into Venetian service. This was Alessandro Grandi, *maestro di cappella* at Ferrara Cathedral, who was willing to enter St Mark's even as a singer (on 31 August 1617). He was soon promoted, first to teach the boys in the choir school, then to be Monteverdi's deputy. Grandi must have been a great help, since he was a prolific composer with considerable experience in writing modern church music.

Monteverdi certainly needed another composer in the *cappella* during these years, since the ceremonial life of the Venetian Republic became as brilliant as it had ever been. In 1617 one of the most splendid of their processions took place, and it is worth while describing it in some detail, since it gives a fascinating idea of the atmosphere in which Monteverdi worked. During April workmen repairing the foundations of St Mark's found a casket with some relics in it. There was an investigation by the ecclesiastical authorities and one relic was declared to be part of the True Cross and to be stained with the blood of Christ. Such a discovery could not go by without a Mass of consecration and a procession, and the Master of Ceremonial in St Mark's, Cesare Vergaro, persuaded the Senate to provide money to meet the necessary expenditure. The preparations

---

[4]Angelo Grillo to Monteverdi, Capo d'Istria, between 2 and 23 August 1614, in Alfred Einstein, 'Abbot Angelo Grillo's Letters as Source Material for Music History', in *id.*, *Essays on Music* (rev. 2/London, 1958), pp. 159–78, at p. 177.
[5]Memorandum of 24 August 1616, ASV Procuratia de Supra, Busta 90, Processo 204, fol. 12v, in Fabbri, *Monteverdi*, p. 190.

involved an incredible amount of work. New robes were made for the priests; new gloves for the people to carry the relics; the biers on which the relics were to be placed were made and covered with various rich stuffs; there was to be a new canopy for the relics. St Mark's Square was decorated by draping cloths from the windows of the Procuratia, and carpets were hired to afford a dignified entry into the basilica.[6] Inside St Mark's a large platform (called a 'theatre' in the descriptions) was built into the middle of the choir, since it was here that the relics were to be exposed to view for three days. Four hundred copies of a booklet by Vergaro were printed and given to the nobility to explain how the relics were found and their significance. Hundreds of candles were made, and extra priests were invited to take part and were paid for the rehearsals of the ceremony.

On Sunday 28 May, the procession took place.[7] The relics were mounted on three biers, and the nobility came out of St Mark's to hear an oration by the dean. Then, says Vergaro, 'there was sung the Mass of the Passion of Our Lord with most exquisite music, at the end of which a procession was formed which, passing in front of the high altar and in front of the Doge and Senate, went round the square'. After this procession the Scuole, or religious confraternities, formed their own processions, each with a number of players and singers to precede the priests and brothers. Some of them had dressed floats, and the Scuola della Misericordia had one in which 'there was a most beautiful youth, dressed to represent the Virgin Mary'. Then came the brothers and monks from each order that had a foundation in Venice, and some of these had decorated floats too. After them came the main procession with the Doge and Senate and the relics, 'preceded by four singers who sang the Litany of the Saints, and after the relics and immediately before the Doge there was the whole body of musicians with their *maestro di cappella*'.

The procession lasted an hour, and there were halts at three places in the square to adore the relics, with suitable music each time, after which the procession returned to St Mark's, where the relics were placed ceremonially on the newly erected platform. This was six feet high with steps up to it made of stone from Verona. In the middle of it was an altar on which the relics were to rest, while orations were given by various notable clerics:

The singers retired to two platforms, one between the two large pillars . . . near the altar, the other directly opposite, singing divine

[6] Payments are recorded in ASV Procuratia de Supra, Cassier Chiesa, Reg. 11.
[7] The following account is taken from G. C. Vergaro, *Racconto dell'apparato et solennità fatta nella Ducal Chiesa* (Venice, 1617).

praise. There was also singing from the theatre [the big platform] by a boy clad as an angel.

On succeeding days there was music to accompany the exposition of the relics, and harp players were given a fee for performing this. The cost of the whole affair was about 800 ducats, an enormous sum.

What exactly Monteverdi had to do is not stated; but since in the following year he described his duties for a similar festival, we can imagine his heavy burden. He writes to Mantua explaining why he cannot promise to send more of his opera *Andromeda*:

on Thursday week, which will be the Feast of the Holy Cross, the Most Holy Blood will be displayed, and I will be required to have ready a concerted Mass and motets for the whole day, given that it will be displayed even for the whole day on an altar erected high in the middle of St Mark's, after which I shall have to put in order [compose or rehearse?] a certain cantata in praise of His Serenity [the Doge] which is designed to be sung every year on the Bucintoro when he goes with all the Signory to marry the sea on Ascension Day, and also put in order a Mass and solemn vespers which at that time are sung in St Mark's . . .[8]

Hard work though it was, Monteverdi was happy. He was financially comfortable, he was famous, he was appreciated both by his employers and by the musical public at large. When an offer came from Striggio to go back to his old job at Mantua (on presumably rather better terms than before), he contemptuously refused:

I will therefore submit in consideration to Your Most Illustrious Lordship how this Most Serene Republic has never before given to any of my predecessors — whether it were Adriano [Willaert], or Cipriano [de Rore], or Zarlino, or anyone else — but 200 ducats in salary, and to me it gives 400, a favour which must not be set aside so lightly without not a little consideration; since (Most Illustrious Lord) this Most Serene Signory does not make an innovation without mature consideration, hence (I repeat) this particular favour should be very favourably viewed by me. Nor having done this for me have they ever regretted it: indeed, they have honoured me and still honour me in this manner, that in the *cappella* they do not admit any singer without first taking the opinion of the *maestro di cappella*, nor do they want any reports in matters of singers other than that of the *maestro di cappella*; nor do

[8]Monteverdi to Prince Vincenzo Gonzaga, Venice, 21 April 1618, in Monteverdi, *Lettere, dediche e prefazioni*, ed. de' Paoli, pp. 106–7 (Stevens, *The Letters of Claudio Monteverdi*, pp. 137–9).

they accept either organists or vice-*maestro* if they do not have the opinion and report of the said *maestro di cappella*; nor is there a gentleman who does not esteem and honour me; and when I go to make some music, whether chamber or church music, I swear to Your Most Illustrious Lordship that the whole city comes running. And then my service is most sweet, because all the *cappella* is under contract except the *maestro di cappella*; indeed, in his hands lies the hiring and firing of singers, and the granting of leave or not; and if he does not go to chapel, there is no one who says anything; and his salary is assured until death, nor does the death of procurators or of a doge interfere with it, and by serving most faithfully and with reverence he stands to gain greatly, and not the opposite; and as regards the money of his salary, if he does not go at his appointed time to collect it, then it is brought even to his house, and this is the first consideration as regards essentials. There are also the incidentals, which are extraordinary, for at my convenience, being begged and begged again by the Lord Guardians of the Scuole, I earn outside St Mark's anything from 200 ducats a year, for those who would have the *maestro di cappella* to make their music, in addition to thirty, nay forty, even up to fifty ducats for two vespers and a mass, do not fail to select him, and they even give him the favours of fine words afterwards.[9]

How different it had been at Mantua, Monteverdi goes on angrily. There the death of a prince or a change in his favour could make a very real difference. There the *maestro di cappella* was treated with no more respect than a favoured singer, either financially or otherwise. Nor had his pay even been very regular when he had had

to go to the Lord Treasurer every day to entreat him to give me what was mine! As God sees me, I have never in my life endured greater affliction in my soul than when I had to go to ask for my due almost for the love of God from the Lord Treasurer . . .

Was it really so bad at Mantua, we are tempted to ask. Were all these slights real or were they imaginary, at least in part? Surely it was not all so depressing there? But what is important is that after the small court atmosphere the change to Venice must have seemed like heaven to Monteverdi. It was a change from a dying civilization to one capable of new life.

[9]Monteverdi to Alessandro Striggio, Venice, 13 March 1620, in Monteverdi, *Lettere, dediche e prefazioni*, ed. de' Paoli, pp. 148–54 (Stevens, *The Letters of Claudio Monteverdi*, pp. 187–93). The Scuole were the guilds-cum-confraternities of Venice, the most notable of which was the Scuola di San Rocco, see, for example, Arnold, 'Music at the Scuola di San Rocco'.

New life is to be found everywhere in the musical activity around Monteverdi. In secular music the popular song-books by Florentine and Roman composers give way to the lively new ariettas of the Venetians. The catalogues of the Vincenti press now contain works not only by Monteverdi and Grandi but also by lesser known composers such as Martino Pesenti, Giovanni Rovetta and Giovanni Pietro Berti, all of whom were part of the Venetian musical scene. When one of the *castrati* of St Mark's, Leonardo Simonetti, made an anthology of solo motets in 1625, he could include works by no fewer than fifteen composers, all living in or around Venice. Six of them were in the employ of the basilica itself. Nor are these pieces perfunctory make-weights; they are written most competently in the latest style.

The manner and quality of the music at St Mark's in the early 1620s are described by Giulio Strozzi in a small pamphlet in which he tells of the memorial service for the late Cosimo II de'Medici, Grand Duke of Tuscany, in 1621. The Florentines living in Venice commissioned the music, which was performed in the great church of SS. Giovanni e Paolo on 25 May of that year:

> The music of the Mass and of the Responsories was newly either composed or concerted by Signor Claudio Monteverdi, *maestro di cappella* of St Mark's, and from the glorious name of the composer one can excellently comprehend the quality of the work, since he committed himself with particular conviction to these compositions because of the devotion which seized him to honour with his virtue our most serene patrons. First, the grieving solemnities were begun with a most plaintive sinfonia apt to draw forth tears, nay excite grief, imitating the ancient Mixolydian mode formerly rediscovered by Sappho. After the sinfonia, Signor Don Francesco Monteverdi, son of Signor Claudio, intoned these lamenting words most sweetly: 'O vos omnes attendite . . .' with the remainder of the Introit . . . The *Dies irae*, the work of the aforesaid Signor Claudio, and a most suave *De profundis* at the Elevation of the Host, by the same, sung as a dialogue as if by souls standing in the torments of Purgatory and visited by angels, produced admiration for the novelty and excellence of the art.[10]

Unhappily, Monteverdi's music and that of his colleagues has been lost, but even the description is invaluable to us since it shows us the way his mind was working. One thing we notice is that his church music is as modern as ever – apparently a dialogue in the dramatic manner. Yet more significant is the mention of the ancients, which

---

[10]Giulio Strozzi, *Esequie fatte in Venetia dalla natione fiorentina al serenissimo d. Cosimo II quarto gran duca di Toscana il dì 25 di maggio 1621* (Venice, 1621), pp. 19–20, in Fabbri, *Monteverdi*, p. 240.

suggests that Monteverdi is still under the spell of the academies. This is quite remarkable, for Venice had never been a centre of academies, at least not those of the kind found at Mantua, Ferrara and Florence. Nor were his younger pupils really interested in interpreting Plato and Aristotle; and even in other centres the composers of opera and monodic madrigals and arias had turned away from these now old-fashioned ideas. This description of his requiem music shows as ever the mixture of the modern and old-fashioned in Monteverdi's music, possible now only for a man of increasing middle age.

Another fruit of his fifty-odd years is the veneration which was accorded to him abroad. In 1620 he visited Bologna to settle his son Francesco's future. After a little time studying law at Bologna Francesco had decided to enter the order of Carmelite friars and came back from Bologna to Venice. There his voice was enough to procure him a post as singer in St Mark's. He had sung in the basilica as early as 1615, and the account books record a payment on 22 April 'to Signor Claudio, *maestro di cappella*, fifty ducats of gold, and ten ducats of gold to Francesco his son for having lent his services on the days of Holy Week and Easter'.[11] Francesco had received a further payment from the procurators in 1618: '15 March: ten ducats paid to Francesco Monteverde, son of the *maestro di cappella*, for having sung the lesson at matins on last Christmas Eve.' His permanent appointment as singer took place in 1623 and he eventually earned eighty ducats a year, which denotes that he was one of the better singers. But to settle all this in 1620 meant a journey to Bologna. Adriano Banchieri, the doyen of the Bolognese musicians, remembered several years later how 'on the day of St Anthony in the year 1620 Your Lordship honoured with your presence the public meeting of the Accademia dei Floridi ['Academy of the Florid Ones'] of S. Michele in Bosco'.[12] Perhaps while Monteverdi was there he discussed his other son's future, for in the following year he made arrangements for Massimiliano to study medicine at Bologna University, carefully writing to the Duchess of Mantua to use her influence with Cardinal Montalto to obtain a place in the Cardinal's College, where Massimiliano would live free from the dangers of bad company and the traditional licentiousness of Bolognese student life.

[11]The payment is recorded in ASV Procuratia de Supra, Cassier Chiesa, Reg. 11. The memorandum noting the award (ASV Procuratia de Supra, Reg. 141, fol. 17r, dated 20 [*sic*] April 1615) is in Fabbri, *Monteverdi*, p. 190.

[12]Banchieri, *Lettere armoniche* (Bologna, 1628), p. 141, in Fabbri, *Monteverdi*, p. 237.

With his sons' education well organized, and the music of St Mark's running smoothly, Monteverdi was free to follow his outside interests. As he was now at the home of music-publishing we find him writing motets for the various anthologies of church music which were so popular. His greatest music for St Mark's was composed for large resources and was not readily saleable; he therefore composed solo motets, duets and other works which could be performed more easily. Another source of income was directing the music at the Scuola di San Rocco, which he did on the day of its patron saint in 1623 and 1628. The accounts of the Scuola tell us that he was paid 620 lire in 1623 – a large sum – but out of this he must have had to pay the other musicians from St Mark's. More revealing is the payment for the second year, when he received a personal fee of 146 lire, or just about the amount shared among the sixteen singers of St Mark's and nearly four times the fee of even the most treasured virtuoso singer.[13]

All this activity as a composer of religious music was counterbalanced by the composition of dramatic works. Monteverdi continued his relationship with the Mantuan court. Agnelli's *favola marittima* had proved no stimulus to his imagination; in its place his friend Striggio suggested another subject, the marriage of Alcestis and Admetus. This was to be a true opera, sung throughout. The only trouble was that he had no libretto early in February 1617, and had only until Easter to complete it. The composer was keen enough to go on with the idea and even obtained leave of absence from Venice to go to Mantua for a fortnight; but even as he made his preparations a letter came cancelling the whole affair.

The next libretto sent him from Mantua was *Andromeda* by Ercole Marigliani. It arrived early in 1618, and quite obviously the idea was to produce it at some time during that year. This was highly optimistic, and from the letters between Monteverdi and Striggio we can gain some idea of why the relationships at the Mantuan court had been strained during the wedding festivities of 1608. Monteverdi was a slow composer, especially of a large-scale work. His first letter to Mantua, after apologizing for delay because of his daily work in St Mark's, shows clearly that he is thinking of the practical details – how many women singers he can count on for the chorus and who is going to sing the part of the Messenger, since he must think about how best to write for the voice?[14] These questions suggest that Monteverdi is about to begin composition in earnest.

[13]The payments are recorded in ASV Scuola di San Rocco, Filze 166 (1623), 168 (1628).
[14]Monteverdi to Prince Vincenzo Gonzaga, 21 April 1618 (see n. 8).

Alas, the next letter, three months later, is full of apologies.[15] The main festivals have gone, so his work in St Mark's is no excuse. This time he has been suffering 'a slight headache caused by the heat which suddenly followed the recent rains', which caused him to lack ideas, and he refuses to send quick but mediocre work rather than good music a little later. In any case he has finished some pieces, has begun others – a chorus of fishermen, for instance – and has planned huge sections. Then there is a large gap. More apologies follow in March 1619, when he has had the libretto for over a year; more apologies still in December. Finally, when pressed to finish the work in time for a performance during the Carnival of 1620, he writes:

I would have sent the enclosed song [for *Apollo*] to Your Most Illustrious Lordship by the last post, but Signor Marigliani made me a most pressing request from Signor Don Vincenzo with a letter direct to me that I should finish the already begun *Andromeda*, the play by the aforesaid Signor Marigliani, so as to be able to stage it before His Most Serene Highness this Carnival on his return from Casale Monferrato. But just as I shall be forced to write it badly in order to finish it in a hurry, so I am thinking that it will be badly declaimed and badly played on account of the very short time, and I am astonished that Signor Marigliani wishes to involve himself in such a dubious enterprise, since it would not have been in good time even if rehearsals, still less learning it, had begun before Christmas. Now consider, Your Most Illustrious Lordship, what you think is to be done given that there are still more than 400 verses to be set to music? I can envisage no other result than bad declamation of the verse, bad playing of the instruments, and a bad musical ensemble. These are not things to be done in such a hurry; and you know *Arianna*, which required five months of very strenuous rehearsal after it was finished and learnt by heart . . .[16]

No wonder he was considered difficult! Even if he had found the libretto to be not to his taste, he might have turned it down earlier. The only excuse there can be for his injured innocence is that at least he had not received his pension from Mantua recently. After many letters asking for it, he dedicated his seventh book of madrigals (1619) to the duchess, obviously with an eye to gaining her

[15]Monteverdi to Prince Vincenzo Gonzaga, Venice, 21 July 1618, in Monteverdi, *Lettere, dediche e prefazioni*, ed. de' Paoli, pp. 108–9 (Stevens, *The Letters of Claudio Monteverdi*, pp. 140–1).

[16]Monteverdi to Alessandro Striggio, Venice, 9 January 1620, in Monteverdi, *Lettere, dediche e prefazioni*, ed. de' Paoli, pp. 124–6 (Stevens, *The Letters of Claudio Monteverdi*, pp. 159–61).

influence in the matter. All he received in return was a necklace, a perfectly suitable token of her appreciation, no doubt, but not what he wanted. It is a wonder that he ever did anything for Mantua again.

In all probability he kept on working for the Gonzagas because in Mantua he could go on producing operas and other entertainments. At Venice there was no opportunity as yet to write dramatic music – or at least only occasionally, for in 1624 he had the chance to have his *Combattimento di Tancredi et Clorinda* produced. This took place in the Palazzo Mocenigo, but we have no means of knowing whether the work was commissioned by Count Girolamo Mocenigo, or whether Monteverdi composed it first and looked round for a chance to perform it. One thing is certain: this time there were no embittering negotiations with a librettist. The poem was by Tasso, a scene from *Gerusalemme liberata*, and Monteverdi had known it for years. This in itself put it outside his normal development as an opera composer, for it was not meant as an opera libretto at all. The result is curious. The work is not really an opera or a ballet. It was performed by only three people, of whom one was a narrator and commentator. Instead of the festival orchestra of Mantua only a group of strings was used. The massive scenic designs were also not available. From this it is clear that Venice had little to offer even the most famous opera composer of the time.

His next commission, then, had to come from elsewhere – from Mantua again. Duke Ferdinando died in October 1626 and was succeeded by Vincenzo II, who was so ill that he spent most of his days in bed. Was it, as has been suggested, that Striggio as court chancellor was really in charge of affairs and could indulge his taste for Monteverdi's operas? Or was it that there was the usual desire for a festival when a new duke came to the throne? Whatever the reason, we find Monteverdi sending to Striggio a play (or a libretto) by Giulio Strozzi that he had been reading. It was called *Licori finta pazza inamorata d'Aminta* (Licori who feigned madness, in love with Aminta) – the composer later styles the work *La finta pazza Licori* – and it is significant that the idea of the opera came from Monteverdi himself. Moreover Strozzi, although a Florentine, was staying in Venice and was willing to adjust his play according to the composer's ideas. This time inspiration visited Monteverdi. He sent the original play to Mantua early in May 1627. By the end of the month he had permission to begin composition, but had to wait for the return of Strozzi from Florence to revise the libretto. Strozzi came back about 3 June and work started. Monteverdi already had the part of Licori planned to fit Margherita Basile, and was thinking of the other virtuosos. By the 20th the play was reorganized into five acts instead of the original three, and by the end of July Monteverdi had almost completed his setting of the first act. But then the project seems to have foundered – it is likely that nothing else was composed – and Monteverdi's initial enthusiasm for the work, which was indeed considerable, passed for naught.[17]

Monteverdi's renewed interest in theatrical entertainment is surprising for a man of sixty. Nor was *La finta pazza Licori* his only project in 1627. He had already set more of Tasso's *Gerusalemme liberata*, probably in some stageable form. And even before he had sent *Licori* to Mantua, he had received a commission from Parma to write music for *intermedi* to be performed during the celebrations of the marriage of Duke Odoardo Farnese and Margherita de' Medici. This time the libretto was sent to him from Parma. The subject of the first *intermedio* he received was the strife between Venus and Diana, and Monteverdi saw the possibilities of the text at once. As usual, he found difficulties of detail, and since he was not conversant with the resources at Parma, nor was he a friend of his librettist, as he had been at Mantua, he decided to go to Parma to discuss the problems at first hand. He already had an invitation from Striggio at Mantua, and having sought leave of absence from the procurators of St Mark's he left Venice immediately after the procession of the Doge and Senate to S. Giustina on 7 October. By the end of the month he was busy at work in Parma and was writing not only *intermedi* but also music for a *torneo* (tournament) to be done during the wedding festivities. He was so busy that he wrote home asking for an extension of his leave. But the procurators were not pleased and wrote back on 27 November, demanding that he should 'come back to the duties of his post' at the earliest opportunity.[18]

No mean year's work, this, and possible only to a composer at the height of his powers. Monteverdi's cup of happiness must have been full when he received yet another invitation to return to Mantua as *maestro di cappella*. The composer's reply (written on 10 September

[17]Monteverdi scholars have long considered that the composer actually finished the score and sent it to Mantua, but a more convincing reading of the surviving letters is presented in Tomlinson, 'Twice Bitten, Thrice Shy'.

[18]The order, dated 27 November 1627, is in ASV Procuratia de Supra, Reg. 194, fol. 40v: 'Molto Mag[nifi]co S[igno]r[e] / Habbiamo inteso da una sua quanto V[ostra] S[ignoria] ci avisa, ma p[er]che la sua absentia da q[ues]ta Capella p[er] diversi rispetti no[n] si può più differire, sciamo necessitati à dirgli, ch[e] quante p[ri]ma si liberi, et ne venghi ad attendere alla sua carica, sapendo massime il termine delle sue obbligationi, et lei beniss[im]o e quanto sij necessaria la sua p[er]sona et car[a]m[en]te la salutiamo.'

1627) is especially revealing if we compare it with his angry refusal of seven years earlier. The anger now has gone. He even leaves his reply to the middle of his letter. No, he says, he is not going to move from Venice where he is secure and happy, where he has no burden of teaching and where his pay is regular and can be augmented with only a little extra work. If Duke Vincenzo really wishes to help him, perhaps he could use his influence to gain for him a canonry at Cremona so that he could return to 'his own earth' in his old age. It is a gentle letter and shows Monteverdi growing more graceful as he grows older. Such happiness was not to last. Even before Monteverdi was home in Venice to direct the Christmas music in St Mark's, disaster had happened. The composer tells us the story in a frantic letter to Striggio:

> As for my coming to Mantua, you will have to excuse me for the present for because of my honour I am unable to come given that my son Massimiliano finds himself in the prison of the Holy Office already for three months past, the reason being his having read a book not known by my son to be prohibited, but accused by the owner of the book, who is similarly imprisoned, having been deceived by the owner that that book dealt only with medicine and astrology. As soon as he was imprisoned, the Lord Father Inquisitor wrote to me that if I gave him a guarantee of 100 ducats that he [Massimiliano] would present himself until the trial was complete, he would release him immediately.[19]

With the aid of his Mantuan friend, Ercole Marigliani, Monteverdi found the bail and Massimiliano was soon out of prison. But the proceedings were by no means over. It was to be more than six months before the final examination proved the younger Monteverdi to be innocent – six months of fear and nervous waiting, with the threat of torture and imprisonment constantly overhead, six months of attempted wire-pulling by the young man's father. In the meantime there was work to be done. Monteverdi went back to Parma in the New Year to finish off the *intermedi* and the *torneo*. With the blessed fortune of a composer of festival music he was able to start rehearsing certain pieces and to try over anything that was doubtful months ahead of the actual performance. This finally took place in December 1628 at the ceremonial entry of Odoardo and his

[19]Monteverdi to Alessandro Striggio, Venice, 18 December 1627, in Monteverdi, *Lettere, dediche e prefazioni*, ed. de' Paoli, pp. 295–7 (Stevens, *The Letters of Claudio Monteverdi*, pp. 377–82).

bride. Alas for the careful preparations – it rained. The firework display planned to take place in the main square was ruined, and Tasso's *Aminta* with Monteverdi's *intermedi* was performed there with a huge cloth acting as a roof.[20] Little wonder that observers have nothing to say about the music, although, as usual, the machines and the *balletto a cavallo* took the eye.

Anyway Monteverdi was not there to hear how his music sounded under such conditions. Again he had tried to stay in Parma for Christmas. Again the procurators refused their permission. They were not going to have any inferior music since 'such solemn days cannot be celebrated without your presence', as they told Monteverdi.[21]

Back in Venice life changed but slowly. In 1627 Monteverdi's deputy at St Mark's, Alessandro Grandi, left to take charge of the music at Santa Maria Maggiore in Bergamo. In his place Giovanni Rovetta, a young man who had been first an instrumentalist and then a singer, was appointed. Less intimately concerning Monteverdi was the death of Duke Vincenzo II at Mantua. His death was hardly unexpected, since he had been ill for some time. What was not so easily foreseen were the consequences. There was no male heir to the dukedom, and the son-in-law of old Duke Francesco Gonzaga assumed the title. Spain and Savoy both protested against the usurper, as they considered him. The Duke of Guastalla also pressed his claims to the throne. The 'usurper' relied on papal influence and Venice. France also took his part. In no time northern Italy was in an uproar. The bitter war which followed needs no description here. It culminated in the invasion of the imperial troops from north of the Alps and the sack of Mantua, with the cruel destruction of the Gonzaga treasures. After this Mantua was no longer a noble and important city. Its days of glory were over.

Monteverdi must have been doubly thankful that he had not returned there. In Venice, at least for the time being, things continued as before. Life seemed stable enough for the German composer

[20]The festivities in Parma in 1628 are described in Nagler, *Theatre Festivals of the Medici, 1539–1637*, pp. 139–42. Details concerning the rehearsals and performances are in Reiner, 'Preparations in Parma'.

[21]The order, dated 13 December 1628, is contained in ASV Procuratia de Supra, Reg. 194, fol. 50: 'Al S[ignor] Claudio Monteverde, Parma./ Siamo alle santiss[im]e feste di Natale, et p[er] honor della Capella di S[an] M[ar]co et satisfat[ion]e n[ost]ra e necess[ari]a la v[ost]ra p[er]sona, vi habbiamo fatto scriver il med[esi]mo dal S[ignor] Rueta, tuttavia habbiamo voluto ancor noi

Heinrich Schütz to come and learn the new art of opera and church music from Monteverdi. Monteverdi himself continued to practise his peaceful art. In 1628 he set to music some verses of Giulio Strozzi for a banquet given by the Venetian state to the visiting Grand Duke of Tuscany in the Arsenal. Two years later he collaborated again with Strozzi (who now seems to have become Striggio's successor as Monteverdi's librettist). This time the work was an opera, *Proserpina rapita*, produced on a grand scale in the palace of the Mocenigo family, with the usual machines and elaborate décor.

The political stability of Venice had protected her citizens from the effects of the war, and life was normal there as late as the summer of 1630. But the imperial troops had not only sacked Mantua; they had brought the plague into northern Italy. Venice took its usual stringent quarantine precautions and this delayed the arrival of the disease. The first cases appeared in the autumn and then it spread rapidly and fearfully. Soon no one would venture out of doors. The procurators of St Mark's even forwent the rents from their houses, for no one would collect them. The fathers of the church of SS. Giovanni e Paolo shut themselves up in their monastery. All their novices had died, and the organist Cavalli sought leave not to attend Mass on festival days for fear of the disease.[22] The school of San Rocco gave up its processions and no longer hired musicians to celebrate Masses for the souls of past wardens. Nor were the musicians of St Mark's spared. Several died, others were broken in health but survived. Monteverdi himself lived to see the end of the plague. So did his son Francesco (we have no news of Massimiliano). Both were almost certainly in St Mark's on 21 November 1631, when the Doge and Senate gave thanks for release from the scourge and 'a most solemn Mass was sung, and during the Gloria and Credo, Claudio Monteverdi, the *maestro di cappella* and the glory of our age, had the singing ring out with *trombe squarciate*, with exquisite and marvellous harmony.'[23]

After the strain of these times, it is not surprising that Monteverdi became ill, even though he had avoided the plague. He was well over sixty, and emotional strain affected him physically. A letter from the

stessi questo tanto farvi sap[er]e p[er]ch[e] vi disponiate subito alla venuta, acciò giorni cosi solenni no[n] si celebrano senza la v[ost]ra assistenza, conforme alla v[ost]ra Carica, et vi aspettiamo co[n] desiderio, co[n] ch[e] vi salutiamo Caram[en]te.'

[22]See the remarks in ASV SS. Giovanni e Paolo, Reg. 12, fol. 206.

[23]Moore, '*Venezia favorita da Maria*', p. 313. Moore gives a full account of the ceremonies staged during the plague in Venice, and speculates on the term 'trombe squarciate' ('loud trumpets', perhaps *buccinae*).

procurators tells us that in 1632 he went away from Venice for a time, perhaps to clear up affairs at Mantua after the destruction of the war. The address to which the letter was sent has been lost, but Monteverdi clearly had overstayed his leave:

> To Signor Don Claudio Monteverdi, *maestro di cappella* to the Most Serene Signory of Venice.
>
> Most Illustrious and Reverend Sir,
>   We have received yours of the 7th instant, but have received no other letter, and we sympathize with your past illness and with the nuisance of the litigations which have kept [you] in those parts, but we rejoice, however, that you are recovered and that you are at the end and settlement of your disputes, wherefore we will be expecting you as soon as possible so that you can return to the service of the church and to your post . . .[24]

The plague and the war which had devastated the two cities where Monteverdi had made his home marked the end of an era, and at first sight it must have seemed like the end of the composer's activity. For the time being there was little enough opportunity for producing opera. Count Alessandro Striggio had died of the plague and the musical establishment in Mantua was sadly reduced. In the 1620s there had been no fewer than thirty musicians, including some famous singers. The roll of employees in 1637 shows that only eight singers were there – mediocrities of no lasting or wide fame.[25] In Venice things did not sink to this level. Monteverdi gradually brought the choir of St Mark's up to strength again, and the records show that the singers were on the whole paid rather better than before the plague. Even so the distinction of these musicians could not approach that of the previous decade. The flourishing school of church music composers had disappeared. And Monteverdi himself seems to have been more lax. Whereas at the beginning of his service in St Mark's he had been keen on daily services attended by the organists and all the singers, we find that several of them now took on outside engagements. One of the organists, Carlo Fillago, even took on the post of organist of SS. Giovanni e Paolo in addition to his own work in St Mark's, for which a few years earlier he had been reprimanded by the procurators.[26]

There are other signs of increasing age. Admittedly Monteverdi

[24]The letter (written between 14 and 18 August 1632) is in ASV Procuratia de Supra, Reg. 194, fol. 81v, given in Fabbri, *Monteverdi*, p. 285.
[25]ASM(G) Busta 395.
[26]ASV SS. Giovanni e Paolo, Reg. 12.

allowed his publishers to collect a volume of his works, the first for thirteen years; but this is a very slim volume of, for the most part, light fashionable airs, popular with both the Venetian process and the public. On the title-page (as from the letter sent by the procurators in this year) we learn that Monteverdi has taken orders, a surprising step for a man of great independence – and one who, after the affair of Massimiliano, had every right to feel a little aloof from clericalism. The only two of his letters from these years which have come down to us show us that his thoughts on music were old-fashioned and had scarcely changed since his youth. The book promised by Giulio Cesare Monteverdi over twenty-five years earlier still occupied his mind:

> The title of the book will be: *Melody, or Second Musical Practice*. 'Second' I understand as considered in the order of the modern style, first in order of the ancient style. I divide the book into three parts corresponding to the three parts of Melody: in the first I discourse about the treatment of the words; in the second, about the harmony; in the third, about the part of rhythm. I am thinking that the book will not be unappreciated by the world, for I discovered in practice that when I was writing the *Lamento d'Arianna*, not finding a book which could open the natural way to imitation, nor even which could illuminate for me what an imitator should be, other than Plato, through so dim a light that with my feeble sight I could scarcely discern from a distance what little he showed me, I discovered, I say, the great effort necessary for me to produce what little I did of imitation, and therefore I hope that it will not displease . . .[27]

We may be reasonably sure that he never completed this book. If he had, one wonders how many people would have been interested in this antiquated academicism.

Just as Monteverdi and Venetian music seemed to be peacefully declining, new life came into both. The immediate inspiration was the arrival of two composers and singers from Rome. Francesco Manelli and Benedetto Ferrari had been producing operas in Rome when political circumstances made it advisable to seek patrons elsewhere. With the illness and approaching death of Pope Urban VIII war looked very likely, and a stable society where opera could be treasured and supported seemed far more probable outside the Papal States – in Venice, in fact, where the two of them came with certain friends late in 1636. Monteverdi, who knew talent when he

[27]Monteverdi to Giovanni Battista Doni, Venice, 22 October 1633, in Monteverdi, *Lettere, dediche e prefazioni*, ed. de' Paoli, pp. 319–24 (Stevens, *The Letters of Claudio Monteverdi*, pp. 406–11).

saw it, snapped them up for the choir of St Mark's,[28] although he must have known that their principal interests were not in church music.

In 1637 an opera house was opened with Manelli's *Andromeda*. The audience was mainly patrician, but since boxes were hired by various nobility and it was possible to buy tickets of admission for the pit, the S. Cassiano theatre can truthfully be said to be the first of the public opera houses. The idea caught on quickly and several others were opened in the succeeding years. Naturally Monteverdi was not to be left out of this feast of dramatic music. *Arianna* was revived in 1640 and he wrote at least two new works – *Il ritorno d'Ulisse in patria* and *Le nozze di Enea con Lavinia*.[29] As if to show that his energy was completely up to any demands upon it he wrote a *balletto* for the Duke of Parma; and published his eighth book of madrigals and a collection of church music. Neither of these books was a slender achievement. The contents of these thick volumes may have been composed earlier, but even the business of seeing them through the press must have been arduous and time-consuming. Finally, at the age of seventy-five, he composed an opera which we may well consider his masterpiece, *L'incoronazione di Poppea*.

What the public thought of these works of Monteverdi's astonishing old age we shall never know. Tangible appreciation of his genius can be found only in the proceedings of the procurators, who twice made him a present of a hundred ducats and finally gave him leave of absence to revisit his old home at Cremona. He spent about six months in 1643 travelling to the places where he had spent his earlier years, not only to Cremona, but to Mantua, where perhaps there were still friends. He returned to Venice only to die. He was taken ill on 20 November and on the 29th the registers of the Public Health tell us of his death: 'The Most Illustrious and Reverend Don Claudio Monte Verde, *maestro di cappella* of the church of St Mark's, aged 73 [*sic*], of malignant fever of 9 days duration: Doctor Rotta.'[30] To quote the obituary written by Caberloti: 'the news of so great a loss disturbed and turned all the city to sadness and mourning, and it was accompanied by the choir of singers not by song but by tears and weeping.'[31] He was buried in the church of the Frari, in the chapel of

[28]See ASV Procuratia de Supra, Chiesa Actorum 144, 3 October 1638.

[29]*L'Adone* (Teatro SS. Giovanni e Paolo, 1640; libretto by Paolo Vendramin), long attributed to Monteverdi, was in fact by Francesco Manelli.

[30]The death certificate is in Fabbri, *Monteverdi*, p. 345.

[31]Matteo Caberloti, *Laconismo delle alte qualità di Claudio Monteverde*, in Giovan Battista Marinoni (ed.), *Fiori poetici raccolti nel funerale del molto illustre e molto reverendo signor Claudio Monteverde* (Venice, 1644), pp. 11–12, given in Fabbri, *Monteverde*, pp. 345–6.

S. Ambrogio, after a requiem with music conducted by his pupil Giovanni Rovetta.

Even in an age which looked to the present rather than the past for its music Monteverdi's music and reputation were too great to die immediately. His publisher, Alessandro Vincenti (perhaps aided by Francesco Cavalli), collected the manuscripts of his unpublished church music and any secular music which could be reconciled with modern taste, and published them in 1650–1. *L'incoronazione di Poppea* was also performed in Naples in the latter year. The procurators of St Mark's found that it was not so easy to replace such a distinguished man. They were careful to make inquiries all over Italy before making their appointment, and tried to persuade a distinguished middle-aged composer, Orazio Benevoli, to come from Rome, before being content to give the post to Rovetta.[32] But gradually memories faded, tastes changed. By the end of the century Monteverdi was forgotten. It is the pride of the modern historian that now we can justly write of his reward; for the reward of the composer of genius is immortality.

[32]See ASV Procuratia de Supra, Busta 90, fol. 43. The appointment is discussed and documented in Arnold, 'The Monteverdian Succession at St. Mark's'; Fabbri, *Monteverdi*, p. 346.

4

The earlier madrigals

The heart of Monteverdi's music lies in his madrigals. There he tackled and solved what he conceived to be the problems of the composer. It is in his madrigal-books that we can observe his spiritual and technical development from his earliest youth to his old age. Just as Haydn's soul is laid bare in his string quartets, so is Monteverdi's in his madrigals; and this fact should make us cautious. No composer works in a medium for fifty years without taking it very seriously. The fact that the madrigal is by its nature a smaller-scale work than an opera or much of the church music does not mean we can dismiss it lightly.

The matter is further complicated by the very nature of the madrigal. The string quartet at least remains for a distinct grouping of players and has a certain unity of purpose from the beginning of its history to the end. The madrigal has not. Some madrigals were written, as we commonly imagine all of them were, for the intimate performance of amateurs, who played or sang their parts for the pleasure of ensemble performance. Others were destined for singing by virtuosos who were made to show off their voices to a highly critical audience. Others were meant as attempts at the revival of the glories of ancient Greece, aiming at the closest of unions between words and music, to be listened to by literati and sophisticated intellectuals. Nor have we exhausted the list. Some madrigals were essentially grandiose choral music, to be performed on a great festival day. Some were the choral episodes in plays and must be accounted dramatic music. Some were essentially light music, using dance rhythms and simple repetitive structures. All could be called madrigals; or, for the lighter music, canzonets. If, then, we are to understand Monteverdi's secular music, we must do more than analyse it in an abstract way. It must be related to the audience or purpose for which it was designed.

Monteverdi's first audience at Cremona can hardly have been made up of the sophisticates and connoisseurs of the larger centres. It wanted pleasing and elegant music rather than anything profound or complicated; and this is precisely what we find in Monteverdi's earliest books of secular music. His first entirely secular publication, which came out in 1584, was a slender book of canzonets for three voices – just the thing for a beginner, not only because its smaller forces made contrapuntal manipulation easier, but because the form was short and clear-cut. By this time the canzonet had lost its earlier connotation of parody and had become virtually a light-hearted, small-scale madrigal – with one difference. Morley tells us what it had become by the 1590s:

> The seconde degree of gravetie in this light musicke is given to Canzonets that is little shorte songs (wherein little arte can be shewed being made in straines, the beginning of which is some point lightlie touched, and everie straine repeated except the middle) which is in composition of the musick a counterfet of the *Madrigal*.[1]

The repetitive nature of the form is very important, for, combined with its small scale, it virtually confined the composer to a simple melodic growth with no complicated counterpoint and to a decidedly harmonic style. There is scant room for word-painting or any complication, not for the tears and pathos of the serious madrigal.

Monteverdi's canzonets are, as we should expect, very like hundreds which were written in the last two decades of the century. Typically enough for a young man, he made his canzonets as complicated as he dared. Out of the score of numbers only two or three have the simple homophony which the more mature or less scrupulous masters of the time used. The close imitations which end 'Io son fenice, e voi sete la fiamma' are typical of his slightly academic attitude:

Ex. 1

(so that to die again I return to life . . .)

---

[1]*A Plaine and Easie Introduction to Practicalle Musike* (London, 1597), p. 180; see *id.*, *A Plain and Easy Introduction to Practical Music*, ed. R. Alec Harman (London, 1952), p. 295.

Conventional 'points' of the sort which filled the textbooks are also common, and Monteverdi does not hesitate to provide some teasing rhythms occasionally, either to express the words or for purely musical excitement. But although these things may indicate his provincial origins, the canzonets are charmingly traditional. Since they are short, the cadences occur frequently and give a clear diatonic harmony. The rhythms of the words suggest a music which constantly repeats short rhythmic patterns, and gives a pleasingly regular structure to each piece. Virtually no difficulties are given to either singer or player, and it can only have been the composer's lack of fame and the rivalry of scores of similar volumes which prevented the book from receiving a reprint.

The same charm appears in Monteverdi's first book of madrigals for five voices, which appeared three years after the canzonets. 'Madrigal' sounds more ambitious than 'canzonet', and from a technical point of view the manipulation of five voices involves a larger scale of writing and a greater challenge to the composer. Emotionally, however, there is no great advance in this book. The beginnings of the madrigals often remind us of the canzonets. 'Se nel partir da voi, vita mia, sento' has an opening phrase identical with 'Chi vuol veder un bosco folto e spesso'; 'Ch'ami la vita mia nel tuo bel nome' is very like 'Già mi credev'un sol esser in cielo'. The canzonet form seems to have remained in the composer's mind too. The traditional repetition of the last line of a madrigal is often interpreted by Monteverdi to mean a fairly strict repetition of a whole lengthy concluding section. Another reminder of the canzonets is the rhythms of the phrases. The gay, regularly accented fragments of melody are constantly used, and sometimes (as in 'La vaga pastorella', the whole madrigal seems to be centred on the rhythm of the music used for the opening words – another sign of small-scale, neat working.

Light-heartedness is the main mood of the madrigals, and the attitude to the poems reflects this. The verse either follows the pastoral convention, with the usual nymphs and shepherds, or it is lyrical, written in the first person with the sighs and tears of (as yet unrequited) love. None of it, except the poems of Tasso and Guarini, can claim any real distinction, and Monteverdi treats it for what it is worth: artificial and pleasing rather than profound. He has obviously learned all the tricks of conventional word-setting, such as the chromatic change to express 'lasso' ('alas'), triple time for 'gioia' ('joy'), the rest which represents a sigh before 'deh' ('ah') or 'sospiro' ('sigh'). More than this, he has learned the art of contrast and has begun to explore the use of dissonance to express the pains of the lover. The strings of suspensions, without ever departing from traditional practice, nevertheless seem rather more prolonged and intense than is usual in madrigals of this time:

Ex. 2

(and yet one dies . . .)

This passage from 'Baci soavi e cari' is magical in the way it excites us with its dominant sevenths, stiffens the tension with the major seventh, frustrates our feeling for tonality with an F natural, and makes it worse by turning this F into a dissonance before sinking helplessly into the cadence.

Such passages are quite common in this book, yet we still feel that the composer has not explored the possibilities of the poems fully. The reason is that the scale of the madrigal is hardly large enough to bear the strength of the passionate sections. He has not succeeded in using the variety of the five voices to develop his phrases to their full power. Too often a voice enters and then disappears after a bar or two without doing anything more than repeat the opening of a motif; and Monteverdi repeats rather than develops. In short, these madrigals are charming but little more, and it is not really surprising that the book had to wait for a reprint until 1607, when the composer's fame would ensure interest in his earlier music.

The second madrigal book also had to wait until 1607 for reprinting,[2] but there is much less justification for this neglect. It

[2]Stattkus, *Claudio Monteverdi: Verzeichnis der erhaltenen Werke*, p. 98, cites a nineteenth-century reference to a reprint in 1593 (C.–F. Becker, *Die Tonwerke des XVI. und XVII. Jahrhunderts*, Leipzig, 1855, col. 206), but its reliability is questionable.

49

came out in 1590, and it is remarkably mature and personal compared with the earlier works. It is not so much that the musical material is different. The canzonet rhythms and phrases permeate many of the madrigals also. The actual harmonies of the pieces contain nothing which cannot be found in his earlier music. Yet everything is slightly changed and more emotionally alive. What has happened is that Monteverdi has seen how to use the full ensemble, how to use the five voices to expand the phrases and sections. The beginning of 'Non giacinti o narcisi', for example, takes two short lines of the poem, opens with the first, overlaps it with the second and finally leaves the second in command. The cadence comes, and the third line takes up and expands the section with duet texture before yet another cadence. At this point Monteverdi would have rested content in his first book; in this one he is just beginning. He takes the melodic fragments already used and expands them. The first phrase, which had lasted only two bars at the beginning of the madrigal and was sung by two voices, is now given to the whole group of five. The phrase is spread over five bars and given a twist which takes it into a foreign key. The same thing happens to the second phrase and the third. A climax comes by bringing in the full group in a homophonic phrase, which is interrupted by two voices and then is itself repeated, slightly altered to make it more powerful. A little polyphonic working-out of new material follows, and then, canzonet-like, the opening phrase comes back and is developed in yet a new way, mingling with the middle section. Canzonet-like in principle this may be; but no canzonet on this scale was ever written, nor of this subtlety. The slight, anacreontic verse is given a new and more powerful meaning by the musician.

This madrigal is typical of the whole book, every number of which gives to its material and form the exact and inevitable working-out needed. To achieve this certainty of form Monteverdi has had to learn about two things. The first is the modern use of harmony. Instead of being little more than a by-product of counterpoint, it is now a very definite part of the musical structure. One symptom of this is the role of the bass part. In the earlier madrigals the bass had taken its place with the others, weaving the imitative fragments into the texture. This happens also in the second book; but there are also long passages where the bass fills in harmonically and does nothing else. In 'Non sono in queste rive' only twice does it take part in the imitation. The rest of the time it provides a foundation to the harmony in a way not very interesting for the singer but absolutely essential for the general effect.

The other development of skill is shown in the way the composer uses the variety of tone colour. Rarely do the voices enter one after another with their melodic points, except for special effects. Instead, Monteverdi brings them in to sing in pairs or threes, using the fifth voice to give a delicious unevenness and unexpectedness. The homophonic *tutti* nearly always comes as the first climax of a madrigal, and is used very sparingly thereafter. More usual are longish homophonic trio sections (such as we find at the beginning of 'Dolcemente dormiva la mia Clori' or 'Intorno a due vermiglie e vaghe labbra'.

Such technical developments are of the utmost importance, for they are precisely what makes possible a new certainty in matching the words. This time Monteverdi was more careful in choosing his poems. Nine of the madrigals are settings of verses by Tasso, and this provided a great stimulus to the composer's imagination. Instead of the rather insipid and negative imagery of inferior lyrics, Tasso nearly always uses concrete images which can suggest music equally picturesque. How much better is the line 'Non si levava ancor l'alba novella' ('The new dawn had not yet risen') than 'Baci soavi e cari' ('Dear, sweet kisses'). It is no coincidence that the most famous madrigal of the book is a nature study where every line has an image in it. 'Ecco mormorar l'onde', indeed, is a gift to the composer. The murmuring of the waves, the rustling of the leaves, the height of mountains are things which naturally give an imaginative composer opportunities. If we quote some fragments of the tenor, we see how Monteverdi was inspired:

Ex. 3

Equally vivid is the suggestion of a hunting scene in the opening of 'S'andasse Amor a caccia' ('If Love went to hunt') with its close canons and quasi-military rhythm. We may recall that the chase, with its opportunities for realism, had been a favourite Italian subject for musical setting as early as the fourteenth century:

Ex. 4

The dawn setting of 'Non si levava ancor l'alba novella', the calm of 'Dolcemente dormiva la mia Clori' similarly inspire the composer to fluent and naturally imitative settings.

With this second book of madrigals Monteverdi spiritually left Cremona; and the difference between it and the first book makes us wonder whether the composer has not been studying more up-to-date models than his teacher Marc' Antonio Ingegneri could provide. The most probable explanation is that some of Giaches de Wert's madrigals had come into his hands, especially Wert's eighth book of madrigals for five voices which had appeared in 1586. There are too many similarities between these two sets of madrigals for a coincidence. Wert was a great friend of Tasso and set many of his poems. He also liked concrete images to make for easy tone painting, and in fact one of his madrigals, 'Vezzosi augelli infra le verdi fronde', resembles 'Ecco mormorar l'onde' very closely, even to the opening phrases setting the words 'mormora l'aura' ('the breeze murmurs') and the melismas for 'cantan' ('sing'):

Ex. 5

Mor-mo-ra l'au - ra   Quan-do can - - - tan'

In another, 'Qual musico gentil, prima che chiara', Wert sets 'sospir' ('sigh') in exactly the way that we find in the second part of 'Non si levava ancor l'alba novella'. The trio sections which Monteverdi finds useful are also clearly derived from Wert's works, as it was he who developed them in writing for the three ladies of Ferrara (see pages 9, 55). The very mood of Wert's madrigals is like those of Monteverdi's second book, never having the artificial gloom of the dissonant passages of Wert's early works, but light, witty and very competent.

More than this, Wert about this time was developing something in which Monteverdi was to interest himself more and more. Wert was an academic composer In the sixteenth-century sense of the word, and was one of the favourite composers of the Accademia degli Intrepidi ('Academy of the Intrepid Ones') of Ferrara. We do not know much about the discussions of this body, as we do about those of the Florentine academies. What is certain is that it too was interested in interpreting the Greek theorists and that it had decided that the vital element in the creation of a modern music was a close relationship between words and music. Although in searching for audibility of the words it did not go so far as advocating monody, there can be no doubt from Wert's madrigals that some form of choral recitative was favoured. So in his eighth book we find constantly lines which repeat notes, less to give musical rhythms than to give exact declamations, and lengthy passages of homophony, not for musical effect, but to allow for the complete clarity of the words to the listener. The results are melodic lines which are quite the opposite of those required by polyphony. Not very interesting in themselves, they are explicable only in terms of the general effect as it appears to the listener.

In addition to these declamatory passages Wert was experimenting with other ways of verbal expression. Unlike many of the Ferrara composers, he had little interest in chromaticism and dissonance. Instead, he sought new effects by deliberately disobeying the tenets of smooth vocal writing and giving the singer huge awkward leaps which naturally conveyed great emotional tension. Sometimes he uses ninths and tenths in this way; at other places he merely arranges ordinary intervals into angular shapes which seem freakish and severe:[3]

[3]Wert's setting of Petrarch's 'Solo e pensoso, i più deserti campi' was published in his *Il settimo libro de madrigali a cinque voci* (Venice, 1581); see Wert, *Opera omnia*, VII, pp. 32–7.

Ex. 6

(Alone and thoughtful, the most deserted plains . . .)

In these new paths Wert was one of the great pioneers, and the musical language of the later madrigal was much indebted to his work.

This extended discussion of Wert's style might seem superfluous if its influence on Monteverdi was apparent only in the second book of madrigals. But the third book is so indebted to Wert that without some knowledge of his work it is impossible to see where Monteverdi was going. The young man's new book was published in 1592. Monteverdi had been about two years at Mantua, and suitably enough the book was dedicated to Duke Vincenzo Gonzaga as a thank-offering. Monteverdi now had a new and more musical audience, a group of composers of the most competent sort to put him on his mettle, and more practised singers to perform his music. This perhaps explains the speed of production of this book. Normally Monteverdi was slow to gather enough works to publish; two years to complete twenty madrigals meant that he was working unusually quickly.

Only two of the madrigals seem to be Cremonese. 'La giovinetta pianta' and 'Sovra tenere herbette e bianchi fiori' are both in a light canzonetta style, with texts by unknown poets, treated with the gay rhythms and repeated sections we have noticed earlier. The rest are quite different in mood and treatment. The poets are largely Tasso or Guarini — both extremely fashionable at Mantua. The musical settings have obviously been influenced by Wert's declamatory technique. Almost all the madrigals in the book have some motifs which are based on a *parlando* monotone. Some begin with a solo voice declaiming the words:

Ex. 7

(If a heart could die of extreme passion . . .)

In 'Vattene pur, crudel, con quella pace' we can see Wert's awkward leaps giving rise to a line which yet reminds us of Monteverdi's most mature writing:

Ex. 8

Vat - te - ne pur, cru - del, con quel - la pa - ce che la - sci̲a me

(Go, cruel one, with that peace which you leave to me . . .)

In fact, throughout the whole of this madrigal and its two succeeding parts Monteverdi is merciless to the singer, using leaps of the octave and of the sixth both ascending and descending, the upper registers of the voices, and chromatic changes both in regular scale-wise passages and in sudden false relations. Add to this the onus on the singer to make the *parlando* phrases alive, and we see how far virtuoso singers have stimulated his imagination. In one madrigal particularly Monteverdi is writing for the virtuosos. This is 'O come è gran martire', inspired (no less a word will do) by the *concerto di donne* of Ferrara (a virtuoso ensemble focussing on soprano voices). The form, with its trio opening and repeated *tutti* sections in the middle, is very like that of 'Non giacinti o narcisi'. But Monteverdi's obvious enjoyment of three virtuoso ladies' voices is reflected in the declamatory phrases, the falling sixths, the top As for the first soprano, the constant delight in crossing the parts to give the same chords new colours:

Ex. 9

E voi se - te il cor mi - o,

E voi se - te il cor mi - o

E voi se - te il cor mi - o,

co - re — E voi se -

(and you are my heart . . .)

One thing we notice in this third book is the widening of the emotional range. Monteverdi still clearly likes the concrete image to give a nature picture. 'O rossignuol, ch'in queste verdi fronde', with its song of the nightingale, suggests delicate melismas; the waves which are the concluding image of 'Vattene pur, crudel, con quella pace' give a charming swirl of sound. But to go with the declamatory lines and chromaticism the dissonant passages have returned. They are not more astringent than in the first book but they are much more effective. With the expansion of the scale these expressions of pain no longer seem exaggerated and out of place. In 'Stracciami pur il core', for example, there are two extended sections of slow-moving dissonance. The first one comes immediately after the beginning and is ushered in while the first, rather jolly theme is still going on. The whole passage is held together by an ascending scale in the bass and the tautest chord involves merely a minor seventh. The atmosphere is relaxed in gentle counterpoint until the words 'Non può morir d'amor' ('cannot die of love') insist on passionate setting. Again we have the rising scale in the bass, and the passage is much shorter than the first one. But this is the climax of the madrigal, and minor seconds and double suspensions give an added burst before the composer finds the cadence and a happy ending.

In this madrigal and others Monteverdi shows how he can move from one emotion to another and mingle them together in a short space of time. This is something that all the great madrigalists of the later sixteenth century could do, Wert included. There is one great difference, however, between Wert and Monteverdi. Wert is more literary, Monteverdi more 'musical'. That is, Wert expects his words to make an appreciable part of the total impression, and music may at times be secondary. Musical forms are less important than the ʀelentless pushing forward of the recitative. Monteverdi, on the contrary, makes the music express the words. He tries to find a musical equivalent, and words are important only in so far as they inspire him to musical forms and textures. A good example of this difference can be found in their two settings of 'O primavera, gioventù dell'anno', from Guarini's *Il pastor fido* (III.1) Wert takes a long section of Guarini's verse and sets it in a recitative-like manner with scarcely a repetition of the words.[4] There is no attempt at finding the image of the poem and setting it in equivalent music. If you cannot hear the words you are lost. Monteverdi's setting, on the other hand, is practically a canzonet. He writes a huge eleven-bar opening on two lines of the verse, and then, in a magical way, gives sixteen bars of expansion and development, using all the possible permutations of motif, phrase and voice combination. One is lucky to hear the words at all – but this does not matter in the least. We know precisely what it is all about from a verbal fragment or two and the very expressive music. Of the two, Wert is the more advanced, Monteverdi the more attractive; and in spite of all Monteverdi's theorizing about the words being master of the music, even at this early stage it is possible to see that it is the composer's musicality which makes his art alive, not his capacity for putting words and music on an equal footing.

The third book today not only seems a great advance on his early music; it was also a success in its own day. It was reprinted in 1594, 1598 and 1600, no mean achievement for a book which clearly was not meant to be popular in the same way that Gastoldi's balletts were; and after Monteverdi had achieved real fame it went through five more editions. His publisher, Ricciardo Amadino, must have been waiting for another collection to send to the press. He had to wait eleven years before the fourth book of madrigals was ready. Why, one wonders, did the composer delay? Would it not have been better to keep his name before the public? Was he too busy to compose? The answer to the mystery seems to be that Monteverdi was peculiarly reluctant to publish his music at this time. When the fourth book did come out he mentions in the preface that he had hoped to dedicate some madrigals to Duke Alfonso II d'Este of Ferrara. Alfonso had died in 1597, so Monteverdi must have been composing before then. We know also from Artusi's criticisms that at least two of the madrigals in the book were composed as early as 1600. This suggests that he was composing continuously in these eleven years. Why, then, was he so loath to see his music in print?

The only explanation we can offer is that Monteverdi felt within

---

[4]Wert's setting was published in his *L'undecimo libro de madrigali a cinque voci* (Venice, 1595); see Wert, *Opera omnia*, XII, pp. 3–15.

himself a sense of progress and movement which made him unsure of his music. Certainly his fourth book is in an 'advanced' style which, although firmly rooted in his older manner, was likely to shock the conservatives. For these eleven years were amongst the most turbulent in the history of music. At Florence the monodists had finally been able to produce an opera, Peri's *Dafne* (1598), and to follow it with the *Euridice* of Peri and Caccini (1600). The latter composer's *Le nuove musiche* came out in 1602, and thereafter the monodic movement was securely launched. Monteverdi must have known all about these events; but we have no need to go even to Florence to find a change of mood and a new revolutionary fervour. In madrigal books published in these vital eleven years both Giaches de Wert and Benedetto Pallavicino showed how they too were concerned in the academic attempt to 'move the affections'. Wert's eleventh book of 1595 is a remarkable achievement for a man of his years. In several numbers, and especially in 'O primavera, gioventù dell'anno', he takes a declamatory style as far as it will go. There are harsh dissonances, and in 'Udite, lagrimosi spirti d'Averno' a knowledge of chromaticism, which we would hardly have expected from him.

More interesting still is Pallavicino's sixth book of madrigals, which came out in 1600. Here a man who had been a reasonably conventional madrigalist a few years earlier suddenly explores chromaticism and dissonance. Many settings are of poems by Guarini also set by Monteverdi; and the older composer shows himself every bit as up to date as the younger. Without ever really doing anything which goes against established practice, Pallavicino manages to express the emotions of the poems with great force. The beginning of his setting of 'Cruda Amarilli, che col nome ancora' (Guarini) is most powerful:[5]

Ex. 10

[5]Pallavicino's setting was published in his *Il sesto libro de madrigali a cinque voci* (Venice, 1600); see Pallavicino, *Opera omnia*, III, pp. 163–71. The madrigal is also in Denis Arnold (ed.), *Vier Madrigale von Mantuaner Komponisten*, 'Das Chorwerk', lxxx (Wolfenbüttel, 1961).

(Cruel Amaryllis . . .)

And he shows in the succeeding bars that he understands the way of building a climax which Monteverdi used in the earlier books, and by different combinations of voices gives breadth to the scale of the madrigal. His use of chromaticism is less satisfactory, for he is more rarely consistent in its use, and, we feel therefore, more experimental. But he is obviously trying to gain something of the quick emotional change of modern music. These are only two of the advanced traits of Pallavicino's madrigals. A further search reveals that the declamatory technique of Wert and the wide melodic intervals (he is even quite fond of the falling sixth we associate with Monteverdi) are also used to fulfil the demands of the verse. He is indeed a composer of the *seconda prattica*.

Did Pallavicino influence Monteverdi or was it the other way round? Or perhaps Wert was the real teacher of them both. We do not know. What we do gain from our knowledge of the work of these Mantuans is a sense of a musical world in turmoil. We need not even think of the work of Carlo Gesualdo in Ferrara (he had married Leonora d'Este in 1594 and must have started his experiments at this time), or Luca Marenzio, to realize that there was a great deal to make Monteverdi unsure of the value of his music, to make him wonder if he was working on the right lines, and so to make him delay the publication of his madrigals. If he had such fears, there was little need of them. His fourth book (1603) is perhaps the most superb and consistent of all of them: it is the work of a complete master. Although the book's greatest achievement may seem to be the added power which dissonance and chromaticism give to the deeply felt sad numbers, there are a number of bright, happy pieces which are superb. Even a sense of quiet bitter-sweet irony can be heard in 'Ohimè, se tanto amate'. There is a completeness of emotional power which touches life at many points, and in each madrigal Monteverdi has a control of the words which means that he can follow their images and feelings in an incredibly exact way.

To show this at work we may take 'A un giro sol de' bell'occhi lucenti'. At first sight it looks like a frothy piece in the manner of the Tasso settings of Book II. The word 'giro' ('turn') produces a picturesque motif, and we begin with a little duet for sopranos with the bass filling in the harmony. The next line of verse is built round the word 'ride' ('smiles') and is worked out accordingly. The next section is an image of the sea and winds lightly moved (most reminiscent of 'Ecco mormorar l'onde'), and Monteverdi again paints delicately. The mood changes: 'Only I have weeping, sad eyes' ('Sol io le luci ho lagrimose e meste'). A sudden change of motion and the harmony is again conventional. Then Monteverdi pushes the shaft home, as the poet does: 'My death is born from your cruelty.' The dissonance here is as harsh as it is unexpected. A declamatory line with two voices on the same note suddenly becomes a slow line of continuous suspensions:

Ex. 11

This movement from unison to dissonance merely by moving one line up a tone or semitone is a favourite device in this book, and always surprises because of its sudden change from the most perfect of consonances to one of the keenest discords. Nevertheless, both in this madrigal and in others, after its use as a weapon of surprise the scale of the piece gradually allows the section to expand, and with its repetition the dissonant phrase loses its sharpness and evaporates into another motif and the peace of the word 'death' ('morte').

Technical perfection, and especially perfection of form, gives Monteverdi a command of this kind; but it is an insight into musical imagery, a knowledge of where to place the emphasis and how to find an equivalent of the inner meanings of words, which gives this fourth book of madrigals a delight hard to find in any madrigal book by any other composer. 'Sì ch'io vorrei morire' is an indecent little piece of verse, in which the love kiss (veiled as usual in the image of 'death') and the way to its climax – now sweet and almost restful, now passionate and energetic – are hinted at, until a state of rest comes at last. It is not a distinguished poem by any standards – little more than a play on words which scarcely arouses our feelings at all. It is indeed a standard of Monteverdi's mastery that he has managed to give added meaning to a poem without any concrete images to inspire him. The neutral opening does not attempt to paint 'morire' – quite deliberately because it is a point of rest. A *tutti*, by a chromatic twist, increases the tension; and then there is a huge section on the 'cara e dolce lingua' ('dear and sweet tongue') in which the lingering weakness and tenseness of love are given memorable expression by the continuous dissonance (usually with three adjacent notes of the scale sounded together), after which comes a falling section of more conventional suspensions as the lover feels himself 'dying'. He has a sudden return to life with a short rhythmic motif, and a feeling of haste is conveyed by a canon at the half-beat and a string of suspensions, repeated in one form or another three times, with a third voice finally exclaiming ecstatically 'Ahi bocca! Ahi baci! Ahi lingua!' ('Ah mouth! Ah kisses! Ah tongue!') until the great climax; and, with a touch of mastery, the peace of the aftermath is given perfect expression by a repetition of the opening.

'Sì ch'io vorrei morire' has an emotional life which could in 1603 be found only in the most intense modern madrigals; yet there is nothing in it which is revolutionary. Even the passage with the three adjacent notes of the scale held together simultaneously can actually be justified by conventional rules. This cannot be said of 'Ohimè, se tanto amate'. The very opening of the madrigal contains harmonies which are impossible by ordinary standards:

Ex. 12

(Alas . . .)

The effect is splendid. Again the subject is the spurned lover; and this time dare we take his sighs too seriously? The dissonance is not extended enough and therefore does not sound too severe. There is merely a tang of desire in these strange unaccented chords. This is carried through the madrigal in a magical way. When we arrive at the climax, 'Alas, why do you wish him who sighs to die?' ('deh perchè fate / chi dice "ohimè" morire?') the dissonances, far from being the astringencies of 'Sì ch'io vorrei morire', are accumulations of passing notes which do not always arrive at their destination and which therefore attract attention to themselves; and they are never prolonged, never harsh. Nor is the ending full of the passion which Monteverdi has at his command. Instead the 'thousands and thousands of sweet 'sighs' ('mill'e mille dolci "ohimè"') are given life by a series of false relations which convey a sense of indeterminate tonality. A pedal note in the final bars gives some light dissonance, and the concluding 'ohimè's gently remind us of the opening. The mood of the music is again the exact mirror of the words. The bantering, never too passionate love of both is a typical offshoot of the pastoral conventions. It is often difficult to believe in the grand amours of Thyrsis and Chlorys. Monteverdi has gone one better: he has written the music of flirtation without becoming purely artificial (for his motifs are anything but conventional), while at the same time remaining always full of feeling.

If I have discussed the emotional life of these madrigals in detail, reading into them perhaps – as is always the danger – things which are not really there, the reason is that the technical resources of this and the fifth book of madrigals are so interesting for the development of music that Monteverdi's masterful psychology is sometimes forgotten. But I cannot leave this book without commenting on its musical resource too, for the volume is a key to Monteverdi's subsequent development. One thing we notice is that the 'academic' traits come to their full expressiveness in these madrigals. Chromaticism, for example, is nowhere better integrated into the madrigal than in the last number of the book, 'Piagn'e sospira, e quand'i caldi raggi'. The rising chromatic scale of the opening acts almost as a *cantus firmus*, around which the different emotions and different musical motifs are wrapped. At the end, when the final chromatic fragment is no longer used, a chromatic change in a chordal passage is as expressive as any harmonic use of chromaticism could be. There is none of the enigmatic suddenness of Gesualdo's chromatics. Everything is musically developed to its fullest extent.

Similarly, Wert's experiments in *parlando* declamation are used perfectly here and no longer seem at all experimental. A great deal of

'Voi pur da me partite, anima dura' is written in homophonic, quickly moving declamation in which the words are perfectly audible. What Monteverdi has done is to make every harmonic change significant, every change of texture contribute to the ebb and flow of tension. More than that, the expressiveness of melody now can be heard at its clearest, for the top lines (usually two of them) use the slides and ornaments, the capacity to hold notes, to make expressive pauses, all of which Monteverdi had learned from the virtuoso singers of Mantua. In 'Sfogava con le stelle' he uses the declamatory style in yet another way. Here is the extreme of verbal clarity in the ensemble madrigal; in six places he does nothing but indicate the chords to be sung, leaving the rhythms to the singers, who must chant them as they would the psalms written in *falsobordone*. Nothing could be simpler; but this is used not just to give clarity to the words, but to make the succeeding passages in counterpoint more overwhelming. As one acute observer has found, the neutral words, the words which have no direct expressive power, are left in chant. Those which are personal, evocative and emotional are given the full power of expressive music – all the modern harmonies, the nervousness of ornaments and strange leaps in melody.

These two madrigals are typical of the whole book in this way. The power of harmony – not necessarily dissonance, but of chromatic changes and modulation – and virtuoso melody have now in fact done away with real counterpoint. There are many passages which could be performed by a solo voice with a keyboard accompaniment – even more by two voices and keyboard. Something would be lost, because the colouring of the voices and the changes of texture are important. Yet the essentials would be there. There is no doubt that Monteverdi is now writing music for the aristocratic listener rather than the aristocratic performer. No groups of dilettantes could possibly perform it adequately. The older ideal of the madrigal is as dead as it is in the madrigals of Gesualdo or in the monodies of the Florentine 'camerata'.

The fourth book of madrigals was successful and had to be reprinted in 1605 and 1607, to go no further (it is interesting to note that a great deal of 'modern music' was seemingly popular, for Pallavicino's sixth book also went through several editions quickly). Perhaps it was this that encouraged Monteverdi to bring out another book soon after. The fifth book appeared in 1605. But it seems that at least part of its contents was composed about the same time as those of the previous collection: Giovanni Maria Artusi had cited passages from 'Cruda Amarilli, che col nome ancora' and 'O Mirtillo, Mirtillo anima mia' in his attack of 1600, and another two,

'Era l'anima mia' and 'Ma se con la pietà non è in te spenta', seem to have been known to him in 1598.[6] There are two changes to note, the first of which might appear a purely technical one. A *basso continuo* part is supplied. For over half the contents it is not necessary; for the last six madrigals it is essential, and these are therefore rather different in technique. We must not exaggerate the immediate effects in sound. Probably madrigals of earlier volumes were performed with instrumental accompaniment and with soloistic decorations such as we find in these new madrigals. Nevertheless the conscious use of an instrumental accompaniment leads to very new conceptions, and these madrigals are original enough to open a new chapter in the history of the genre. The other novelty for a Monteverdi madrigal book was the complete elimination of the canzonet style. Even the highly serious fourth book had its lighter numbers, for instance 'Io mi son giovinetta'. The 'conventional' madrigals (as we may call those which do not use the *basso continuo* as an essential ingredient) of Book V are all sad. Some of them seem almost emotionally overwrought. The laments of the various lovers in Guarini's *Il pastor fido* are the main choice of verse, and they are treated as vehicles for great musical intensity, without any suggestion of that teasing not-too-serious pastoralism of which Monteverdi is sometimes capable.

The immediate result of this emotionalism is that the harmony of some of the madrigals is more dissonant, and stranger in the way it uses false relations; and it was these things that Artusi attacked in his various books and pamphlets. It was to be expected that he would direct an attack on 'Cruda Amarilli, che col nome ancora', for there is one bar which is very unconventional (see Ex. 13). Even so, Artusi's attack is more on a paper reading than on the actual sound. If we compare Monteverdi's opening, it is much less dissonant than Pallavicino's. It is unusual for its ornaments, fully written out; but Artusi must have heard things like that many times from singers adding improvisatory embellishments. There are other pin-pricks of harmony, but again they are more 'difficult' on paper than in sound. For the most part, the madrigal is more conventional than many in the fourth book, both in its melodic motifs and in its treatment of them.

More worthy of Artusi's attack, for it is one of the greatest of Monteverdi's madrigals, was 'Era l'anima mia'. Guarini's first image is of the soul at its last hour. Its double meaning is so ordinary in the verse of the period that we hardly think about it. Monteverdi seems to take it at its face value, and using the lower voices (and the lowest

[6]On the dating of the Book V madrigals, see Fabbri, *Monteverdi*, p. 81; Fabbri would go so far as to date all the pieces in the book before 1601.

Ex. 13

(ahi ala . . .)

registers of them) he gives a picture of frightening intensity. Long-held pedal notes, over which two voices in thirds give the effect of modern dominant preparation, and frequent false relations never allow the tension to drop. If we wish to feel how intense this is, it is only necessary to compare the passage with a setting by Pallavicino:[7]

Ex. 14

[7]Pallavicino's setting of 'Era l'anima mia' was published in his *Il sesto libro de madrigali a cinque voci* (Venice, 1600); see Pallavicino, *Opera omnia*, III, pp. 142–6.

(and languishes as a dying soul languishes . . .)

The soul is reprieved by a glimpse from a more blessed spirit and Monteverdi brings in his upper voices with almost angelic effect. Thereafter the verse proceeds by a series of double meanings, by sighs and threatened deaths. The music breathes life into the conventions, and by long pedals and dissonant passing notes comes to a memorable climax. These two madrigals could well have come from the fourth book; in psychological power and emotional grandeur they seem to complete a phase in Monteverdi's work.

The other 'conventional' madrigals, with one exception, seem less interesting and, for Monteverdi, more experimental. There are two long cycles of linked madrigals to verse from *Il pastor fido*, both of which seem to have gone back to the ideals of Wert. Both are obviously concerned less with madrigalian expressiveness than with the audibility of the words. Almost the whole of the first part of 'Ecco, Silvio, colei che in odio hai tanto' is written in homophonic declamation. There are varied groupings of voices and some striking harmonic changes; but the sacrifice of expressiveness has been great. In the subsequent sections the texture is adhered to less severely, but nowhere in the works is there anything of the sheer magic we find in some of the earlier madrigals. What we do notice is a great interest in the development of the melodic line – by now the upper melody throughout. The lower parts often consist of filling in of little independent interest. Monteverdi is developing a definite attitude to this, and a number of personal mannerisms have appeared. One is the use of a descending leap of a sixth which comes at moments of crisis. It is possible to find this in earlier works (even in Book III), but it now happens so often as to become almost a cliché. Another is a suspension which resolves irregularly and draws attention to itself by leaping to an unexpected note of the new chord. Another is the use of sequence to press home a phrase; and another an occasional expressive ornament. The beginning of 'Dorinda, ah dirò mia se mia non sei' is a good example. First a short phrase; then a repetition of it higher up; then an ornamental repetition and an obsessional development of the three notes of the scale before the section is complete – these are the stages of melody building:

Ex. 15

(Dorinda, ah! shall I call you mine if you are not mine . . .)

This is more skilful and more deeply felt than anything we find in Wert's recitative madrigals; yet it is little compensation for the splendours of Monteverdi's natural madrigal style. There is, however, one exception: 'O Mirtillo, Mirtillo anima mia'. It is certainly written in the recitative madrigal style, and with little trouble it could be reduced to a monody, for the important melody is always in the top part and there is always a clear bass part, even in the trio sections. The melody is of the most expressive kind of declamation. The downward sixth leap begins the madrigal and sets the atmosphere at once. The suspension which resolves irregularly comes several times. But more than this, Monteverdi uses the complete resources of the madrigal. The chains of suspensions which we have seen in earlier books now dominate the first climax. Words and phrases are repeated to give scale to the madrigal, which never seems restricted or in the least experimental. As several observers have pointed out, it is the first of the great laments and the true model for the *Lamento d'Arianna*, which was in turn to set a fashion for many years and many composers. Although rather simpler in psychology than some of the madrigals of the fourth book, it is a good example of what can be done with the new manner.

The continuo madrigals seem to demand a new chapter. Typically enough they start in the middle of a madrigal book, for Monteverdi's music progresses so naturally that any division is artificial. The division of his madrigals into two is merely for our convenience, since the introduction of the *basso continuo* is a suitable place for us to recapitulate the excitement of the 'new music' which had been so proudly proclaimed by the Florentines a few years earlier, and which used this new device as an integral part of its nature. Yet if the glories of Greece had been re-created by anyone it was by Monteverdi, using the older techniques or extensions of them. His claim to be a descendant of Cipriano de Rore and the rest was quite justified, and already he could claim to be by no means the least of the moderns.

As a writer of conventional madrigals Monteverdi stays somewhere between Marenzio and Gesualdo. He is a less polished composer than the former, whose music is often the accurate mirror of the anacreontic verse he sets. Monteverdi is too rugged, too interested in human beings to be able to believe in the pastoral convention. Yet he is too much a musician to be a purely psychological composer like Gesualdo, who seems to have no interest in musical device. In one way he excels both of them. In his range of emotion he is greater than either. He can be passionate and pessimistic, gently ironic or supremely gay in turn. We have no right to be surprised when he turns out to be a great opera composer. His madrigals, with their range of human interest and their variety, from introversion to almost pure objectivity, have prepared the way thoroughly; and if at times we seem to undervalue these works, the only reason can be that we do not devote to their performance the virtuosity which their composer expected. There is no other barrier to our understanding.

5

Madrigals with basso continuo

The *basso continuo* was one of those inventions which had an influence on the history of music far beyond any expectations of its originators. It came out of the specific needs of certain composers. Some of them were mundane. Lodovico Grossi da Viadana, sometime *maestro di cappella* at Mantua Cathedral, had the need for a notation which would allow the organist to fill in gaps in the harmony when the singers were few. Motets written deliberately for one or two or three solo voices required a well-organized accompaniment if the music was not to sound thin and weak. A notation which allowed for the cheap production of keyboard parts was a godsend to him and many another musician working in difficult conditions.

There were also more noble reasons, especially those of the Florentine academics, who, in their attempt at reviving the glories of Greek music, came to the conclusion that the decadence of modern music was really caused by polyphony, since it 'lacerated the poetry' (as one of them put it),[1] and that the only way of uniting words and music on equal terms was for a single voice to be used. The words would then be clear and the singer could 'move the spirit', or appeal to both the intellect (through the words) and the emotions (through the music). Unwilling to sacrifice the power of harmony altogether, they too sought a notation which would make quite clear the subordinate role of the accompaniment. Their attempt was a revival of Greek music; their success, a new kind of music for the court. It is no coincidence that some of the first composers of the 'new music' were singers. The very nature of monody was to glorify the virtuoso, and since for some time the tastes of Ferrara, Mantua and the other courts had been for the nimble throats of Laura Peverara, Adriana Basile and the rest, it is no wonder that the 'new music' became fashionable. The first song-books came out in 1602, and within ten years monody was in constant demand.

The earliest monody books contained two types of song. One, the

[1] The most trenchant criticisms of contemporary madrigals are made in Vincenzo Galilei's *Dialogo della musica antica, et della moderna* (Florence, 1581); see the extracts translated in Strunk, *Source Readings in Music History*, pp. 302–22.

most important in the first fifteen years or so, preserved the name 'madrigal'; and with good reason, for it followed the main principle of the later polyphonic madrigal – that the words were to be expressed in the greatest possible detail. The new methods were admittedly a little different, although they too had their origins in the older style. In some madrigals the conception was to provide an exact declamation for most of the song, repeating the words little, if at all, and saving expressive music for important words or phrases. This expressiveness often took the form of virtuoso ornamentation, which now became surpassingly involved and demanding. In other madrigals exact declamation was sacrificed a little for a continuous *arioso* movement with climaxes brought about by jagged intervals and dissonant harmonies. Some of these *arioso* madrigals are really very like the more advanced madrigals in Monteverdi's fourth and fifth books, in that these would have sounded very similar if performed with a single voice and instrumental participation. But the newer style, as it was first conceived, had several disadvantages. Whereas the lightly contrapuntal texture of Monteverdi enforces both a fairly strict rhythm and a sense of formal development, these *continuo* madrigals had a tendency to be a little amorphous and uninteresting, especially if sung with the free *rubato* which some of the composers advocated. Admittedly this followed up the ideas of the theorists in so far as it threw emphasis on the words; but as time went on the music conquered, and the repeating of verbal phrases, the use of refrains and other devices began to give a new attractiveness.

The *continuo* madrigal was inconceivable without the taste for splendid virtuoso singing. The second type of monody was designed for broader popularity. The aria, as it was called, had nothing to do with the ancient Greeks. It was the natural descendant of the ballett and the canzonet, both of which were sold by the score (Monteverdi's among them) in the latter decades of the sixteenth century. The simplest arias are sharp in rhythm, clear-cut in harmony and tonality, and – so that they should be unforgettable – strophic in their treatment of the words. They set verse which one writer has aptly characterized as 'amorous baby talk' to the lightest of tuneful music.[2] Some arias were, it is true, a little more complicated. These were written in the form which we know as the strophic variation. Each verse of the poem was set to slightly changed music, but the bass is kept the same throughout – a tether by which the melody maintains its general shape. The composer may manage to get in

[2]Compare the discussion in Fortune, 'Italian Secular Monody from 1600 to 1635'.

more detail of word-painting, but the general mood is still gay and it is no surprise that these two types of aria eventually defeated the more serious madrigal and drove it from the song-books.

What had Monteverdi to do with such new ideas? Not much, is the answer: or rather, not much while the ideas were really new. Certainly he was interested in the Greek philosophers and in the possibilities of monody. But the glories of the ancients were not necessarily to be found in this music of singers and dilettantes. Like most professional composers, he was slow to take to the solo madrigal and aria. When he did use the *continuo*, it is typical that it should interest him more as a new technical means, rather in the practical way of Viadana than in the experimental way of the Florentines; typical also that when he finally took the plunge, in the last six madrigals of Book V, the general effect is perhaps more conservative than some of the daring numbers of his Book IV. The first of the *continuo* madrigals, 'Ahi come a un vago sol cortese giro', is a masterpiece. The poem belongs to the usual kind of love verse, with all the conventionally affective words – sighs, wounds and so on. Monteverdi writes music which gives them vivid expression. In a *continuo* madrigal, melody is especially important, and the opening duet for tenors uses all the resources of florid ornamentation in much the same way that Caccini's madrigals of his

Ex. 16

(As if towards a sweet and gentle sun . . .)

Le nuove musiche use them. With a second voice to enrich both harmony and sonority, the effect is superb and much more powerful than anything Caccini ever wrote (see Ex. 16 on previous page).

The phrasing, too, is magical – now long and sustained, then suddenly quickened emotionally with short, more broken fragments of melody. The bass moves comparatively slowly as the interest lies completely in the tenor parts, but because of the continuous movement in these there is never any feeling that the rhythm has collapsed, as there sometimes is in early monody. This tenor duet is in four sections, the first very long and culminating in a splendid decorative climax, the second still decorated but somewhat shorter, the last two becoming progressively more direct in melody and more concentrated. To separate them is a *tutti* – a refrain which happens four times in all, slightly altered each time in texture but otherwise the same, with the final *tutti* extended by a coda using harmonies over a pedal note, reminiscent of earlier madrigals. Indeed, the refrain is altogether like part of one of the madrigals from the fourth book, contrasting with the tenor duet by its rhythmic directness and mobile bass. Nor is any part of the madrigal very different from the earlier madrigals which use the trio texture freely. There are just two significant changes. One is the rondo form – a form which is clearly melodic, and much more obvious than the earlier developments from the canzonet. The other is the sectionalism which results from giving all the trio sections to one group of voices and from decisive cadences at each change of texture. This interest in forms, which derives from Monteverdi's earliest days, stands him in good stead. We have only to look at the motets of his Mantuan colleague Viadana, who was trying to solve the same problems at the same time, to see how well Monteverdi has avoided the amorphousness which was the trouble in much early *concertato* music.

In '"T'amo mia vita", la mia cara vita' we find the same inventiveness in the face of this problem. The verse is simple enough. The beloved says 'I love you', and the lover is happy. Here Monteverdi gives the words of the beloved to a soprano, who sings them several times, while each time the lover, represented by the three lower voices, gives a different cry of joy and tenderness. The sections are short and the bass is more consistently in motion, so that everything sounds quite conventional. Yet the way the upper voice is used leaves no room for doubt that a soloist is needed, a soprano who can hold a note and make it expressive. The lower voices are full of chromatic changes, effective if perhaps less subtle than those used in Book IV; and the declamatory chattering in quavers, although at first sight not interesting in itself or very exactly matching the rhythm of the words, is psychologically right. The amplification of the opening motifs into a concluding *tutti* rounds off the piece perfectly.

After these successes (the fifth book went through eight editions in fifteen years) we might expect another madrigal book to follow; but between the Mantuan operas of 1607–8 and his emotional troubles Monteverdi can have had little time, and indeed the only volume of any sort to appear was a collection of trios made by his brother, Giulio Cesare. These are called *Scherzi musicali* and came out in 1607. Scholars have devoted a great deal of attention to the volume, mainly in trying to find out what Giulio Cesare meant by referring in the preface to 'canto alla francese' – a term which turns up again in some of Monteverdi's motets. To relate these slight trios to *musique mesurée* and French academic ideas is to take these songs too seriously. They belong to an Italian tradition – a Mantuan tradition even. They are the natural successors of Gastoldi's *balletti*, which were popular as early as the 1580s. In particular, Gastoldi's *Balletti a tre voci*, which came out in 1594, are very near in atmosphere, texture and phrasing to Monteverdi's *Scherzi musicali*; and since they were designed for playing and singing together, they may well have sounded like the later works. Typically, Monteverdi is rather more complicated. He likes the *hemiola* rhythms, which indeed intrigued some of the writers of the monodic ariettas and were to become increasingly fashionable:

Ex. 17

(Da-mi-gel-la Tut-ta bel-la, Ver-sa, ver-sa quel bel vi-no. Fa che ca-da La ru-gia-da Di-stil-la-ta di ru-bi-no.)

(Pretty maiden, pour forth the fine wine, let drop the crimson distilled from the ruby.)

Monteverdi also provides a short instrumental *ritornello* between the verses of each song, in most pieces seeming to develop the themes of the song lightly. Some of the songs are very charming, especially 'Lidia, spina del mio core' with its appealing little ending alternating between major and minor. Others are too regular and too short-breathed to satisfy. In this sort of light music many composers were as good as Monteverdi, and we must look elsewhere for his true development.

The sixth book of madrigals appeared in 1614 when Monteverdi was firmly installed in Venice, but its contents are the work of his

Mantuan years. A madrigal book for five voices looked old-fashioned in 1614, even if there was a *basso continuo* part; and it is not surprising that (to judge by the reprints) there was not the tremendous success for it that there had been for the fifth book. Even so, it is a splendid volume. The two main works are a madrigalesque arrangement of the *Lamento d'Arianna* and 'Incenerite spoglie, avara tomba', the lament of a shepherd on the death of his nymph. There are also two Petrarch settings, both in a reasonably conventional, almost *a cappella* style, and a number of *concertato* madrigals after the manner of the last six in Book V.

The laments are both examples of Monteverdi's finest music. The *Arianna* arrangement was criticized by Giovanni Battista Doni on the grounds that it spoiled a work which was essentially expressive solo music.[3] Be that as it may (and we must remember that we neither have seen the opera nor possess the complete score of the *scena*), it is easier for us to understand the popularity of the piece from the madrigal version than from the monody. The scale of the madrigal is nearer our expectations; the monody, as later printed by the Gardano press, with its chorus interpolations cut out, seems too small. Again, the harmony which the composer uses in the madrigal is more powerful than any we can conjure up from the *basso continuo* part of the monody, if only because the sustaining power of the voices is so much greater than on any accompanying instrument; and this is important, for the madrigals are clearly very much in the tradition of Book V. Moreover, the arrangement is a great deal more than a thickening out of the monody. In the very first section, for example, the refrain, 'Lasciatemi morire' ('Leave me to die'), with its acid dissonance, comes twice in the monody to make up a neat *da capo* form which is entirely satisfactory. In the madrigal version, it bursts in yet another time. After the opening (slightly lengthened to allow all five voices to enter and expand the phrases) the second section, 'E chi volete voi' ('and whom do you wish') acts as an episode for three voices with a dissonant climax of its own. Then the first phrase of 'Lasciatemi morire' returns, but is never allowed to complete itself, as 'E chi volete voi' comes in with renewed tone on the full ensemble. Only then is a *da capo* allowed to bring a state of despair and rest. In a way this is more expressive than the original, and although the very complex rhythms of the later parts of the lament hardly seem appropriate for domestic music-making, it is one of the heights of Monteverdi's madrigal writing.

---

[3]For Doni's comments and criticisms (made in the *Trattato della musica scenica*, written 1633–5), see Fabbri, *Monteverdi*, pp. 193, 382 (n. 27).

Monteverdi's arrangement of the piece is so good that there is only one thing which might make us suspect that the lament is part of a longer work. It is too intense. From its dissonant beginning to the turbulent final section there is scarcely a relaxed moment, and this robs the piece of some of the pathos which may well have been part of the original *scena*. In arranging the lament Monteverdi has clearly kept the moments of highest tension and cut away the rest. From this point of view, the other lament, 'Incenerite spoglie, avara tomba', is formally better, for it works towards its climaxes from points of rest and alternates the tragic exclamations with less subjective phrases. Several observers have pointed out that it would be possible to arrange the piece as a monody without much alteration, and this is certainly true of the first section, in which the tenor stands out against the *tutti* and in declamatory phrases sings of the shepherd's grief.

But this, after all, is something which would be said of many of the declamatory madrigals of Wert and a number of the madrigals from Monteverdi's earlier books, and it is as the successor of these that we must discuss 'Incenerite spoglie'. It opens rather like 'Era l'anima mia' with a chant setting the scene – the shepherd weeping beside the tomb of his beloved. His cry 'Ahi lasso' ('Ah! alas') breaks in on the chant with a madrigalian symbol which is all the more effective for its context:

Ex. 18

Then in a manner very similar to the madrigals in Book IV the declamation returns, but with varied vocal colouring in different trio combinations. In one way these trios are very different from the earlier madrigals. There is no attempt to make the words clear, and often the bass part of the trio sings a completely different phrase from the others.

The mastery of Book IV, however, is in evidence. Using but a single line of the poem, Monteverdi builds up a tense atmosphere, now allowing the phrase to complete itself, now breaking it off, now giving it a new ending or speeding it up to bring it to the cadence. In the later sections Monteverdi adds a device most affecting in its simplicity. While most of the voices declaim continuously, one or two voices break off to exclaim 'Ahi morte' ('Ah death') or 'Ahi Corinna', so insistently that the other voices too in the end take up the plaint. Also unlike the earlier madrigals is the comparative lack of dissonance. Nor is chromaticism used a great deal, either for sudden changes or large-scale modulations. Only towards the end of the fourth section is there anything like the harmonic astringency which is often associated with Monteverdi, and here again the very restraint in the rest of the cycle makes the moment of anguish even more agonized, as the double suspensions and pedal notes bring the musical climax. The result is very different from the *Lamento d'Arianna*. Less obviously powerful, the cycle is by no means inferior, and it is as moving in its pathetic helplessness as any of Monteverdi's madrigals.

These two laments, with two shorter numbers in much the same mood, take up about two-thirds of the book. It is tempting to see reflected in them the emotions of Monteverdi's later troubled years at Mantua (and 'Incenerite spoglie' does indeed commemorate the death of Caterina Martinelli). But just as Beethoven could write an *Eroica* and a fourth symphony together, so we find in this sixth book of madrigals a lighter vein which shows that Monteverdi was still the complete master of all expressive music. In one of the conventional madrigals he even returns to the development of the canzonet. 'Zefiro torna e'l bel tempo rimena' goes back to Petrarch for its poem, and to an *a cappella* texture for its music. Conventional, however, is not quite the word for it, because its first section is in triple time, something very rare in *a cappella* madrigals, and the decorations in the upper voices which round off each section never happened in former times. Both are reflections of the newer monodies – the triple time now a favourite for ariettas, the ornaments conventional for all music. All the old skill is there, with the contrasts of the poem brought out between lengthy sections as always, and the ending 'Sono un deserto e fere aspr'e selvagge' ('are a desert and rough, wild animals') is a recollection of Wert's setting of another Petrarch sonnet, 'Solo e pensoso, i più deserti campi'.

There are no such backward glances in the style of 'Qui rise, o Tirsi, e qui ver me rivolse', a joyous *concertato* madrigal and a proper successor to 'Ahi come a un vago sol cortese giro'. The form again is a series of duets and trios separated by the *tutti* singing an ecstatic refrain, 'O happy memory, o happy day' ('O memoria felice, o lieto giorno'). This little refrain is in the style of the *tutti* sections of the madrigals of the earlier books (it is very like 'O Mirtillo, Mirtillo anima mia'). The duet sections, on the other hand, are modern and show an increasing grasp of the new medium. Instead of the mainly declamatory style of 'Ahi come a un vago sol', Monteverdi enjoys the resources of florid melody to the full, using dotted rhythms and roulades with the greatest freedom. These ornaments appear consistently throughout the phrases, forming sequences which give a firm shape to the melody. The duet texture itself is used splendidly. Plain writing in thirds and sixths which fills out the harmony is the staple fare; but instead of the rather dull results which come through the excessive use of these cloying intervals in the *Scherzi musicali*, Monteverdi now knows exactly how to offset them by breaking forth into counterpoint. How effective, for example, is the following climax to a duet section for tenors after about eight bars of movement in thirds; it comes about not just because of the florid melody but also because the second tenor has simply moved one beat later than the first:

Ex. 19

(. . . a bosom gathers.)

In spite of this more cheerful music the total impression of the volume is one of tragic power, which seems to be Monteverdi's more familiar vein. To this period we must also ascribe yet another monodic lament, the *Lamento di Olimpia*.[4] Written in three sections to words inspired by a scene in Ariosto's *Orlando furioso*, it is clearly an offshoot of the success made by the *Lamento d'Arianna*. The same short, memorable phrases, the same use of emotional falling intervals, the same tendency for the harmony and melody to be slightly at odds make it a fine piece. It is a worthy companion to the similar laments of contemporary composers such as Sigismondo d'India.

Yet pure monody of this sort still seems to have interested Monteverdi comparatively little. Admittedly the title of the next madrigal book is *Concerto: settimo libro de madrigali a 1, 2, 3, 4 & sei voci, con altri generi de canti* (1619). We might expect now, only seventeen years after Caccini's *Le nuove musiche* appeared, to see Monteverdi's contribution to the history of monody. The contents reveal that we are likely to be disappointed. Only four out of over thirty works are for solo voice and only two of these are for the simple combination of voice and keyboard. The other two demand some form of instrumental accompaniment or intervention. The rest of these madrigals are duets, trios and ensemble music of various kinds, including the ballet *Tirsi e Clori*, which, as we shall see in a later chapter, belongs to the madrigalesque genre only in the way that some of the great choruses for plays which appeared in other composers' madrigal books throughout the sixteenth century did. The very shape of the book is most unusual, and although we can find a similar *mélange* in the work of another senior composer – Marco da Gagliano's *Musiche a una, dua e tre voci* (Venice, 1615), which also contains monodies, duets and a *balletto* – even in this there is not quite the rich diversity of Monteverdi's set.

The works for solo voice are emotionally the least significant, although all are interesting in some way. The two most difficult for the twentieth-century musician to understand are the *lettera amorosa* and *partenza amorosa*, written in the recitative-style *genere rappresentativo* (or theatrical manner) and designed to be sung in a free rhythm. These are 'academic' monodies of the most severe kind, and it is rather surprising to find that they are so different from the climaxes of the operas. More ingratiating is the first work in the volume, 'Tempro la cetra, e per cantar gli honori'. This is an aria in a sense that the word had been used by the Florentines – a set of

[4]On the attribution, see page 203.

strophic variations. There are four verses to be set, and the bass part of each is kept roughly the same (there are minor changes of rhythm). Over this the singer develops his theme. He has taken the lyre to sing to the glory of Mars, but as the first verse ends, he declares that all he can sing of is love. Each verse contrasts the images of war and love and gives the singer the opportunity for varying the melody. In each verse he increases the expressiveness of the ornaments, until the last stanza brings forth the *trillo* and the whole repertory of *gorgie*. To offset this, Monteverdi provides a little *ritornello* for five unnamed instruments, in the manner of *Orfeo*. As it is repeated between the verses, it seems little more than a conventional device; and then, as it seems to be about to bring the piece to an end, Monteverdi adds a little dance which is given twice before the *ritornello* finally does end the piece. The work is obviously an offshoot of Orpheus' aria to Charon, although more simple in its decoration and less intense, more playful in mood.

The fourth solo work is unique. 'Con che soavità, labbra adorate' is written for a soprano accompanied by three groups of instruments. The first consists only of *continuo* instruments – two *chitarroni*, a harpsichord and a spinet; the second, three upper string instruments and a harpsichord; the third, three lower strings with an organ. The conception is based on the dialogues which were so popular in both church music and chamber monody; but instead of a voice with each group of instruments Monteverdi gives the words to a single voice, which sings virtually continuously. As usual when he grafts a new idea on to old forms, his inspiration runs high. The comparatively slow-moving harmonies traditional in dialogues, to accommodate the large forces performing them, fit exactly the work's mood suggested by the word 'soavità' ('sweetness') in the opening phrase. But then the passion of the lover's kisses comes to life suddenly and powerfully in the contrasts which can be conjured up with the three instrumental groups. The vocal melody, by using the repetitions which are so much part of the dialogue form, is magically organized, always *arioso* rather than recitative in its steady rhythms and tight phrase structure. There is no need for extravagant decoration or severe dissonance. As a result the piece is one of the most contented of love madrigals, never violent yet never frivolous. It is a pity it is not more widely known, though perhaps understandable since the resources needed for its performance are not easy to come by.

The most notable masterpieces of the book, however, are the duets. They take up about half the volume and several of them seem in their emotional richness to hark back to the greatness of Book IV. It is not surprising that Monteverdi took to the medium so well. As we have seen, much of his earlier work had used the duet texture for long stretches even though it retained the variety inherent in larger resources; and duets suited him better than pure monodic writing. Fullness of harmony and expanded forms came out of the duet more easily than from the solo. Monteverdi borrowed what he required from the monody, but these duets are essentially a development of his earlier quasi-contrapuntal style. This will be clearer if we compare his duets with some by Marco da Gagliano. There are several in Gagliano's *Musiche*, and they divide quite naturally into slightly built strophic songs and more serious and complicated *continuo* madrigals. The strophic songs are clearly ariettas, with a melody, a bass, and the second voice filling in. Short phrases and regular harmonic changes give a pleasant tunefulness, and variety is worked in by the instrumental interludes, which, however, never break up the phrase structure and seem to belong to the melody of the voice. The serious duets are another matter. They are declamatory, use the *gorgia* for the normal monodic expressiveness and have slower moving harmony. Here again, there are repeated sections where the voices change parts as had been customary in canzonets and balletts for a long time.

To compare Gagliano's slighter duets with Monteverdi's 'Chiome d'oro' is perhaps unfair, since Monteverdi's work seems on a so much more extended scale; but the works are similar, and 'Chiome d'oro' is really an extension of the style of the *Scherzi musicali*, which certainly are comparable. The idea of instrumental *ritornelli* has been taken from the *Scherzi musicali* and the actual form of the duet also reminds us of them for it is in essence a strophic song with everything repeated twice. But there are some important differences. The *ritornello* is quite a complicated piece with three closely related strains, and instead of using all of it between the sung verses, Monteverdi uses the strains separately in between various lines of the poem. The vocal melody itself is superb, using the dotted rhythms which had previously been ornaments so consistently that they became the whole springboard of the tune. Typically for Monteverdi, though much of the time the voices sing in thirds with one another, they interchange occasionally and add little roulades which mean that both are entirely necessary and that the piece is thus a genuine duet. Typical too are the two little cadenzas, as they seem to be, at the end of each stanza – typical, for they insert into a song of flirtation a touch of deeper feeling, without ever being heavy or sentimental.

The more serious works explore the resources of the duet even more thoroughly. The one which at first sight seems nearest to monody is 'Interrotte speranze, eterna fede'; and yet this is a work far away from Florence. It is a song of a spurned lover whose hope and faith merely raise his desire. It begins with a pedal note in the bass. Over this two tenors begin the plaint, chanting on the same note. In a way which Monteverdi had used in his earlier madrigals, dissonances are produced by the upper part moving up a tone and thrusting the lower part down. These dissonances and the rise in the melody, the sustained pedal note, the broken phrases, the low *tessitura* for the voices, all establish the psychology of the despairing, desiring lover in a very powerful way. And then, when the pedal note has changed and the cadence has provided relief, Monteverdi repeats all this nervous material, only with altered, even more intense declamation. This cannot be kept up, and the music relaxes with a dialogue and more sober thoughts about the beloved. Only at the end are the dissonances resumed to twist the knife in our hearts:

Ex. 20

(and my funeral pyre.)

In this duet it is the declamatory opening with the static bass that gives the appearance of monody; and it is possible to find many similar places in the duets of this volume. The expressive ornamentation also seems 'monodic' at first sight, and so do the sudden changes of harmony. But in fact the real power of these emotionally rich works lies in their derivation from older sources. The scale is achieved essentially by the methods of the older madrigal books, that is by repeating sections of varying lengths with new tone colouring. In 'Perchè fuggi tra salci, ritrosetta', for example, almost every melodic phrase is repeated – not with a sterile one-voice-after-the-other method, but by using the second voice in the repetitions to add new counterpoints, enriching the harmony and timbre. As for the ornamentation, it is less 'monodic', or based on the expression of a single word or phrase, than an integral part of the melody – a dotted rhythm repeated again and again to balance the phrase, or a *portamento* which comes in each voice in turn to become a memorable fragment to shape the melody (as in 'Ecco vicine, o bella tigre, l'hore'). This is nearer the continuous application of ornament which was so common in the sixteenth century, though, it must be said, with the application of much more purpose and skill than the improvising singers can ever have achieved. Out of virtuosity has come a rhythmical melody which can truly be called tuneful.

All these duets are fine, and they show a very wide emotional range. The flirtatious 'Tornate, o cari baci' with its refrain of kisses, the richly decorated 'O come sei gentile' for two virtuoso ladies or the more serious kisses of 'Perchè fuggi tra salci' form a splendid treasure which is every bit as deserving of revival as the early polyphonic madrigals. All are rewarding and only one of them can be mentioned as standing out from the rest – the set of variations on the *romanesca* theme, 'Ohimè, dov'è il mio ben, dov'è il mio core?' The idea is borrowed from the song-books, for the duet is a set of strophic variations. There are four sections, each with the same stock bass, over which two tenors sing the lament, 'Where has my beloved gone, where is my heart?' The words remind us of the *Lamento d'Arianna*, and so does the music. The first section, with its short, stabbing phrases intensified with dissonance between the voices, has the same bitter agony. If anything, the agony is greater, as the imitations between the voices expand the scale and make pure declamation unnecessary by their overlapping rhythms. As in the earlier work, Monteverdi uses a refrain technique to make the music highly taut. The bass itself suggests this by a repeated cadential figure, but the repetitions in the melody are of greater length than those of the bass, and Monteverdi glories in the clashes which necessarily arise. Even more remarkable is the command of harmony which gives the piece its emotional variety. The final cadence in each successive verse expresses in turn despair, agony, the sweetness of hope and the finality of death:

Ex. 21

(and who takes her from me?)

(. . . trifling wishes.)

It was another thirteen years before a new madrigal book of Monteverdi's appeared. They were years in which the nature of secular music changed completely. The serious monodic madrigals of the Florentine and Roman virtuosos went out of fashion, and a taste arose for the simpler, more obviously popular songs. Monteverdi's younger assistants at St Mark's were especially good at composing these. Giovanni Pietro Berti and Alessandro Grandi published some song-books in which tunefulness is all. Light rhythms, regular phrases, clear-cut diatonic harmonies became the order of the day. The verse was if anything even more trivial than the canzonet verse of the sixteenth century. In the more serious songs there are sometimes passages in the older declamatory style, but they often end with a gay triple-time section to provide easily memorable music (giving a division into recitative and aria, which became familiar later on). When more complicated music was required, it was usually given the form of the strophic variation, with the bass repeated in the manner of Caccini; or else an *ostinato* bass was employed. It is doubtful whether Monteverdi really cared very much for this frothy music, in which the academic theories of the earlier composers of monody had completely disappeared. Yet it was too important and popular for him to be able to ignore it. He contributed some eight pieces to various Venetian anthologies; and the book of *Scherzi musicali* which came out in 1632 (significantly with a dedication by the publisher Bartolomeo Magni, who clearly had gathered the collection together himself, a sign perhaps of Monteverdi's indifference) is in fact a book of arias in this new style.

The simplest of these songs are as near as Monteverdi ever went to writing in a purely conventional style. Catchy little tunes to insignificant verses, they have the charm of their genre but little individuality. The only way they can be said to differ from the works of many lesser composers is that Monteverdi can never resist the temptation to 'paint' the words, even if it breaks up the balance of phrases and the general mood of the song. A little chromatic passage to illustrate the word 'dying' or a succession of dissonances to express the cruelty of the lady intrude themselves. The strophic-variation arias can accommodate these old-fashioned methods better, allowing for melodic variety in each verse, and Monteverdi usually adds a little *ritornello* for instruments in between, to give still more subtle emotional opportunities. 'Et è pur dunque vero' is a good example of the style, the same bass allowing ample scope for melodic devices to express the weeping of the lover and the triumph and apparent indifference of the beloved, interspersed with a host of natural images such as the murmuring of the wind.

But as usual, Monteverdi's full inspiration is best found in ensemble music and especially in the duets, now clearly his favourite medium. The editor of one anthology published in 1624, Giovanni

Battista Anselmi, was very lucky to be given such a fine piece as 'O come vaghi, o come'. The poem is the conventional nonsense about Lydia and her eyes being wounding darts; but Monteverdi draws from it all its meaning and gives it a depth it scarcely deserves. First there comes the rich sound of two tenors singing in thirds, and then as the lover is bewitched they split up, and in alert, lightly imitative phrases build up a climax. As the rays from Lydia's eyes become little arrows Monteverdi invents a motif which in pure sound, a dental consonant followed by a smooth vowel melisma, shoots out in a strikingly realistic way, multiplies in imitations between the voices and then, as the lover is wounded, is lost in dissonances. The harmonies become astringent as the pain increases:

Ex. 22

(you kill them with pain and grief.)

Then quite suddenly the sweetness of love is felt, and with a motif reminiscent of the beginning of 'O Mirtillo, Mirtillo anima mia' a consonant and still section ends the duet, disturbed only by the cadential dissonance, as the 'dying' of the lover is mentioned in the poem. This is a subtle piece of erotic music, which, like some of the earlier madrigals from Book IV, is effortless in passing from flirtation to true love, from love's climax to perfect peace.

Of the other duets from this period, 'Zefiro torna, e di soavi accenti' (in the 1632 *Scherzi musicali*) is deservedly famous. The poem is not the usual one by Petrarch, which Monteverdi had set in Book VI. It is a sort of 'parody' (in the sixteenth-century sense) of it by Ottavio Rinuccini and, most important, keeps the same contrast between joyful nature and the lover abandoned to his doleful thoughts. Monteverdi sets this as a chaconne, using an *ostinato* bass pattern very popular about this time:

Ex. 23

The form is a difficult one. The shortness of the bass pattern (compared with others such as the *romanesca*) means short phrase-lengths which can become tiresome, and the harmonies are not easily varied enough for an extended piece. Monteverdi conquers these problems magnificently. His first paragraph lasts a dozen bars, as each voice replies with a variant of the initial theme; and then the sweetness of the breeze, slightly syncopated, is expressed by a succession of pure consonances. There are gentle roulades for the murmuring waves, pictorial motifs for the valleys and mountains (complete with the echo device), in fact all the imagery of 'Ecco mormorar l'onde' in the form of a duet. Then, as the lover speaks of his plight, a piece of recitative with dissonances is ushered in with a great chromatic change, brought to a peaceful end as the lover sings praise of his lady's eyes in an ornamental, sonorous passage with trills and scales in thirds. The technical mastery of the piece is astonishing. Out of conventional features – the *ostinato* bass, the by now customary division into speech-rhythm recitative and dance-rhythm aria, echo music and so on – Monteverdi builds up a vivid picture, and one which proves him to be a composer by no means *semper dolens*.

The remainder of his vernacular settings appeared in three collections, an eighth book of madrigals (1638), the *Selva morale e spirituale* (1640–1) and a posthumous collection put out by Alessandro Vincenti in 1651. It is impossible to date the individual numbers. All that can be certain is that they were composed over a considerable space of time, probably between about 1625 and 1635.

Those of the trios which Vincenti put out in 1651 seem to belong in atmosphere to the lightest of the 1632 *Scherzi musicali*. They are gay dance songs with strong rhythms and tonalities typical of the trivia common in Venice around 1630. They are usually strophic songs, sometimes given a little variety by each of the three singers in turn having a little solo at the beginning of the verse, sometimes plainly repetitive. Most of them are either written completely or for a large part in triple time, although one or two divide into recitative and dance-song as in so many arias of Giovanni Pietro Berti, Tarquinio Merula and other minor composers of the time.

These works might make us believe that Monteverdi had surrendered the high ideals of music gained in the academies of his youth. He had certainly not followed blindly the ideas of the Florentine 'camerata' composers and the 'advanced' madrigalists; but the old ideas were in his mind to the end. The eighth book of madrigals has a new title: *Madrigali guerrieri, et amorosi*, not forgetting a preface which carefully explained the contents:

> I have reflected that the principal passions or affections of our mind are three, namely, anger, moderation and humility or supplication; so the best philosophers declare, and the very nature of our voice indicates this in having high, low and middle registers. The art of music also points clearly to these three in its terms 'agitated', 'soft' and 'moderate' [*concitato, molle* and *temperato*]. In all the works of former composers I have indeed found examples of the 'soft' and the 'moderate', but never of the 'agitated', a genus nevertheless described by Plato in the third book of his *Rhetoric* in these words: 'Take that harmony that would fittingly imitate the utterances and the accents of a brave man who is engaged in warfare.' And since I was aware that it is contraries which greatly move our mind, and that this is the purpose which all good music should have – as Boethius asserts, saying; 'Music is related to us and either ennobles or corrupts the character' – for this reason I have applied myself with no small diligence and toil to rediscover this genus.
>
> After reflecting that according to all the best philosophers the fast pyrrhic measure was used for lively and warlike dances, and the slow spondaic measure for their opposites, I considered the semibreve, and proposed that a single semibreve should correspond to one spondaic beat; when this was reduced to sixteen semiquavers struck one after the other and combined with words expressing anger and disdain, I recognized in this brief sample a resemblance to the passion which I sought, although the words did not follow metrically the rapidity of the instrument.
>
> To obtain a better proof I took the divine Tasso as a poet who expresses with the greatest propriety and naturalness the qualities

which he wishes to describe, and selected his description of the combat of Tancred and Clorinda as an opportunity of describing in music contrary passions, namely, warfare and entreaty and death. In the year 1624 I caused this composition to be performed in the noble house of my especial patron and indulgent protector the Most Illustrious and Excellent Signor Girolamo Mocenigo, an eminent dignitary in the service of the Most Serene Republic, and it was received by the best citizens of the noble city of Venice with much applause and praise . . .

My rediscovery of this warlike genus has given me occasion to write certain madrigals which I have called *guerrieri*. And since the music played before great princes at their courts to please their delicate taste is of three kinds according to the method of performance – theatre music, chamber music and dance music – I have indicated these in my present work with the titles *guerriera*, *amorosa* and *rappresentativa*.[5]

If ever a madrigal book required some sort of explanation it is this one. It puzzles us today; it probably puzzled Monteverdi's contemporaries nearly as much. Instead of the usual chamber music for a few voices and instruments this one contains some big choral works and three dramatic ones (one, a ballet written thirty years earlier) as well as duets and trios. Then the arrangement into madrigals of war and those of love was unique. All madrigals (more or less) dealt with love: but what were warlike madrigals? No wonder the volume was never reprinted.

We might well dismiss the warlike part of the volume as speculative compositions to demonstrate a theory if it were not for two things. One is that Monteverdi had always liked concrete imagery in the verse he set and managed to put it into realistic music. Then warlike music was not by any means new, although the audience of the 1620s and 1630s may not have remembered it. In the sixteenth century there had been a vogue of battle pieces, started by Clément Janequin's *La Bataille de Marignan*. By the second half of the century the vogue had reached Venice and two of the St Mark's musicians, Annibale Padovano and Andrea Gabrieli, wrote instrumental pieces called *arie della battaglia* for the Venetian wind band. Fanfares and military calls of various kinds were the stuff of this music, which was a form of elementary realism; and these pieces had an immense popularity in the 1590s. Monteverdi must have known them, but he would only use their methods after he had justified himself on theoretical grounds.

The works for a few voices from the 'warlike' part of the eighth book are the nearest to his normal style. One of them, 'Armato il cor

---

[5]Translated in Strunk, *Source Readings in Music History*, pp. 413–15. For Plato's *Rhetoric*, read *Republic* (399a).

d'adamantina fede' had been included by Magni in the 1632 *Scherzi musicali*, where it hardly seems out of place; and the other duet, 'Se vittorie sì belle', also seems at first sight reasonably normal. Neither piece is a description of a battle. Both are settings of love poems with conventional warlike metaphors (as had been 'Non più guerra, pietate' in Book IV); and both have the natural division between a fight and possible victory, and defeat and the wounds of death. There is no novelty in this, and seemingly not much in the music with its extended triple-time passages and contrasting, less rhythmic sections; and if there is some realistic musical imagery, this is, as we have seen, quite normal for Monteverdi.

Nevertheless there are differences. The warlike sections, built up from melodic fanfare arpeggios, are much simpler than anything we find in such duets as 'Interrotte speranze, eterna fede' and 'Tornate, o cari baci' from the seventh book. The harmonies are almost completely consonant and huge sections use two or three common chords, tonic and dominant predominating. Syncopations are rare, the rhythms being very straightforward and dance-like. The supposedly contrasting sections, where victory is in doubt and the poet is preoccupied with love's wounds, are equally unusual. Instead of the normal dissonances, Monteverdi maintains a remarkably pure harmony (again full of sequences and other devices which emphasize a diatonic key structure). 'Se vittorie sì belle' ends with a peaceful passage which completely ignores the implication of 'morir' ('death'):

Ex. 24

(it is glorious to die for the desire of victory.)

The result is curiously new. These works are completely Monteverdian, with all the old skills of creating a live, large-scale music which closely follows the sense of the words, but it is Monteverdi without the eroticism of his earlier works. In action or calmness, the works are extrovert, the images of the verse accepted at their face value rather than intensified as symbols of the lover's inner feelings.

Much the same may be said about the madrigals for six or more voices and instruments, although here the interest is often intensified by the splendid sonorities which are possible with a large group. 'Ardo, avvampo, mi struggo, ardo: accorrete', for example, builds up a tremendous power in its first section, starting with two tenors, then adding two sopranos and finally four more voices and two violins. The first twenty-seven bars are simple repetitions of the G major chord, and the rest of this section is built from the simplest harmonic and melodic material. In 'Altri canti d'Amor, tenero arciero' a similar effect is used in a big choral section, the fanfare material again well to the fore. These passages are thrilling, and yet the total effect of the madrigals is a little disappointing. They are too loosely organized, unlike Monteverdi's earlier *continuo* madrigals. It is customary to call them cantatas rather than madrigals, which means that they are sectional in construction. 'Altri canti d'Amor', for example, has an overture, a trio, a central chorus, a bass solo accompanied by strings and a final chorus, all reasonably independent, though the final section grows out of the bass aria. The basic idea behind this kind of work came from the *concertato* motet, and like many of these it has too little sense of unity and climax for the form to be entirely satisfactory. The sections are not in themselves complete or well enough organized to stand as entities, but they seem to have distracted the composer from a satisfying overall construction. The problem is exactly the same one that Monteverdi had failed to solve completely in his first madrigal book. Clearly it took him a little time to gain the necessary experience with a new form.

The most successful piece in this style is one which approaches his earlier madrigals. 'Hor che'l ciel e la terra e'l vento tace' is a setting of a poem by Petrarch, a sonnet which Monteverdi might have set at any time in his life. The lover cannot sleep, although heaven, earth and the wind are all silent. But his mind is at war within itself and only the thought of his beloved can bring peace. The image of war is only incidental to the theme, and so it appears in the music. The madrigal opens with a *parlando* section expressing the stillness of nature, very like those in the madrigals of Wert which had influenced Monteverdi in his youth. The colour of the voices – low in range – gives a magical, dark touch; and suddenly from this comes the dissonant, strident, curt lover's plaint, intensified in a duet for tenors. This is again very much in Monteverdi's older vein, and the only sign of the *stile concitato* comes in the passage actually setting the word 'guerra' ('war'). The passage is transient and gives way to a homophony expressive of the lover's peace while thinking about his lady. The madrigal which forms the second part of the setting is even more old-fashioned. For long passages the *basso continuo* could be removed and the harmony would remain complete. The eroticism is back, too, with chromatic scales imitated throughout the parts and declamatory sections repeated again and again to give the meaning to the words 'a thousand times a day I die, and a thousand I am reborn' ('mille volte il dì moro, e mille nasco').

'Hor che'l ciel e la terra' is successful because it really belongs to the *canti amorosi*, and in fact it is the second part of the eighth book that contains the most rewarding works. The madrigals for five or more voices are, as in the first part, less emotionally rich than the duets and trios, but they have a charm of their own. The two pieces marked 'alla Francese' are especially fresh, and 'Dolcissimo uscignolo' is very effective, a charming melody given strength by the firm organization of alternating solo and *tutti* passages; and with some episodes tending towards the minor there is a touch of wistfulness which adds flavour to an otherwise contented and sweet-sounding piece. The same thing can be said of 'Vago augelletto che cantando vai', in which a small group of strings is added to the seven voices. The solo-tutti relationship is kept up and turned into a rondo form, and although there are some symbolic and more passionate bars for the words 'weeping over times past' ('piangendo il tuo tempo passato'), the same anacreontic spirit permeates the music.

The more intimate pieces – duets, trios and one quartet – are very different, and it is in these that Monteverdi's madrigalian art reaches its second climax. The trios are the lightest of the music – triple-time dance-songs in the manner of a Venetian arietta but very deliberately handled and among the best of the genre. 'Ninfa che scalza il piede e sciolto il crine' is a splendid example. One tenor first sings an arietta, with happy, regular rhythm organized into short repetitive motifs that remind us of *Tirsi e Clori*. A second tenor joins in for a new section as the lovers come together: and a touch of syncopation livens up the dance. Finally a bass is introduced and the dance continues, made more exciting by the gentle imitations in which the parts tumble one after another. And then, without interrupting the triple rhythm, a typically Monteverdian touch, the voices turn to the minor to proclaim the harshness of the beloved, and with a dissonance here and there one voice or another anticipates the harmonies of the others.

The trios show one side of Monteverdi's musical character; the duets are equally typical of others. One of them, 'Mentre vaga Angioletta', is a setting of a poem in praise of music and gives the composer every chance of showing off the clever external manner well known from 'Zefiro torna, e di soavi accenti'. 'Murmuring' ('mormorando'), 'alternating flights' ('alternando fughe'), 'tremulous and wandering passages' ('modi tremoli e vaganti') – one can imagine Monteverdi's delight in these opportunities for word-painting. He takes them all and gives the voices their opportunities in richly ornamented lines. The most deeply felt duets, on the other hand, are two which are shorter and in the erotic tradition. 'Ardo e scoprir, ahi lasso, io non ardisco', and 'O sia tranquillo il mare, o pien d'orgoglio' are such fine works that it is not surprising that Alessandro Vincenti printed them again in his volume of 1651. 'Ardo e scoprir' is in the tradition of 'O come vaghi, o come' and 'Interrotte speranze, eterna fede'. 'I burn', cries the poet, 'but I burn more since I dare not tell of my passion.' Monteverdi sets this with an expansive

Ex. 25

gesture, the harmonies remaining on the chord of D minor as the voices rise to an immediate climax. They die away in dissonance (as usual arrived at by separating the voices in an imitative section) as courage fails (see Ex. 25). The poet dares to call for help and the music surges to the upper register of the voices. It is useless, for when he is with his lady he would like to speak (a repeated fragment which breaks off suddenly) and dare not. He only trembles, and as he starts to tell of his love the words are broken on his lips:

Ex. 26

There is realism in this madrigal, but it is an inner psychological reality, an expansion of the verbal imagery made vivid especially by the sudden changes of vocal range, the growth and breaking off of the melody. 'O sia tranquillo il mare, o pien d'orgoglio' is cast in the same emotional mould, although its technique is different. The poet never leaves the cliff top, whether the sea is calm or troubled, as he laments the loss of his beloved; but Phyllis never returns, and his laments and prayers are carried away on the wind. Monteverdi, again following the Venetian aria composers, divides the piece into a recitative followed by a triple-time aria. The recitative (not perhaps a truly accurate description of it since it is always rhythmic; but it is declamatory) sets the scene: calm chords for the tranquil sea, dissonance for the lament, a cry of agony as he weeps: then the aria, not a cheerful dance as so often in these triple-time pieces, rather a lost bewailing in the words 'You do not return, my Phyllis, oh, you do not return' ('Ma tu non torni, o Filli'), which are repeated again and again – sometimes in a continuous flowing melody, sometimes broken short and left to suggest mere exhaustion.

These duets are masterpieces, and there is one more great work in the book. This is the *Lamento della ninfa*, written for a soprano and three male voices. Monteverdi calls it a work in the *stile rappresenta-tivo* or theatrical style, but it needs no acting, any more than did the madrigal comedies by Orazio Vecchi and Adriano Banchieri of earlier years. The men tell us the story. A nymph is lamenting outside her dwelling the loss of her lover. They are objective, though sympathetic, and their music is there only to prepare for the second stage, the nymph's lament. This is a piece which defies description or quotation. It is a chaconne with a short bass pattern (a descending tetrachord) repeated thirty-four times. Over this the nymph cries out against her fate and the lover who has deserted her. Sometimes the men commiserate with her, one by one, or all together. They never join in her song, which is too heartfelt for anyone but her. At the end she is left by herself. Always the bass figure goes on as before, reminding her and us that her fate is eternal and that she will always be alone. There is dissonance and marvellously expressive melody, the more passionate because it is in the triple time of the dance measure, while always avoiding the strong accents of the aria, and Monteverdi tells the singer to sing it not in strict time but 'according to the emotion' ('a tempo del'affetto del animo'). None of these devices is in itself remarkable but together they make the piece unforgettable; and when the epilogue is sung by the men in the same objective style as the prologue, the contrast is sharp, the lament being made almost unbearably intense.

The eighth book is a worthy end to the series. Like the other volumes, it is never purely fashionable, nor artificially difficult or experimental. It is impossible to discuss the madrigal as a single form, for Monteverdi managed to adapt it to a variety of purposes; and it is not very helpful to call these later works cantatas, as though they were quite different from the earlier music. It is equally unsatisfactory to assume that Monteverdi's development is in fact the development of all music over the half-century. There is one principle which informs all Monteverdi's madrigals. He would have called it 'imitation'. We may call it fidelity to the truth of the poetry. Taught him in the academies of Mantua, he never forgot it, even when his younger contemporaries bothered about it very little. It made him take the madrigal seriously to the end of his life, even in the lightest of canzonets and arias. In the madrigal there was freedom to choose the verse which music could enhance, to give an even greater variety than was possible in opera, much less in church music. For his madrigals Monteverdi deserves a proud title: a great humanist.

6

The dramatic music

Opera was very new in 1607. *Orfeo* was to be the sixth *dramma per musica* ever written.[1] To Monteverdi the form was even newer. He may have seen one of the first Florentine operas, Peri's *Euridice* (1600), or he may have studied its score – that was all. But if opera was new, dramatic music was not; plays with music were extremely common, especially in the free courts of northern Italy. Mantua was famed for its players, Ferrara and Venice for their court entertainments. The fashionable plays at these courts by the early years of the seventeenth century were the pastorals. To the English the pastoral idiom is best known through the lyric poetry of *Comus* and *Lycidas*; or in the dramatic form in *As You Like It*, where Shakespeare gently pokes fun at its conventions. The scene is always an idealized countryside, the characters are shepherds and shepherdesses. The main subject-matter is love, at first frustrated by circumstance but eventually brought to a happy ending. The shepherdess Sylvia refuses to love the shepherd Amyntas who loves her. At the climax of the play Sylvia will be reported dead, killed by a wolf, or in some other accident. Amyntas, given this news by a messenger, will despair and go away to commit suicide; whereupon Sylvia will reappear and realize on hearing of her lover's fate that she really loves him. Finally, Amyntas will come back, having failed to kill himself, and the pair will be happily united. Add to this a host of confidants, some gods and goddesses to speak a prologue and intervene at vital moments, and we have the recipe for the pastoral play.

Taken as drama the pastoral is usually far too slow and often preposterous. It is quite impossible to believe in these idealized shepherds who speak in beautiful lyrical verse and whose main interest is to convey hopeless passion at some length. When Shakespeare borrowed the pastoral idea he took care to insert some

[1]*Orfeo* was preceded by Jacopo Peri's *Dafne* (Florence, 1598), Emilio de' Cavalieri's *Rappresentatione di anima, et di corpo* (Rome, 1600), Peri's *Euridice* (Florence, 1600; performed with some music by Giulio Caccini), Caccini's *Euridice* (published 1600; first performed Florence, 1602), and Agostino Agazzari's *Eumelio* (Rome, 1606).

real yokels, who at least have some action in them. But such criticisms are rather beside the point. The pastorals were not considered purely as drama, and in reading them today we have only the bare bones of the entertainment. Its flesh was ornate scenery, machines and a great deal of elaborate music. The spectacle was especially important, and no expense was spared. Today it is difficult to imagine the splendour of the scene. How can we re-create in our minds the wonder and delight of the audience when they saw 'a vast and most lovely canvas painted with various animals hunted and taken in divers ways, which, upheld by a great cornice and concealing the prospect scene' took up the whole of one end of a great hall? Or their amazement at the perspective scenes in which the woods and fields seemed to stretch back to the distant horizon? Or the gorgeousness of the machines – clouds which opened to reveal gods and goddesses in the sky and which moved high across the stage?[2]

The music for these pastorals was almost as splendid. We never possess it in its entirety, for full scores were unknown, but some of the numbers appeared in the madrigal books. The choruses, in which the voices were joined by instrumental ensembles must have sounded magnificent. There were solo songs and some dances – as we know from one stage designer who insisted that the stage must be made solid enough to take the strain of the energetic *moresche*. And as if this spectacle in the play were not enough, there were the *intermedi* which came during the intervals and at the end of the play itself. The *intermedi* had little dramatic action and their whole interest lay in the scenic designs and the machines. The gods here came into their own, and their cloud machines were ornate beyond belief. Infernal scenes where smoke and fire effects could be used were quite common. The allegorical figures of Hope and Fear and so on were carried on the stage in floats, splendidly decorated to illustrate the theme.

Speech was less important than songs, for there was no action to be made clear. The orchestra was often large – forty players were not uncommon – and it was used dramatically. Trombones for infernal scenes, recorders for the zephyrs, and similar effects, were the stock-in-trade of the composer. Here too there were large-scale choruses and elaborate dances. Such magnificence was bound to take up the energies of composers, not to mention the attention of the audience.

[2]The best accounts of such scenic spectacles are in Nagler, *Theatre Festivals of the Medici, 1539–1637*; Pirrotta, *Music and Theatre from Poliziano to Monteverdi*.

'Once', said one playwright ruefully, '*intermedi* were made to serve the comedy, but now comedies are made to serve the *intermedi*.'[3] Someone interested mainly in drama could have said much the same about the French court ballet at the time.[4] Here again there was some dramatic action completely swamped by the interest in the spectacle. Naturally dances were of the first importance, but both drama and music had to be subordinated to the demands of the eye.

Monteverdi knew all these genres well; he was to write music for every one of them by the end of his life. But before his *Orfeo* came into existence there were the other five operas to make possible a drama set in continuous music. It is easy to see why Florentine composers and theorists were dissatisfied with dramatic music in its conventional form. The plays with music mixed up with the *intermedi* and the French court ballet were essentially distracted by spectacle from their principal aim – a truly dramatic action It is also easy to see why Jacopo Peri and Giulio Caccini used recitative, for though it is true that they misinterpreted the ideas of the Greeks, their instinct was sound. If the full power of music was given only to the static moments of the play, interest would naturally concentrate there, and the conflict of action which is the basis of drama would inevitably be lost.

To regain a sense of drama in the new form, the Florentines – the poet Ottavio Rinuccini and the composers Peri and Caccini – took to a process of simplification. In place of the complications of the pastoral play, with its sub-plots and large casts, they set the simple story of Orpheus and Eurydice to music. Admittedly they retained the pastoral idiom with a great deal of lyricism and the conventional happy ending. Orpheus finds his wife in Hades and thereafter there is no complication of losing her again. There is a prologue by an allegorical figure, Tragedy, which as we have seen was a common feature of the pastoral plays; and a messenger scene when the news of Eurydice's death is given is equally conventional. Some of the songs and choruses must also have seemed quite normal to the Florentine audience. Two features, on the other hand, are new. There is no sign of important orchestral music or the large number of instrumentalists assembled for the plays and *intermedi*. Most important of all is the recitative in which the story is carried on.

[3] Antonfrancesco Grazzini, prologue to *La strega* (1566), in Solerti, *Gli albori del melodramma*, I, p. 9.
[4] The obvious example is *Le Balet comique de la royne* of 1581: see Carol and Lander MacClintock (trans.), *Le Balet comique de la royne (1581)*, 'Musicological Studies and Documents', xxv (American Institute of Musicology, 1971).

The Florentine recitative has been much maligned. It has admittedly little variety of phrase length, since the composers nearly always stop at the end of each line of verse with a cadence. Even so, some of it is highly expressive and in the hands of intelligent singers and actors must have had an excellent effect. A juster criticism is that the composers seem to have had little conception of musical form on a broader scale. Believing that the drama must be left to do its own work, they made no attempt to build up climaxes in musical terms. There can have been little in the music that the audience found really memorable, and none of the effects which can be brought about by organizing the music into the repetitive forms which give it its great emotional possibilities. In parts the audience may well have been deeply moved by the total effect of acting and music, but it is difficult to believe that it was continuously interested.

Given this background and Monteverdi's gift for intelligent borrowing, the form and manner of his new opera were almost predictable. Alessandro Striggio, the librettist of *Orfeo*, must have known the poet Giovanni Battista Guarini, the most famous writer of pastorals, quite well, and the idiom of pastoral verse was second nature to him. In borrowing the idea of the Orpheus story in a pastoral version from the Florentines there may have been more than a small element of rivalry. What is interesting is that Striggio retained much more of the dramatic flavour in the story than Rinuccini had done.

First there is a prologue, sung by an allegorical figure, Music. The first act and a half are taken up with the rejoicing of shepherds and shepherdesses, including the hero and the heroine. This is purely in the pastoral lyrical tradition, and so is the first element of drama, the arrival of the messenger bearing the news of Eurydice's death. Orpheus' reaction is again in terms of pastoral, a lyrical despair from which he emerges only slowly when he resolves to seek her in Hades. The beginning of Act III introduces another allegorical figure, Hope, who seems to have been brought in from an *intermedio*, and Orpheus is led to the banks of the River Styx. There he is given an opportunity to persuade Charon to ferry him across to Hades. Charon eventually goes to sleep and Orpheus crosses the Styx. In the next act we see Orpheus in Hades. After a discussion between Pluto and Proserpine he is allowed to return to earth with his wife.

At this point Striggio, instead of surrendering the drama of the story as the Florentines had done, continues with it, in spite of the difficulty of ending it in the pastoral tradition. Orpheus must not look back on his journey; but 'that which Pluto forbids, Love commands' ('ciò che vieta Pluton comanda Amore'), sings Orpheus.

He looks behind him at Eurydice and his beloved wife is claimed by death. The final act presented Striggio with a problem. A pastoral had a happy ending, the Greek story its inevitable, tragic one. Striggio instinctively preferred the strength of the original to a watered-down tragi-comedy dénouement. His first version (as we learn from the printed libretto of 1607) begins the fifth act with Orpheus in the fields of Thrace, singing a song which is echoed from a rock. This is again pure pastoral; Guarini has a splendid echo scene in *Il pastor fido*. After this, Striggio leaves the pastoral convention and becomes a purist. The Bacchantes enter, and with solo and choruses bring the play to its macabre end. This, however, was too strong for Monteverdi.[5] Orpheus' echoed lament in the fields was just what he wanted. But after that he took the easier course and either wrote himself, or made Striggio write, a happy ending. The god Apollo takes pity on Orpheus and descending on a cloud takes him up to heaven, to the satisfaction of the chorus.

If this ending seems to us unsatisfactory, we must remember that it was no more preposterous than the ending of Tasso's pastoral *Aminta*, whose hero, having thrown himself over a cliff, has his fall most luckily broken half way down. Further, the last thing which the audience of a play usually saw was not the final act of the play itself, but the allegorical *intermedio* which followed it. The new ending of *Orfeo* is clearly an *intermedio*, with the stage-designer finding good use for his cloud machine. Indeed the whole opera libretto is a mixture of *intermedio* and pastoral. The first two acts and the first half of the last one are completely pastoral. The prologue, the infernal scenes and the dénouement are *intermedi*, all of them with splendid scenic opportunities. It is Striggio's achievement that the drama is still remarkably unified and in the third and fourth acts comes to a dramatic climax.

It is Monteverdi's achievement too, for he also welds the diverse musical elements which were suggested by Striggio's play into a unified structure. The first sign that he imagines opera in terms of the *intermedio* and pastoral comes in the overture, a 'toccata' to be played on the complete orchestra. The orchestra is a large one, having fifteen string players, about a dozen brass and wind, and nine *continuo* instruments – harpsichords, a harp, *chitarroni*, organs, and

[5]The sources for and implications of the two endings are discussed in Whenham (ed.), *Claudio Monteverdi: 'Orfeo'*, and see page 15, n. 13. In the first edition of this book, Denis Arnold noted the possible parallels with the situation between Giambattista Varesco and Mozart over *Idomeneo*, where the composer's emendations were sung but the librettist's original verses printed so that the honour of both should be satisfied.

a regal or reed organ. The strings are violins, violas and cellos (though there are bass viols and a contrabass viol as well), and two players have to be prepared to double on little violins (tuned an octave higher than those used today). The toccata must have sounded well, even though it is really a conventional flourish on a single chord.

When the curtain goes up to reveal the figure of Music (probably seated on some marvellously elaborate float) we hear Monteverdi's conception of monody. He uses not the pure recitative style of the Florentine operas but the *arioso* of the song-books such as Caccini's *Le nuove musiche*. Music's song is in fact an aria (in the monodists' sense), a set of strophic variations, the bass kept mainly the same for each verse while the voice varies the melody over it. The vocal melody is comparatively plain and gives its effects by different phrase-lengths and some 'affective' leaps which remind us of Monteverdi's madrigals. Intervening between each verse is a *ritornello*, a short instrumental piece rather like a pavane, to give a rondo form. There is nothing amorphous here. The music is as tightly organized as it can be, and could be played as a separate piece (it is very like 'Tempro la cetra, e per cantar gli honori' in the seventh book of madrigals).

The prologue, on the other hand, is no test of the dramatic composer. The play itself is another matter. From the beginning of the first act we can see Monteverdi's strong desire for musical variety and form. A shepherd sets the scene with some recitative. His role is narrative and he cannot be allowed a full *continuo* madrigal. Nevertheless his recitative is well organized, and two phrases catch our attention with their brevity and isolation by rests:

Ex. 27

(Let us sing, shepherds, in such sweet tones that our harmonies are worthy of Orpheus.)

When Monteverdi repeats his opening section to make a miniature *da capo* aria, it is these fragments that concentrate our attention on his formal pattern.

Then, broken only by short pieces of recitative, the shepherds' rejoicing is expressed in choruses. These are delightful. One could hardly have supposed Monteverdi capable of such charm and light-heartedness; for there is nothing like these lyrical dance-songs in the madrigal books. They are real canzonets, and are ornamental with a splendid lightness of touch which beats Gastoldi on his own ground. Orpheus breaks into them with an *arioso* – a hymn to the sun ('Rosa del ciel'). Again there is the same feeling of organization brought about, not this time by refrains, but by a balance of phrases, a similarity of rhythms and a large leap downwards to end each section. Then, to create the larger entity, Monteverdi repeats the choruses in the reverse order. As a coda he writes a chamber aria, setting three verses, one as a duet, the next as a trio and then a duet again, the bass each time kept roughly the same, with the melodies clutched by ornaments and a masterly variety of texture. And since the audience may not recognize the unity given by the bass, a *ritornello* again separates the verses to complete yet another rondo. The act ends with another chorus.

This act, lyrical in style and using established forms, must have been the easiest to write. The second act was perhaps much harder. The arrival of the messenger breaks the lyricism and demands a complete change of mood. The first part of the act continues with the shepherds' rejoicing in the same manner as before; but it is clear that some climax must be brought about, if only to strengthen the contrast with the arrival of the tragic news. Monteverdi chooses an essentially modern means to bring it about – an aria. It is an aria in both the seventeenth-century and our modern sense of the word – a strophic song with a clear-cut melody, a strong rhythm and moving bass part to provide harmonic change. It is a *hemiola* song, in much the same style as the *Scherzi musicali* of 1607, and like them provided with a *ritornello*. It has a splendid tune and could stand by itself as music; but, like all the best operatic music, it achieves its full significance only in its context. There is just time for a shepherd to praise the song and then the fateful messenger arrives.

Recitative is inevitable, for the messenger's news is narrative and must be understood; yet there is no loss of expressive power, rather the contrary. Monteverdi writes in a style quite different from that of the recitatives earlier in the opera. He reverts to the harmonic language of his madrigals and to the dissonance which seems to arise from a conflict between the movement of the upper part and the tardiness of the bass and its harmonies. Here his deliberate awkwardness of melody is at its finest:

Ex. 28

(Ah bitter event, ah harsh and cruel fate, ah malevolent stars, ah greedy heaven.)

The development of the scene follows the practice of Greek tragedy. The messenger at first tells the shepherds only of disaster, not of its nature. It is a shepherd who first asks her meaning. The messenger still tells only of sorrow. Orpheus himself asks her more sharply what she means. Only then in shorter and shorter phrases does she tell that Eurydice is dead. This is real musical dialogue, and the music with its curt sections and its changes of harmony as the messenger and Orpheus converse has the authentic accents of tragedy. The details of the messenger's story inevitably form a little of an anticlimax, for Monteverdi is preparing for Orpheus' own expression of grief. The description of Eurydice's death, crying 'Orfeo, Orfeo', makes one of the shepherds break out with the theme 'Ahi caso acerbo' with which the messenger had entered – a masterly touch. Orpheus' cry of despair comes in an *arioso* which ends with the helpless realization of his fate (see Ex. 29).

The dramatic action is now cast aside, and pastoral returns. The chorus of shepherds begin an elaborate *continuo* madrigal, in form like those of Book V, with duets and solos held together by a

Ex. 29

(Farewell earth, farewell sky, and sun, farewell.)

refrain for the full choir; and as a final stroke of genius, Monteverdi uses the messenger's entry theme as the bass of the refrain. Finally, the *ritornello* of the prologue returns to give the only hint that all may yet be saved.

This superb act is a remarkable achievement, the more so since so much of it had to be written in recitative and still had to avoid a lack of tension. The act which follows was so like an *intermedio* in Striggio's libretto that Monteverdi probably found it more familiar. The figure of Hope leading Orpheus, the arrival at the Styx (with a boat to be pulled across) and the infernal chorus to end the scene, all offer the producer opportunities, so that such recitative as is necessary need not be so emotionally charged (though again it is well organized with refrains and never seems amorphous). The difficult moment must have been the song in which Orpheus used all the powers of music to persuade the boatman to ferry him across. Again Monteverdi uses a solo chamber aria with several verses held together by the same bass and separated from one another by instrumental interludes. With sure insight he starts his song with a virtuoso strophe, full of opulent ornamentation; and then finding the boatman still unyielding, tries even harder in a second and then a third verse, each richer in ornament than the last. This compels admiration, not pity; and as if realizing this, Orpheus sings a simpler and more natural melody, till his plea becomes a pathetic *arioso*. This in itself would be moving. The instrumental interludes make it more so. First violins, then cornetts, and then a *ritornello* from the harp reinforce the plea, until, in keeping with the general plan, the virtuosity of the soloist gives way to a small string ensemble which plays simple echoes of the voice.

The infernal scenes which take up the second part of this act and all the succeeding ones are musically less splendid, though with the smoke and fire of hell which the producer must have provided the total effect was probably impressive enough.[6] There is a lilting song for Orpheus to sing as he reclaims his beloved Eurydice ('Qual onor di te fia degno' in Act IV) and a very dramatic recitative when he fails to conquer his desire to see her again. The last act is less of a dramatic entity, but, as we have seen, an audience used to *intermedi* would scarcely have noticed this. The first part is an echo song – a fashionable device of which scores were written in the years round 1600, but none the worse for that. Then, after Orpheus' *arioso* has reached its climax, a short instrumental piece allows Apollo to descend on a cloud machine, and the pair ascend to heaven singing an ornamental duet. A chorus and dancing (the inevitable *moresca*) end the evening's entertainment.

Orfeo has been called the first real opera, and with justice; for it was not an experimental work or the result of theorizing, as the Florentine operas had been. At the same time in using the term 'opera' there are dangers that we may expect the interests of later opera composers to be Monteverdi's also. He clearly made little attempt to produce a set of characters seen in the round, as Mozart did, or to provide vivid dramatic action. His interest was more in a series of moods, in setting poetry in a lyrical rather than a dramatic way and in preserving a basic unity of musical forms.

The score of his second opera, *Arianna*, is lost,[7] although the libretto and several versions of its greatest scene have been preserved. From Rinuccini's poem we can see the way opera was to change. He was still working in the medium of pastoral, and the prologue and the final scene, where Ariadne joins the gods as the wife of Bacchus, are pure *intermedio*. Even so, there seems to be much more emphasis on the human beings, especially Ariadne herself. Her lament is one of Monteverdi's most moving compositions. Originally it was a solo interrupted by a chorus of fishermen, who moralize on the theme of her sadness, and again it seems likely to have been an offshoot of the *continuo* madrigals in the style of those in Book V. The recitative-arioso (which is all we have left) is clearly written in the style of the greatest moments of *Orfeo*, with strong dissonances arising between

---

[6]There are close parallels with the inferno scenes common in Florentine *intermedi*, for example the fifth *intermedio* for the wedding of Prince Francesco de'Medici and Johanna of Austria in Florence, December 1565, where Psyche is led to the inferno, replete with smoke and fire, and sings a lament accompanied by trombones and bass viols, see Nagler, *Theatre Festivals of the Medici, 1539–1637*, p. 20; Pirrotta, *Music and Theatre from Poliziano to Monteverdi*, pp. 180–2. Note, too, the comments below, page 132.

[7]For a full synopsis of the plot, see Westrup, 'Monteverdi's "Lamento d'Arianna"'.

voice and harmony instruments, 'affective' intervals and refrains. Monteverdi had no compunction about repeating words (the repetitions are already present in Rinuccini's verse), and right from the start he uses this to create balanced phrases and a natural development of the melody as melody (not just as declamation), which makes the first section of the lament, at least, unforgettable:

Ex. 30

(Let me die, let me die.)

The loss of *Arianna* is irreparable, not merely for the historian but for music itself. The *Ballo delle ingrate* written at the same time is not consistently good – it was written under considerable pressure – but its moments of beauty are intense enough to make us regret the loss of any music which Monteverdi wrote in this fecund time of 1608. It is an interesting work, the more so because it gives us some idea of the roots of *Orfeo*, since it is a ballet in the French style, a form known to Monteverdi perhaps since 1598. The scene, the jaws of hell, grimly lit with internal fire, is similar to that of Acts III and IV of *Orfeo*. The opening action of the ballet is a dialogue between Venus and Cupid, in which Cupid asks Venus to plead with Pluto to allow the *ingrate* (women who have preserved hard hearts against their lovers) to come up to earth. The resemblance to *Orfeo* becomes still more pronounced when Pluto eventually allows the *ingrate* to come to earth, to warn the ladies of the audience against a similar fate. The dialogue recitative during this part of the ballet is more interesting than moving, in spite of an attractive little *continuo* madrigal with *ritornelli* sung by Venus, and some very effective *arioso* using the deep register of Pluto's voice.

Then, quite suddenly, Monteverdi's inspiration returns. As the *ingrate* come from the fires of Hades, even Cupid (whose reason for wishing to see them had been the malicious desire to gloat over them) is moved to pity, and in a short but moving duet Cupid and Venus express their horror at the fate of these unloving ones. Dances in the

French style ensue and at the end of them Pluto points the moral in a long *arioso* with a recurring instrumental interlude. Then, as he bids the *ingrate* return to Hades, one of the unfortunates sings a final lament, as pathetic and as powerful as Ariadne's. The ladies of the fashionable audience were moved to tears, and no wonder. For the 'cruel fate' which is so wonderfully expressed in Monteverdi's dissonant and broken *arioso* is given added point as he contrasts it with the consonance and smoothness and simplicity of the 'serene and pure air' which now the *ingrate* must leave behind for ever:

Ex. 31

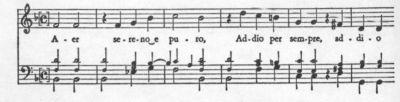

This marvellous scene would probably have been lost with so much of Monteverdi's dramatic music if he had not included the whole *ballo* (as revised for Vienna in 1628) in his eighth madrigal book in 1638.

The next piece of music for the stage also survived in a madrigal book. This was the ballet *Tirsi e Clori*, written for Mantua in 1615. It is music for the stage – but hardly dramatic music, for it is purely dance-song with the minimum of action. It begins with a dialogue, with Thyrsis trying to persuade Chlorys to dance and Chlorys resisting him. Thyrsis sings in a cheerful dance measure, his beloved replies in a less exuberant *arioso*, and a chorus of shepherds combine with a small group of strings in a series of dances. It is a charming piece but not one of the first importance, significant mainly because it shows Monteverdi's lessening interest in recitative and his growing control of the light aria style which replaced the new music with still newer music in Venice.

In the succeeding ten years Monteverdi wrote a number of dramatic works, none of which exists today. In 1616 he was composing a *favola marittima*, *Le nozze di Tetide* – in no way different from a pastoral except that it was to be performed on the water, perhaps on the Mincio at Mantua. The correspondence about this is fascinating. Monteverdi obviously believed when he received the libretto that it was to be an opera 'sung and represented in music as was *Arianna*'.[8] From this point of view the poem was highly unsatisfactory, and in one striking passage we gain a good idea of his approach to the aesthetics of opera:

> Furthermore, I have observed that the interlocutors are Winds, little Cupids, little Zephyrs and Sirens, and as a result many sopranos will be necessary, and moreover, that the Winds, that is, the Zephyrs and the Boreals, have to sing. How, dear Sir, will I be able to imitate the speech of the winds if they do not speak? And how will I be able by their means to move the passions? Ariadne moved us because she was a woman, and equally Orpheus moved us because he was a man, and not a wind. Harmonies themselves imitate, and without words, the noise of winds, the bleating of sheep, the neighing of horses, and so on and so forth, but they do not imitate the speech of winds, which does not exist . . . As for the tale as a whole, as far as my no little ignorance goes, I do not feel that it moves me one jot, and indeed I understand it with difficulty, nor do I feel that it leads me in a natural manner to an end that moves me. *Arianna* led me to a just lament, and *Orfeo* to a just prayer, but this leads me I do not know to what end.[9]

This serious view of opera is confirmed in subsequent letters, for when Monteverdi was told by Striggio that this 'maritime tale' was really a series of *intermedi* he settled down to write it, and bothered only about severely practical details, though it is significant that he never finished it. But it is clear that for him opera involved certain principles. *Intermedi* were much less important, for they did not involve characterization in the same way. And the demand for an inspired climax – some set piece which will act as a focal point – shows that he understood the nature of opera far better than most of his contemporaries.

The letters on *Andromeda* and the eclogue on Apollo (both 1620) reveal more about Monteverdi's character than about his thinking on opera; and the fragment of music for the sacred drama *La Maddalena* (1617) is also unimportant. The next work, however, we possess in its entirety, and although it is unique in form, neither opera nor *intermedio*, it is of the utmost importance in his development. This is the *Combattimento di Tancredi et Clorinda*

---

[8]Monteverdi to Alessandro Striggio, Venice, 6 January 1617, in Monteverdi, *Lettere, dediche e prefazioni*, ed. de' Paoli, pp. 95–7 (Stevens, *The Letters of Claudio Monteverdi*, pp. 124–7).
[9]Monteverdi to Alessandro Striggio, Venice, 9 December 1616, in Monteverdi, *Lettere, dediche e prefazioni*, ed. de' Paoli, pp. 85–9 (Stevens, *The Letters of Claudio Monteverdi*, pp. 113–18).

('The Fight of Tancred and Clorinda'), which was produced in Girolamo Mocenigo's palace in 1624 and published in the eighth book of madrigals. In the madrigal book Monteverdi tells us that it was intended to be performed during a musical evening after madrigals had been sung in the normal way, without any scenery or action to distract the eye. Clearly then, the *Combattimento* was not meant to be like any of the other music for the stage. It demands a small orchestra of strings and only three voices. The poem was not a specially written libretto, but part of Tasso's *Gerusalemme liberata*, a description of a fight between Clorinda, who disguised as a man assaults the Christian encampment, and Tancred, a crusader, with whom, finding herself cut off, she fights in single combat. Having mortally wounded her, Tancred unlooses her armour and finds that his adversary is a woman. He is stricken with grief as she dies.

The difficulty of making the piece a success as a dramatic scene lies largely in the inhibiting necessity for a narrator who is rather more important than the two characters. The attraction, on the other hand, was the great one of demonstrating the new *stile concitato*. The result is that the voice parts are comparatively inexpressive, except for the final part of the work where Clorinda dies and where the recitative blossoms forth in the way we expect from Monteverdi at moments of climax. Elsewhere the interest is in the realistic sounds of battle – fanfares, clashing of swords and Tancred's horse galloping on to the scene – rendered by all the tricks of the trade such as pizzicatos, tremolandi, sudden changes from loud to soft. For these tricks alone it is an interesting work; and for the biographer it is more so, as it reveals Monteverdi's tendency to realism which we have noticed in his letters about the *favola marittima* above (not an uncommon feature of opera composers). But in itself the *Combattimento* is not entirely a success, as the sympathy for its characters is rarely imparted to the audience. As a form, this kind of dramatic scene is a dead end – but Monteverdi, as so often, used the experience gained to good advantage in another context.

No music at all has survived of the various pageants for Mantua and Parma in which Monteverdi was engaged during the later 1620s. The abandoned *La finta pazza Licori* is undoubtedly a great loss; and since we have no trace even of Strozzi's libretto, it is difficult to know precisely the sort of problems which faced the composer. From his letters on the opera, however, we can see how his interests were developing. First, he was still trying out a theory of the affections and was trying to divide the human emotions in the way which we find in the eighth book of madrigals. Secondly, he was even more interested in characterization, and he wanted a principal figure who would be capable of several emotions within a brief space of time – hence his liking for a mad person who could simulate this in a natural way. This is an important step forward, and the results of such thinking are evident in his last operas.

After this Monteverdi had little opportunity for opera for over ten years, and by that time he was an old man of seventy. He would probably have never composed a big work again if the new opera companies of Venice had not been so successful. If the new audience was not socially very different from that to which Monteverdi was accustomed in Mantua, it was different in one significant way. It was not in the least interested in the old academic ideas. It was out for entertainment, and found it where it had always been found – in the spectacle. The scenery and the machines became even more important than before. *Orfeo* could have been produced with about five or six scenic changes. A score of them was not an uncommon number for a Venetian opera. As for the music, the audience had never heard of the discussion about the audibility of the words and the total impression of meaning and emotional sense which had resulted in the recitative style. The Venetian patricians were better acquainted with the arias in the song-books of the last two decades. As for the highly symbolic stories of the earliest operas, they were less interested in mythology and more concerned with human characters, at least in so far as the pastoral drama made them possible.

The two Venetian operas by Monteverdi which have come down to us both show the new style very well. The first of them, *Il ritorno d'Ulisse in patria* ('The Home-Coming of Ulysses'), has been held by some scholars to be a spurious work, so different is it from his earlier operas; and admittedly there are difficulties connected with it. The manuscript is now in the National Library in Vienna and no one knows when or how it came to be there. Then the libretto (in St Mark's Library in Venice) and the score are different in many particulars. Finally, it is held to be an inferior work (although this is surely flimsy evidence on which to come to any conclusion). In reply it must be said that stylistically the music is too like Monteverdi to be rejected on this evidence. There are passages in the *stile concitato* – very like the warlike madrigals of Book VIII – a plethora of duets in Monteverdi's style, the *arioso* laments and his general feeling for organization in writing recitative, and, above all, a sense of serious interest in the drama. If the work is not by Monteverdi himself, it is by someone who knew his music extremely well – not a very sensible conclusion to come to.

The story is taken from Homer. Ulysses has spent many years wandering over land and sea. His wife Penelope, though near to despair, is still waiting for him. But now he is near at hand, guided home to Ithaca by the goddess Minerva. Disguised as a beggar, he meets an old shepherd Eumaeus, who helps him towards his home, although he does not as yet recognize the king. Ulysses' son, Telemachus, is also brought to meet Eumaeus by Minerva, and Ulysses reveals himself. They plan to return to the court and rid Penelope of the unwanted attentions of her suitors, anxious to inherit the king's wealth. Telemachus is sent on ahead and warns Penelope that Ulysses is near. The suitors gather for a final attempt to persuade her to marry one of them, and Penelope suggests that whoever can bend Ulysses' bow shall be her husband. They try, and fail. And then Ulysses himself comes to try – as yet unrecognized by anyone at court. He kills them all with his arrows. Penelope at first cannot believe that the old man is Ulysses, in spite of the assurances of Eumaeus and Telemachus; but eventually the opera ends with a triumphant recognition.

This has all the hallmarks of a Monteverdi libretto (and we know from his librettist, Giacomo Badoaro, that he moulded its shape himself in many particulars).[10] There is the great dramatic climax of the trial scene, the situations of Penelope and of Ulysses himself which are so like that which inspired the lament in *Arianna*, a messenger scene when Telemachus arrives at court and a happy duet at the end (there is a similar one in *L'incoronazione di Poppea*). No less Monteverdian are the complicating features. The audience's need of the grand spectacle suggested to him the use of the old form of *intermedi*. So we find a prologue with the allegorical figures of Human Frailty, Fortune and Cupid, who sing their rather irrelevant introduction in the form of a set of strophic variations (in exactly the same way that Music had introduced *Orfeo*). And at various points in the drama there are interpolations from the gods – especially from Neptune, who gives some excellent opportunities for spectacular sea machines (to make it almost a *favola marittima* like *Le nozze di Tetide*). As usual there had to be some link between gods and humans, and this is provided by Minerva, who carries out the wishes of the gods by turning from time to time into human form. In other words, the opera is again a story with *intermedi*, as *Orfeo* had been. From the point

[10]See Badoaro's dedication to Monteverdi in the manuscript libretto of *Il ritorno d'Ulisse in patria* at the Museo Civico Correr, Venice, given in Osthoff, 'Zu den Quellen von Monteverdis "Ritorno di Ulisse in patria"', pp. 73–4.

of view of the stage manager, this form offers tremendous opportunities, and the score abounds with directions for machines and stage business of one kind and another. From the audience's point of view, it makes the basic progress of the opera a little too diffuse to be really satisfactory. This is a pity since it means that some of Monteverdi's most splendid music will rarely be heard in its proper surroundings.

The outstanding feature of *Orfeo* was the way Monteverdi crowded into it all the musical forms known in 1607 to express a totality of human emotion. *Il ritorno d'Ulisse in patria* does exactly the same thing in terms of 1640. The Venetian ariettas, the older virtuoso *arioso*, the *madrigali guerrieri*, the strophic-variation songs, the chamber duets – all are used to express the varied situations. There even seems to be a rather rough but effective idea of characterization in music. The gods, for example, usually maintain their dignity in the *arioso*-recitative of the older operas and *intermedi*. Neptune in fact is the natural successor both of Charon and of Pluto (in the *Ballo delle ingrate*), a deep bass whose words are ponderously painted in conventional musical images, with sudden changes of register. All the gods have highly ornamented and virtuoso parts and are deliberately denied the smoother aria rhythms which would rob them of their superhumanity. Only Minerva is allowed to sing pretty tunes, and only when she appears in human clothes.

Similarly Penelope, unhappy and beset with troubles until the very last scene, is given her character in highly charged emotional recitative. In the first scene we have a re-creation of the glories of Ariadne's lament. Not so dissonant as the model, Penelope's plaint at the absence of Ulysses gains its effects by changes in tempo, variations of phrase length and repetitions of phrases. The first climax with its rising sequences of despair and fall of a sixth reminds us so strongly of Monteverdi's earlier music that it is difficult to believe it is by any other composer:

Ex. 32

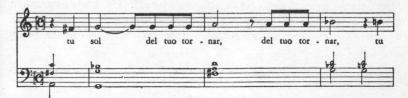

(you alone have lost sight of the day of your return.)

The whole scene is as tightly organized as ever, with the occasional use of memorable fragments to make refrains and give musical power to the recitative. Ulysses is introduced in a similar *scena*, and with recitative scarcely less poignant and powerful. But since in subsequent scenes he is led homewards by Minerva and therefore given hope and a purpose for living, he tends to interrupt the recitative with songs – rarely complete in themselves but expressive of his mood. His music is precisely what Monteverdi had planned in setting the libretto of *La finta pazza Licori*, full of sudden changes to express the detail of the words.

This shows the fine concern for the drama which had been Monteverdi's all his life; and it is confirmed in yet another way. The soliloquy is now less important than the dialogue. Every scene, even

Ex. 33

([T.] O my delight . . . [U.] I embrace you . . .)

if it contains an important aria, manages to weave in an interplay of characters and gives them conversation which is significant dramatically. People talk to people, rather than as in *Orfeo* to the world in general; and this makes it an opera of ensembles (as all successful operas are). Not for nothing had Monteverdi written so many duet madrigals. *Il ritorno d'Ulisse in patria* adds to their number. Perhaps the most beautiful of them is the one where Ulysses meets his son Telemachus (Act II Scene 3). It begins in a passionate recitative style and gradually becomes *arioso*, full of the melting suspensions which Monteverdi uses in his most magical chamber duets (see Ex. 33 on previous page). Scarcely less beautiful are the duets between Eumaeus and Ulysses in Act II Scene 2 and the final love duet. Both are written mellifluously in triple time, and the first of these is a chaconne of impeccable technique:

Ex. 34

(Sweet hope delights the heart but [a waiting soul] cannot be assuaged . . .)

Although these pieces and the arias could come straight out of the song-books of the 1630s, they never caused Monteverdi to lose sight of the larger formal patterns required in each scene, and he seeks out every opportunity to give large-scale organization to the music as he had done in *Orfeo*. The scene where the suitors plead with Penelope to marry them is a gift to the composer, who can repeat her refusals and punctuate their individual appeals with a thrice repeated *continuo* madrigal. In the scene where Penelope tests them with

Ulysses' bow the relationship of aria and recitative is especially useful. In each case the suitor's aria comes first, to express his confidence. It is only when he tries and fails that the recitative comes – usually broken into short phrases to give the impression of breathlessness. Ulysses, on the other hand, starts in recitative and then breaks into aria as he succeeds; and a 'sinfonia da guerra' as he deals with his foes is a particularly effective way of using the *stile concitato*.

Even now we have not mentioned half the beauties or the variety of character to be found in the opera – Penelope's maid Melantho, for example, who sings a lovely duet with her lover in the first act, using all the arts of the chamber duet; long-held notes on the voices while the harmonies go on underneath, quasi-recitative, *arioso* and triple-time aria, the last for a particularly seductive refrain; or Irus, the suitors' toady, who has to run away after Ulysses has returned to court and who parodies all the passionate tricks of the virtuoso singer in a scene (Act III Scene 1) which deliberately offsets the climax of the opera. Yet, in a way, this very variety is a weakness. The plot never develops steadily as *Orfeo* had done. It is too fussy, and lacks that overwhelming central point which Monteverdi had sought for in his earlier operas. Though it is always dangerous to condemn an opera which one has never seen on the grounds that its drama is not strong enough, it is not too much to say that if *Il ritorno d'Ulisse in patria* is rarely produced today, the libretto is responsible more than the music.

There is no such excuse for neglecting Monteverdi's last opera, *L'incoronazione di Poppea* ('The Coronation of Poppaea'), however complex its status (see pages 164–5). Monteverdi and his librettist, Giovanni Francesco Busenello, chose a historical subject – for the first time in the history of opera. This has some significance for the development of the genre; but it was not so important to Monteverdi, to whom Ariadne and Penelope were just as real as Poppaea. What is really significant is that in *L'incoronazione di Poppea* the *intermedio* elements have been considerably reduced. There is the customary allegorical prologue, and allegorical figures appear in the body of the opera. Yet they are interwoven into the progress of the play and never stand completely outside it as the gods do in *Il ritorno d'Ulisse in patria*. Similarly, although, there are many possibilities for scenic changes and a splendid production, the drama is developed in longer sections, scene leading into scene in a natural way. There is far less of the fussiness which mars the earlier work, and the dramatic unity is never abandoned merely for the glories of the producer. It is, in fact, a libretto which conforms to most of the criteria which we apply today, and in spite of a large cast there is never over-complication either of plot or character. Variety of human emotion was Monteverdi's

principal aim in all his later operas, and in *L'incoronazione di Poppea*
he finds the most dramatic method for exploiting it. In this libretto the
same situations affect different characters in different ways. There is a
real conflict and hence a real opportunity for the musician to build up
characters in a consistent way. The story is taken from Tacitus,
Suetonius and perhaps Seneca, and moulded into significant scenes,
each carefully chosen for its musical possibilities.

Otho, returning from a journey of state, comes home to find
soldiers guarding his house. He guesses what has happened. Nero is
in love with his betrothed Poppaea and is visiting her. This is
confirmed by the soldiers' conversation and, as the day dawns, by the
appearance of Nero with Poppaea herself in the garden. Nero is loath
to leave her, but dare not risk a scandal as yet. He declares that he
will divorce his wife Octavia and then all will be well. Left alone,
Poppaea becomes less the loving woman and shows her vicious
ambition. 'Love and Fortune fight on my side' ('Per me guerreggia
Amor e la Fortuna'), she sings. Her nurse, Arnalta, who has joined
her in the garden, warns her that these are not the best of allies. We
now have a companion scene where Octavia, far from being
confident and ambitious, regrets Nero's infidelities. She consults
Seneca about her possible courses of action, but his counsel is merely
to bear her burden stoically – little comfort indeed either to Octavia
or to her page who is standing by her. These two depart, leaving
Seneca alone; and suddenly the goddess Pallas Athene is heard (no
doubt from some great cloud machine) telling Seneca that he will die
that day. He is unmoved by this and looks forward to a better life.

At this point Nero enters (and we notice how Seneca acts as a focal
point for several consecutive scenes). Nero tells Seneca that he has
resolved to divorce Octavia and marry Poppaea. Seneca warns him
that the people will be displeased. Nero becomes petulant and shouts
that he cares nothing for the people or for anyone else. He tells Seneca
sharply to go away. Poppaea enters (Nero acting as the link between
scenes this time) and the two of them sing another love duet. Having
put Nero in a good mood, Poppaea then whispers slanders against
Seneca, who she fears is an obstacle to her ambitions. Nero orders a
soldier to go to Seneca with the sentence of death. Nero departs and
Otho enters to make a last attempt at reconciliation with Poppaea
(now the linking personality in her turn). She will have nothing to do
with him and Otho thinks darkly of murdering her. After his soliloquy
Drusilla, one of the ladies of the court and in love with Otho, comes in
and manages to make him say that he loves her. But, 'Drusilla's name is
on my lips, Poppaea's is in my heart' ('Drusilla ho in bocca, ed ho
Poppea in core'), he sings. With this the first act ends.

Act II is in three main sections. The first is constructed around Seneca, who receives warning of his impending death from Mercury (the cloud machine again), and then the death sentence comes, borne by Nero's captain. Seneca's friends plead with him not to die, but he bids them prepare his bath, in which he will open his veins and bleed to death. Before the second section there is an intermezzo (in the modern sense) – a flirtation between the page-boy and a young girl; this is clearly to allow for the passage of time. Then we see Nero again with some friends, now celebrating Seneca's death with ribald glee. The third part of the act is taken up with Otho, now almost determined upon the murder of his betrothed. His doubts are finally overcome by Octavia, who equally wants Poppaea out of the way. They plot to dress up Otho as a woman: in this disguise he is to gain entrance to Poppaea's room. They leave, and we next see Drusilla, happily confident in the love of Otho. He enters to borrow her clothes, which she gives him quite willingly. Now the moment of murder approaches. The scene is again Poppaea's garden, where she falls asleep while her nurse sings a lullaby. Then the god of love enters and sings yet another lullaby. The disguised Otho comes in and is just about to strike when the god (perhaps with an intricate movement of the cloud machine) stops him. Poppaea wakes up, and seeing the prospective murderer running away thinks it was Drusilla.

The final act begins with an aria by Drusilla. She is interrupted by Poppaea's nurse, who comes in with guards and identifies her as the attacker. Drusilla protests her innocence but Nero enters and threatens her with tortures if she does not tell the plot. She confesses to the crime to save her beloved Otho. Nero is ordering an exceptionally cruel death for her as Otho himself arrives, to confess his own guilt and Octavia's. Nero, realizing that it is Octavia who is ultimately to blame, banishes Otho, who departs with Drusilla. Nero announces his divorce and the banishment of Octavia. The final scene is the brilliant coronation of the new empress, Poppaea.

This detailed synopsis of the plot reveals some of the reasons why it is a masterpiece. The excellence of the libretto lies in the way it avoids unnecessary explanations and makes the reasons of the heart compelling. Nero, for example, acts in a predictable way in every situation and is seen in enough differing situations to appear as a complete man. He is amorous but sad on leaving Poppaea, petulant when Seneca disagrees with him, cruel with Drusilla, revoltingly jolly with his friends, and amorous and content at the end of the opera. Equally, Poppaea is flirtatious, ambitious and hard, triumphant and sensuously happy in turn. Monteverdi's power in expressing these differing emotions is beyond all praise. At the places where we expect him to be good he is magnificent – as in the love duets which derive from the madrigal books and yet outdo them in sensuousness. And it is the music which gives great variety to the love-making. The opening duet between Nero and Poppaea is full of longing, dissonances and minor harmonies predominating, and fragments of aria always being interrupted by recitative. The two voices never sing together, and their motif 'addio' ('farewell') is repeated time after time in harmonies which do not resolve, as they cannot break away from one another. Their final duet, on the contrary, is a smooth chaconne, the dissonances always resolving promptly and the melody continuous even when shared between the voices. The harmony has the usual richness of Monteverdi's duets, and as the bass repeats itself so their happy love seems endless.

Neither of these is like the duet between Nero and Lucan when, Seneca dead, the bachelor party thinks lustfully of Poppaea's charms. Again Monteverdi writes a triple-time chaconne, but this time while Lucan sings a *bel canto* melody, Nero can do no more than gasp, 'Ah destiny!', in single notes or short phrases:

Ex. 35

([N.] Ah destiny! [L.] Mouth, mouth which enticingly offers me the tender ruby . . .)

The love duet between the page and the girl which comes just before this in Act II is also completely different. This is light-hearted flirtation, the boy singing a song which might have come out of the 1632 *Scherzi musicali*, the girl taking it more seriously and more confidently in a smooth triple-time aria before they finally join rapturously together.

As always, there are laments, and very fine ones. Of the several set pieces the one sung in Act III by Octavia, leaving Rome for ever ('Addio Roma'), inevitably reminds us of *Arianna*. Compounded of short pregnant phrases, it makes the same use of dissonance and has the same power of changing its mood rapidly, by changing from declamation to *arioso*. Drusilla's agony when falsely accused is shorter and part of a dialogue but is no less taut and gripping. Otho's opening scene of the opera is equally expressive. He starts in happy *arioso* as he asks Poppaea to open the door of the balcony,

Ex. 36

(You force me to anger . . .)

even breaking into a felicitous aria. Then he sees the soldiers. The recitative at once becomes agonized, broken and dissonant, and at its climax becomes obsessed with a tiny motif as the librettist piles up the appealing phrases: 'I am that Otho who followed you, who longed for you, who served you – that Otho who adored you' ('Io son quel'Ottone che ti segui, che ti bramò, che ti servì; quell'Otton che t'adorò'). These are offshoots of Monteverdi's earlier music. There are other moments which are quite unexpected. The use of the *stile concitato* is new, for it not only occurs to express the usual external

Cremona Cathedral (from Antonio Campo, *Cremona, fedelissima città, et nobilissima colonia de Romani rappresentata in disegno col suo contado, et illustrata d'una breve historia delle cose piu notabili appartenenti ad essa,* Cremona, 1585)

Monteverdi in middle age (portrait by or after Bernardo Strozzi,
Gesellschaft der Musikfreunde, Vienna)

Monteverdi in old age (engraving on
title-page of Giovan Battista Marinoni (ed.),
*Fiori poetici raccolti nel funerale del molto
illustre e molto reverendo signor Claudio
Monteverde*, Venice, 1644)

Mantua (seventeenth-century engraving)

St Mark's, Venice (seventeenth-century engraving, Victoria and Albert Museum)

Venetian serenaders (sixteenth-century engraving, Victoria and Albert Museum)

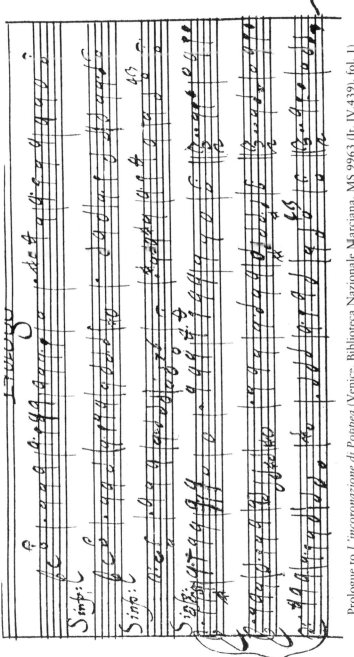

Prologue to *L'incoronazione di Poppea* (Venice, Biblioteca Nazionale Marciana, MS 9963 (It. IV.439), fol. 1)

SELVA
MORALE E SPIRITVALE
DI CLAVDIO MONTEVERDE

Maeſtro Di Capella della Sereniſſima
Republica Di Venetia

DEDICATA

ALLA SACRA CESAREA MAESTA DELL' IMPERATRICE

ELEONORA

GONZAGA

Con Licenza de Superiori & Priuilegio.

• SOPRANO  Primo

IN VENETIA MDCXXXX

Appreſſo Bartolomeo Magni

Title-page of Monteverdi's *Selva morale e spirituale* (Venice, 1640-1)

images of war (as when the soldiers are talking in Act I) but also to conjure up the emotions of wrath and cruelty. Nero's anger when Seneca refuses to fall in with his wishes provokes an outburst which shows very clearly the immaturity of a monarch who has always had his own way (see Ex. 36 on previous page). A similarly pungent passage comes when Drusilla is interrogated in the last act.

The trio in Act II is also unusual for Venetian opera. Sung by Seneca's friends imploring him not to commit suicide, it is a most moving chromatic piece which culminates in a series of agonized cries: 'Non morir, non morir, Seneca, no!' ('Do not die, do not die, Seneca, no!').[11] The final surprise, perhaps, is the memorability of the melodies. Not that Monteverdi had ever been untuneful, but in this opera he surrenders a number of times to the charms of the Venetian song-books. Poppaea's aria after Nero has gone in Act I, Drusilla's song (a perfect *da capo* aria) as she awaits Otho, and the two lullabies in Act II are extremely attractive in themselves. These and the others are mainly in triple time, and because of their clear rhythm and lucid diatonic melody (although Monteverdi has a mannerism of juggling with alternate major and minor thirds), they stick effortlessly in the mind.

'Ariadne moved us because she was a woman, and equally Orpheus moved us because he was a man, and not a wind' (see page 107). This philosophy reaches its most practical realization in *L'incoronazione di Poppea*. Like Mozart and Verdi, Monteverdi saw that it was necessary to have a sufficiently large and contrasting cross-section of humanity with which to create the world of opera, and that all the resources of music would be needed to bring these characters to life. The only larger criticism which can be brought against the opera is that the strange morality of ancient Rome is too vividly drawn. The characters and situations are so alive that to end with the glorification of an evil couple at first sight seems rather revolting. And yet it is satisfying. As Wagner said of the ending of *Götterdämmerung*, when it was pointed out to him that with the gold returned to the Rhine-maidens there was no reason why the gods should perish, the emotional logic of art demands the destruction of Valhalla. Monteverdi also knew this kind of logic. *L'incoronazione di Poppea* is a great opera.

---

[11]The chorus bears striking similarities to 'Non partir, ritrosetta' in the *Madrigali guerrieri, et amorosi* (1638).

7

The church music

The obsession of the last hundred and fifty years with the music of Palestrina and his followers has almost completely obscured the complexity of church music in the later sixteenth century. Counter-Reformation church music has the same complications as the Counter-Reformation itself. The Roman Church could have within its ranks evangelists with such differing methods as the Oratorians of St Philip Neri and the Jesuits. Its church musicians contain equally diverse figures. Palestrina, Victoria, the Gabrielis, Lassus and the host of cathedral musicians seem at times to have little in common with one another. To try to see them as part of a single movement is to despair of finding a general pattern. If there is a common denominator to be found, it is one of principle rather than of style or technique. The principle is a familiar one – that the words must fertilize the music and not act merely as its excuse. This was the demand of the Council of Trent no less than of the humanists who helped opera to come into being. But principle is one thing; its application is another. Just as the interpretations of the Greek theorists gave rise to a host of differing musical styles, so in church music we can find several interpretations of the basic idea, all of them valid and defensible.

There was, first of all, the demand that the words should be audible. The church had its own monody ready made in plainsong. Palestrina and a colleague, Annibale Zoilo, were commissioned to revise the chant for Mass and Office. Then as now, plainsong was not always sung unaccompanied. The support of the organ was quite often needed, and this gave rise to yet another sort of music in which the words were heard clearly – the harmonized chanting known as *falsobordone*. Here the composer provided some simple chords and left the words to be chanted in speech rhythm, breaking into polyphony only at the end of each section of the text. This, at least, was the theory. In practice, singers found it far too elementary to satisfy their desires and they often added ornaments to the chant in an ornate, not to say extravagant, manner.[1] *Falsobordone* was the

[1] The Sistine Chapel's singing of Gregorio Allegri's *Miserere* in Holy Week is a good example of how it was done. Useful examples are also in Francesco Severi, *Salmi passaggiati (1615)*, ed. Murray C. Bradshaw, 'Recent Researches in the Music of the Baroque Era', xxxviii (Madison, 1981).

favoured medium in setting the psalms for vespers. Its popularity probably rested on simplicity of performance, and scores of books were published in the later years of the century.

Audibility was a prime consideration in the other popular outlet for composition, the *missa brevis*. Here the composer admittedly imposed a musical rhythm on the words, but in the *Gloria* and *Credo* at least he generally followed the injunction 'to every syllable a note' (the phrase is Archbishop Cranmer's, and it is interesting to see similar ideas developing in the music of the liturgies of the Roman and Anglican faiths). Elsewhere in the Mass the composer was allowed imitative counterpoint and melismatic melody. Even so, the *missa brevis* shows a strong tendency towards homophonic writing and therefore an increased interest in harmonic devices. All this is not to say that the tradition of conventional polyphony disappeared, merely that it was not alone. Yet it too shows some effect of counter-reform in the widening gap between secular and religious music. Gone were the parody Masses on secular songs. Thematic material was now taken from plainsong or polyphonic motets. Palestrina's conscious attempts to produce consonant harmony from smoothly flowing melodic lines contrast powerfully with the growing dissonance and rugged melody of the madrigal. The asceticism of the Jesuits has its counterpart in this music.

But the asceticism of the Jesuits was achieved through the sensuous *Spiritual Exercises* of St Ignatius Loyola.[2] Nor were they averse to using the sensuousness of art to impress and overwhelm the common people. This too has its counterpart in the splendid church music written for the ducal chapels of northern Italy. These had the resources to give church music a glamour which, if it reflected the glory of the prince or doge, was not unsuitable for praising an all-powerful God. *Castrati*, a big choir and a large group of instrumentalists could stimulate the church composer's imagination as well as that of an opera composer or madrigalist.

Wert's church music, for example, shows that he made virtually no distinction between secular and religious music. When in his early life he was composing in a predominantly Netherlandish style, his church music was contrapuntal in the traditional way. But there is none of the asceticism of Palestrina about it. It is full of rhythmic life, with jaunty syncopations and cross-rhythms, and its harmony has that lively roughness which disappears from contrapuntal

[2]On the Jesuits and the arts, see Rudolf Wittkower, *Art and Architecture in Italy, 1600–1750* (London, 1958), p. 4. A useful introduction is also offered by T. Frank Kennedy, 'Jesuits and Music: Reconsidering the Early Years', *Studi Musicali*, xvii (1988), 71–100.

music only when the Roman school has become the chosen model. When Wert's madrigal style changes, about 1580, his church music changes with it. The expression of the words becomes all important, and dissonance and chromaticism are as essential a part of his church music as of his madrigals, as in the motet, 'Vox in Rama':[3]

Ex. 37

(Rachel weeping . . .)

The large awkward leaps which we have seen in such madrigals as 'Solo e pensoso, i più deserti campi' appear in the motets too, and for the same purpose. And for joyful moments Wert's natural virility of rhythm turns almost to dance music, as rolling sequential phrases

[3]In Wert's *Il secondo libro de motetti a cinque voci* (Venice, 1581); see Wert, *Opera omnia*, XIII, pp. 81–4.

produce clear-cut strong accents, as in 'Amen, amen dico vobis':[4]

Ex 38

[*Cantus* silent]

(is turned into joy . . .)

In this later music of Wert and in the motets of the younger men, Pallavicino and Gastoldi, the Venetian style begins to predominate. This is based on the *cori spezzati* – two or more choirs sometimes widely separated in the church and alternating with one another throughout a motet or Mass. In the first place this means of expression, based as it was on ancient Jewish practice and simple in its homophonic declamation of the words (necessary to ensure ensemble at all), might well have been ordered by the reformers of Trent. By the 1580s, however, it had become rather debased. The

[4]In Wert's *Il secondo libro de motetti a cinque voci* (Venice, 1581); see Wert, *Opera omnia*, XIII, pp. 53–60.

Venetian love of vocal and instrumental colour saw that the emphasis was placed less on the words than on the grandeur of effect. Some of the 'choirs' now became groups of instruments with soloists placed among them. From these special effects were produced. Echo music was one favourite, even though it almost blasphemously turned 'clamor' to 'amor' and 'clamat' to 'amat'. Dialogue motets dramatizing the speeches of saints and apostles were also popular. As for the instrumentalists, they took their part in sumptuous canzonas and sonatas played during the Mass or vespers. There was, then, a tremendously varied choice before the composer of church music. In practice his style was conditioned as always by the resources to hand. At Cremona, for example, Ingegneri hardly needed to concern himself with the grand manner. He had instrumentalists for some of the greater festivals, but of necessity his music grew out of small resources. His music naturally follows the contrapuntal school, rather less austere than Palestrina's and more like the earlier church music of Wert. He is not averse to an occasional chromaticism, but expressiveness is not his main consideration.

Monteverdi's *Sacrae cantiunculae* (1582), the work of a boy of fifteen, are an offshoot of such conservatism. They are *tricinia*, that is, motets for three voices; and this, coupled with the fact that the texts in question are for the most part unliturgical, suggests that they were probably meant for private devotions rather than for public peformance. For domestic singing they are ideal. The melodic lines are always interesting – a thing not to be taken for granted at a time when composers were becoming more concerned with the total effect of vocal colour. Nor are they ever really difficult, for they remain largely diatonic and are constructed from the more familiar motifs and decorative figures. Monteverdi at this stage in his career was rather inconsistent in the way that he decorated unimportant words with melismas while often ignoring expressive ones; but this is something we might expect of a boy, for the manipulation of words is often no little embarrassment to a beginner whose main concern is making the counterpoint fit together. As for the counterpoint itself, it is very efficient indeed, with a pure consonant harmony and the skilfully overlapping phrases which maintain the contrapuntal flow. The *Sacrae cantiunculae* are not works of genius. It is enough that they are indistinguishable from countless other *tricinia* of the epoch.

At Mantua the choice of style and scoring became a real one. Everything was known there. We know from the descriptions of Duke Vincenzo's coronation that Wert commanded resources of Venetian sumptuousness.[5] From the publications of Pallavicino and

[5]See Fenlon, *Music and Patronage in Sixteenth-Century Mantua*, I, p. 121.

Gastoldi we learn that *falsobordone*, separated choirs and large contrapuntal music were used in the Church of S. Barbara. Whether Monteverdi added to these works is not known. It seems probable that until Gastoldi's death in 1609 his duties led him only to compose chamber music and opera. By the time that he did come to compose church music, the choice had widened even further, for the *basso continuo* altered church music just as much as it had changed the madrigal. Not that it altered the spirit of church music very much. Lodovico Grossi da Viadana's *Cento concerti ecclesiastici* of 1602 are very like the older motets in their melodic writing and their harmonies. They spread the melodic writing among fewer voices and rid themselves of constant imitations. Apart from this they can have sounded very little different from some of the more harmonically conceived *a cappella* motets.

In the larger-scale works much the same thing happened. The Venetian composers now accompanied their soloists with the organ and added groups of soloists to the possible variety of groupings. By the ingenious positioning of these groups the soloists were not drowned by the *ripieno* voices and instruments, and sudden dramatic contrasts were obtained. The only novelty in technique was the increasing sectionalism which soloists engendered. One or two composers took advantage of the contrast between solo passages and *tutti* to insert duets and trios which were more or less complete in themselves and were punctuated by refrains sung by the choir. Finally, there was a continuation of the tradition of secularized church music and the spiritual madrigal. Naturally enough the modern equivalent was to introduce monodic techniques into motets – declamatory lines, virtuoso ornaments, rich dissonant harmonies and the rest. This happened rather slowly, largely because the early composers of monody were courtiers and singers, while the church musicians were professional composers; but by about 1608 true sacred monodies were appearing, usually under titles like *Sacri affetti* or *Ghirlanda sacra*, deliberately non-commital about liturgical usage. The texts of these sacred songs come mainly from biblical sources rather than from the liturgy, and mirror the secular song in emotional richness. Like Monteverdi's *Sacrae cantiunculae* they were probably more often heard in the private chambers of the nobility and such members of the higher clergy who had virtuoso singers among their retinue.

The new never replaces the old suddenly, especially in church music, where traditions have always been treasured more than elsewhere. Even so, to find the profusion of styles and techniques that we have in Monteverdi's volume of 1610 is surprising. A Mass in the old polyphonic style, a set of vesper psalms in the grand manner, and a group of monodic *sacri affetti* – these are unusual bedfellows even for this period of change.[6] The explanation is not hard to seek. Trying to find a job outside Mantua he determined to show that he was competent in all fields and was fit for a post either in conservative Rome or scintillating Venice. It is no surprise that the collection was never reprinted. Its size and contents suggest that it was a presentation volume, not meant for ordinary practical use.

That the *Missa 'In illo tempore'* should be written in *a cappella* polyphony is not surprising in a book to please the Roman taste. The form the polyphony takes is a little overwhelming. Monteverdi takes ten themes from a motet by Nicolas Gombert (nothing recent or popular, we notice) and then works these out in the strictest possible way.[7] The work is thick with imitative points. Voices are given rests only to emphasize new imitations, regardless of their breath capacity or proneness to be tired. But there are signs of modern tastes. The choral writing is deliberately brilliant in sonorities, not unlike that in Palestrina's *Missa 'Assumpta est Maria'*. The old modal system is largely replaced by diatonic scales and sequences, while the rhythms have a regularity distinct from the plasticity of the Roman school. What seems most strange, in view of Monteverdi's normal manner, is his steadfast refusal to paint the words, even when it was quite conventional to stress the contrasts of 'Crucifixus' and 'Et resurrexit' in the *Credo*, for example. It is as though the composer was determined to make it an undoubtedly *prima prattica* piece, with the music the mistress of the words. It is for this reason that it seems so untypical of its time and composer. Nevertheless, it has its excitements and will reward a choir that is not daunted by its technical demands.

But it is the vespers music which reveals Monteverdi's real inclination. This is indeed the work of a North Italian court musician. The big orchestra, the solo singers and the choir are all there, and the music reflects the worldly grandeur of prince and

[6]The contents are described as follows on the title-page of the *bassus generalis* partbook: 'Of the Most Blessed Virgin, Mass for six voices suitable for church choirs, and Vespers to be performed by larger forces, together with some motets, suitable for chapels or apartments of princes' (for the original, see Appendix B). Latin usage allows 'accommodata' to go with both 'Missa' and 'Vespere'.

[7]Gombert's 'In illo tempore loquente Jesu' is edited in Nicolas Gombert, *Opera omnia*, ed. Joseph Schmidt-Görg, 'Corpus Mensurabilis Musicae', vi (American Institute of Musicology, 1951–), IX, pp. 13–19. For the 'great studiousness and difficulty' of the Mass, see the letter from Bassano Cassola to Ferdinando Gonzaga, 26 July 1610, in Fabbri, *Monteverdi*, p. 154. Monteverdi delivered a copy of the Mass to Rome.

doge.[8] And whereas no one could find anything Monteverdian in the
Missa 'In illo tempore', the *Vespers* bear the imprint of his style,
above all in the taste for compromise – the interest in putting old
means to new uses. Separated choirs, *falsobordone*, the traditional
Venetian canzona are the materials. Every one of them is given a new
twist. The opening versicle and response, 'Domine ad adiuvandum',
for example, is really written in *falsobordone*. The choir chants on a
single chord except at the very end. This is conventional enough. If
the instruments had doubled them in some way it would have been
completely conventional. But Monteverdi has given them music of
their own to play – an adaptation of the toccata which had opened
Orfeo. As an instrumental piece it is sonorous; with a choir adding
sonority but not any thematic material to distract the ear from it, its
splendour is increased.

The five psalm settings use an equally traditional technique, that of
the *cantus firmus*. Each is founded on a psalm-tone, which is
repeated several times, often altered very freely in rhythm. Superim-
posed on this pattern is one of the common techniques of the early
seventeenth century. In the first one, 'Dixit Dominus', the predomin-
ant method is to mingle passages in *falsobordone* with duets and
trios for solo voices. The organ bass over which these solos develop is
the *cantus firmus*, giving the effect of strophic variation in the
manner of the *continuo* madrigal. Each *falsobordone* section flowers
into the traditional polyphony, which is expanded by instrumental
repetition. These sections at first sight seem more revolutionary than
they really are. One dance-like passage is in fact almost identical
with Wert's motet 'Amen, amen dico vobis' quoted above
(page 123); another is a common contrapuntal tag; yet another,
highly ornamented, merely writes down what had been improvised
by singers for many years, as a glance at the treatises on ornamentation shows us. Even the solo sections are restrained – Viadana-like
rather than secular in origin.

The first page of 'Laudate pueri Dominum' looks quite conservative. It develops in the manner of a large contrapuntal piece by
Andrea Gabrieli, announcing its plainsong theme with a jaunty
rhythm and working it to a climax in polyphony. Only then does
Monteverdi start with the *concertato* technique which reminds us of

[8]As Denis Arnold noted in the first edition, the word 'big' is relative: if, as is
possible, the vesper psalms were later used as his test pieces for St Mark's,
Venice, it is of interest to note that the account books show that he had an
orchestra of six resident players and twenty specially hired for the occasion, and
a choir of about twenty-five (two extra organs also had to be brought in from St
Mark's Seminary).

the fifth book of madrigals. A series of trios ensues, one part singing the plainsong, the others decorating extravagantly. This is really secular in style; and after some double-choir interjections in triple time there is a voluptuous duet which is very like parts of 'Ahi come a un vago sol cortese giro':

Ex. 39

'Laetatus sum' uses a similar technique, except that here Monteverdi gives an added importance to the organ bass, which gives out a theme in crotchets and acts as an anchor in much the same way that the plainsong had done in 'Dixit Dominus'. The actual chant is split up among the voices as the piece proceeds. Again Monteverdi draws clear contrasts, this time between the quasi-contrapuntal trios and quartets and sections in which *falsobordone* is left either as a simple chant or as the basis for voluptuous improvisation.

The other two psalms are more conventional. 'Nisi Dominus' is a big double-choir setting in which the *cantus firmus* appears in long notes in the tenor part of each choir. Although the use of *cori spezzati* hardly ever fails to fascinate, the piece is constructed in too long sections, with a great deal of repetition, and lacks the cut and thrust of Gabrielian dialogue. The sonorities of the final climax are magnificent, but it is not consistently interesting. 'Lauda Jerusalem' on the other hand, is very exciting throughout. Though it uses contrasting groups from time to time, it is really a piece in the manner of Wert. The smooth unexciting rhythms of Palestrina are quite foreign to it, and the syncopations are given added force by a regularly changing harmony.

To match the grandeur of these psalms in the hymn 'Ave maris stella' presented Monteverdi with a new problem. Hymns were normally sung in plainsong in Venice, and the only models to hand were the rather old-fashioned settings by Wert. Monteverdi's setting of the first verse is rather like these, with its eight independent lines following their own rhythms to give a complicated texture in which the rhythmicized plainsong in the *cantus* part is sometimes a little obscured. Then he has a brilliant new idea. He turns the plainsong, one of the most beautiful of hymn melodies, into a song in triple time, engagingly serene in its balanced, *hemiola* accentuation. One choir sings a simple harmonization of it; the other repeats it; and then three soloists (the bass as usual being left out) sing in their turn, accompanied by the organ. In between these middle verses a *ritornello* in triple time is given to the instruments to provide a rest from the tune. The opening contrapuntal setting rounds off the piece in the final verse.

All this music is liturgical. The *Sonata sopra 'Sancta Maria, ora pro nobis'* is only loosely so. The words 'Sancta Maria, ora pro nobis' ('Holy Mary, pray for us') come from the litany of the Blessed Virgin, but the idea of an instrumental piece around them is purely north Italian. Monteverdi borrowed it from a Ferrarese composer, Archangelo Crotti. A fragment of plainsong is sung by a soloist eleven times. Around it the instruments play a *canzona francese* complete with the stereotyped rhythm and *da capo* form which are its hallmarks. These are the bare bones of the piece; but such a bald description does no justice to the tremendous invention that Monteverdi brings to it. Whereas Crotti's piece had been a small-scale chamber *canzona*, Monteverdi turns it into a splendid sonata in the Venetian manner – in fact, one of the largest orchestral pieces of its time. We have a swinging tune which turns into a triple-time variation in the way in which a pavane becomes a galliard, a series of ensembles in which each separate element of the instrumental group is exploited to the full, virtuoso dotted rhythms and sequential phrases, and the initial *canzona* tune forming a climax by being played simultaneously with the plainsong *cantus firmus* at the end. Here is a magnificence which Crotti never knew.

Magnificence and splendour are recurring words in any account of this vespers music. They represent something quite new in Monteverdi's work. In the madrigals it is an intimate power which he commands, and grandeur is an extension of this range. The natural continuation of his earlier style is to be found in the *sacri affetti* (interspersed among the psalms) and the Magnificats which complete this volume of church music. The four motets for solists were the first chamber music by Monteverdi in the style of the 'new music' to be published, and they show that the seventh book of madrigals of almost ten years later was given lengthy preparation.

Ex. 40

et di - xit mi - hi: Sur -

ge, sur - ge, sur -

ge, sur - ge a - mi - ca, sur - ge, a-mi-ca me-a

The one solo motet, 'Nigra sum sed formosa', is a setting of some voluptuous verses from the *Song of Songs*:[9] 'I am black, but comely, O ye daughters of Jerusalem. Therefore the king hath loved me and hath brought me into his chambers and hath said to me: "Rise up, my love, and come away."' The relationship of the text to the words of Monteverdi's secular music needs no explanation. He puts on his finest *seconda prattica* manner and writes a monody which might

[9] The text conflates Song of Solomon, i.4–5 and ii.10–12.

well come from an opera. His capacity for inventing the memorable phrase, for fitting the music to the detail of the words, is displayed at its best. This can hardly be shown more completely than in the way Monteverdi isolates the king's words, 'Rise up, my love', with a preliminary rest, and then writes rapturously persuasive music for the constant repetition of the word 'surge', the shortening phrases melting into the continuous climactic phrase (see Ex. 40 on previous page). As in the recitatives of *Orfeo*, the musical shape is always of primary importance. The motif set to the words 'Nigra sum' inevitably comes again, and the final section of the motet is repeated, even though there is no reason for it in the words.

The duet, 'Pulchra es amica mea', is another setting of verses from the *Song of Songs* (vi. 3–4). It is Monteverdi's first chamber duet and it needs little description here simply because it shows complete mastery of all the technical devices of the duets in the later madrigal books. The second voice amplifies the phrases, gives harmonic fullness and expands the scale of the music in just the same way. There is the same ability to organize the ornaments of the melody into satisfying patterns, and to change the mood abruptly with an alteration of harmony or a move from *arioso* to declamation. This is fine music and is capped only by a yet finer motet, 'Duo seraphim clamabant'. If it were not for its tenor clefs, this would look like a piece for the Ferrara ladies who so bored Ambassador Urbani. All the resources of ornamentation are deployed – sobbing trills, dotted notes and scale-wise melismas – and given to all the three voices they produce a marvellously rich effect. We are meant to admire the virtuosity, and we do. But true greatness is given to the piece by other things: the way the third voice, brought in to express the mystery of the Three (a triad) in One (a unison), is then retained for the repetition of the word 'Sanctus', making it still richer and more flowing; and the opening of the motet itself with its wonderful series of suspensions:

Ex. 41

(cried one unto the other . . .)

With 'Audi coelum' we come to the almost inevitable echo piece. But this does not remind us of the Venetian choral dialogues. It is a descendant of Jacopo Peri's 'Dunque fra torbid'onde' for the fifth of the Florentine *intermedi* of 1589 (which was also a model for 'Possente spirto' in Act III of *Orfeo*).[10] The descending sixth in the melody, the passionate reiteration of the word 'Maria' each time decorated anew and the careful declamation are the results of *seconda prattica* thinking. Nor are the echoes ever applied mechanically, for they are used to expand the phrases and add emphasis. Even when the full choral group is brought in at the end to express the words 'Let us all therefore follow her' ('Omnes hanc ergo sequamur'), the solo and its echo maintain the sensuous mood as they sing the words 'miseris solamen' ('comfort for the afflicted'; the last word producing the echo 'amen', to lead music and words towards the ending).

Monteverdi provides two Magnificats, one for the large group of instrumentalists and voices needed for the psalm settings, the other

[10]Peri's 'Dunque fra torbid'onde' is in D. P. Walker (ed.), *Les Fêtes du mariage de Ferdinand de Médicis et de Christine de Lorraine, Florence 1589: i, Musique des intermèdes de 'La pellegrina'* (Paris, 1963; repr. Paris, 1986), pp. 98–106.

simply for voices and organ. Both use the same techniques, and if we discuss the larger one it is because it is easier to see in this the union of the grand manner and the sacred monody. The Magnificat was traditionally a sectional work, with duets and trios interspersed between sections for the *tutti* of five or six voices. No doubt these contrasts were accentuated further when instruments took part. Where Monteverdi is original is in conceiving the work in such a way that instruments, solo and *ripieno* voices are each given something to do which only they can do well. He turns the Magnificat into twelve sections (ten verses and two sections for the doxology), and each of them is treated in a different way. The only common feature to them all is the plainsong *cantus firmus* which appears in long notes throughout. A choral setting of the first one gives way to a soprano, who sings the plainsong while the organ decorates. Two tenors

Ex. 42

133

weave their dotted notes and roulades round the alto in the next one, and then as a tenor sings out the plainsong, duets of instruments – flutes followed by trombones for the words 'the lowliness of his handmaiden' ('humilitatem ancillae suae'), and recorders for the angelic 'call me blessed' ('beatam me dicent') – enrich the texture. Violins with ornamental figuration are included in the next section. The fifth section returns to the voices alone, who sing a choral dialogue with contrasting upper and lower groups in the manner of a motet by Giovanni Gabrieli, 'Beata es Virgo Maria'.[11]

After this first climax the humanity of the Virgin's song increasingly infects the music. The seventh section is in fact an operatic *scena*. The tenor sings of the abasement of the mighty ('Deposuit potentes'); and cornetts and violins each in pairs, echo one another with the same magic that Orpheus used to bewitch Charon. After more duets and trios the two tenors sing another echo song, to the glory of the Father, Son and Holy Ghost. Their fine disregard for accurate declamation and their splendidly virtuoso phrases make this one of the most passionate moments in a passionate work (see Ex. 42 on page 133). Then, and only then, are the instruments allowed to double the voices to give a noble conclusion to the work.

Passion and magnificence – these two are inseparable words in describing this music; and their peculiar mixture makes it quite unlike anything else either in Monteverdi's works or in those of his contemporaries. Ostensibly it is in the Venetian manner, and should be performed, as the late Thurston Dart so perceptibly saw, as *musica spezzata*, with the singers and players placed in diverse parts of the church.[12] Yet its emotional life is not Venetian. The use of plainchant as *cantus firmi* means that the modern harmonic simplicity of Giovanni Croce and the Gabrielis is not possible, and the result is much more highly spiced than their works in the grand manner. Nor could any Venetian provide such a diversity of style. When the motets, psalms, hymn, Sonata and Magnificat are given, as they usually are today, as an entity (and for this there is a strong case to be made out),[13] the total concept appears to inhabit a world of its own. It is indeed very personal music, and can only be understood as the statement of a highly complex composer, who has come through the ruin of his peace by worldly events to a position of some faith. It is

[11]In Giovanni Gabrieli's *Sacrae symphoniae* (Venice, 1597); see Giovanni Gabrieli, *Opera omnia*, I, pp. 57–62.

[12]See Thurston Dart, *The Interpretation of Music* (London, Hutchinson, 1954, 4/1967), pp. 107–8.

[13]On the 'unity' of the 1610 *Vespers*, see pages 161–2. Of course, this does not preclude the separate performance of individual items.

no wonder that it has no equivalent in his later church music written for Venice, where he was both highly esteemed and relatively stable emotionally.

Even so, the seeds of his later style are all to be found in the volume of 1610, with passion and magnificence as basic aims, if not in its exclusive *mélange*. In Venice he developed passion in more *sacri affetti* and magnificence in the motets for festival days, not to mention the *a cappella* polyphony for ordinary use in St Mark's. The publishers sought the first of these, and sacred songs and duets by Monteverdi appeared in most of the anthologies of the time. He maintains in them a complete stylistic unity with his secular chamber music, never becoming deliberately conservative in any way. The four motets published in Leonardo Simonetti's *Ghirlanda sacra* in 1625 are typical. Two of them, 'Ecce sacrum paratum convivium' and 'Currite populi, psallite timpanis' are Venetian arias, both having extended triple-time passages interrupted by recitatives. The triple-time sections are completely diatonic, and the 'alleluia' refrain of 'Currite populi' is a lively tune which Berti or Grandi would have been pleased to write for their song-books:

Ex. 43

This was an especially popular style, and Monteverdi wrote several of these lighter works, of which two solo motets, 'Exulta filia Sion' and 'Venite videte martirem', are very attractive.[14]

[14]Published in Lorenzo Calvi's *Quarta raccolta de sacri canti* (Venice, 1629) and in the *Motetti a voce sola de diversi eccelentissimi autori* (Venice, 1645) respectively.

The other two motets from Simonetti's *Ghirlanda sacra*, 'O quam pulchra es' and 'Salve Regina', are among the most beautiful of solo madrigals. Both are *arioso* contemplations, and rapturous ones, of womanhood, settings of texts which were especially popular in Venice, where the Blessed Virgin was specially venerated. 'O quam pulchra es' begins with Monteverdi's favourite downward sixth in the melody and then lavishes the extravagances of trill and melisma to express the beauty of the beloved. As usual, Monteverdi seizes on the chance to give his melody shape. The short phrases, 'amica mea, colomba mea, formosa mea' ('my love, my dove, my beauty'), suggest the repetition of a motif; and each time the opening words, 'O how beautiful you are', come round the *gorgie* return. The climax comes as the lover 'languishes of love' ('quia amore langueo') with a chromatic bass pushing the belated melody down to form voluptuous dissonances.

'Salve Regina' is more serene, although it too has a touch of chromatic desire as the singer sends up 'our sighs, mourning and weeping' ('ad te suspiramus gementes et flentes') in his prayer to the Virgin. It is a piece of long phrases (not so usual for Monteverdi) organized at the beginning by a rhythm suggested by the repetition of the word 'salve' ('hail') and given variety by sudden bursts of rhythmic energy – 'ad te clamamus' ('We call to thee') or 'eja ergo, o advocata nostra' ('O thee, our advocate'). Dissonance is reserved for the climax and the inevitable downward sixth comes in the very last phrase.

These motets are fine because they draw out the inner meaning of the words. But Monteverdi is not averse to painting the outer meaning any more than he was in the Tasso settings of his madrigal books. The motet for solo bass, 'Ab aeterno ordinata sum' (in the *Selva morale e spirituale* of 1640–1), with its description of the creation of the world, is reminiscent of the recitatives of Charon and Pluto in its leaps to the depths for words such as 'abissos' (abysses') and runs for 'aquis' ('waters'). The first 'Laudate Dominum omnes gentes' in the same volume follows up the mood of 'Zefiro torna, e di soavi accenti' and 'Armato il cor d'adamantina fede'. Some details are painted in the *stile concitato* (suggested by the warlike instruments mentioned in the psalm), and both the chaconne bass and the melody which develops over it – with *hemiola*, held notes and descriptive melismas – are very like the secular duets. Even the sudden change from triple time to the quasi-recitative (not really justifiable in the psalm setting) brings 'Zefiro torna' to our minds.

There is also some attractive choral music, though, in an age when the soloist was supreme, it naturally did not take up a large part of Monteverdi's energies, at least in its non-concertante forms. He contributed an especially fine group of four motets to an anthology collected by a former Mantuan colleague, Giulio Cesare Bianchi, in 1620. One is a grave setting of words from a penitential psalm 'Domine ne in furore tuo' in a sonorous manner. Of the others, 'Cantate Domino canticum novum' is a splendid frolic, with much strongly accented triple time and some madrigalian phrases (one closely resembling a passage from 'Ecco mormorar l'onde' in his second book) well worked out. More remarkable still are two ecstatic works, 'Christe adoramus te' and 'Adoramus te Christe', probably written for the festival of the Holy Cross, for which, as he wrote to Striggio (see page 31 above), he had to provide ample music each year. These speak the language of the mature madrigals, using chromaticism and some luscious dissonances, yet never allowing such sensuous devices to overwhelm the dignity which seemingly comes naturally in his Venetian music.

These works, then, are recognizably Monteverdian. This certainly cannot be said of the *prima pruttica* Masses and psalms which we find in the two Venetian collected editions of Monteverdi's church music. Here he limits dissonance to suspensions and passing notes on the weak beats, and writes smooth melodic lines in the overlapping phrases which necessarily preclude any dynamic contrasts. These works are consciously archaic; but they are not self-consciously learned as the *Missa 'In illo tempore'* had been. Monteverdi composes in an idiom familiar to his age. Completely tonal melody, rhythms which are moulded by the bar-line, the harmonic language of the *missa brevis* rather than the exaggerated imitative counter-point of 1610 – all these give him plenty of scope for writing expressive music. The *Crucifixus* of the Mass published in 1650 uses suspensions most beautifully to express the words 'Passus et sepultus est' ('suffered . . . and was buried'), and there is genuine excitement in the triple-time 'Et resurrexit' ('He rose again') and the sequential phrases of the 'Hosanna'.

The same is true of the psalms for double choir, which bear little relationship to the idiom of the Gabrielis. The dialogue interplay of the older Venetians is there, but the rhythms are rather square and the harmony is deliberately more consonant, more Roman than Venetian. The interest in sheer sonority is restricted to the effects which can be obtained from two equally balanced choirs which never use the extremes of the voice. Even so, the idiom is consistent and has a dignity of its own, though it remains impersonal. But the true successors of the grand Venetian motets are to be found in the works written in the *stile concertato*. The grandeur, like Venice's own, becomes slightly diminished as the century proceeds. The huge variety of the Gabrielian orchestra is reduced in Monteverdi's work to a body of strings, sometimes with trombones brought in to support the voices. At the same time he develops the idiomatic use of this orchestra in the way we have seen in the large 1610 Magnificat. The instruments rarely double the voices, and then only at climaxes. They add material which is not really suitable for the voices, or else use the vocal material separately to contrast with the choral colour.

It is often said of these works that they are truly secular, and it is certainly true that they often use the same kind of material as Monteverdi's later *continuo* madrigals. One setting of the psalm 'Beatus vir' (the first of two in the 1640–1 *Selva morale e spirituale*), for example, uses 'Chiome d'oro' from the seventh book of madrigals as its basic material. The warlike phrases of the eighth book appear a number of times in the church music – in the 'Nisi Dominus' for six voices (in the *Messa . . . et salmi*, 1650) and, delightfully, to express the words 'He hath shown strength with his arm' ('Fecit potentiam in brachio suo') in the first Magnificat in the *Selva morale e spirituale*, to exactly the same figure that appears in the 'sinfonia da guerra' when Ulysses has equally shown the strength of his arm (*Il ritorno d'Ulisse in patria*, Act II Scene 12). Yet these works do not have the same inner spirit as Monteverdi's madrigals and they do not have the same power of expression. The reason is not, as has been suggested, a spiritual so much as a musical one. With the liturgical music which was needed for St Mark's there was no question of specially choosing or reorganizing the words as in the madrigals. Many of the texts to be set were long, and as yet the new *basso continuo* motet had not evolved a form suited to making such settings continuously interesting. Some of the younger men were working on the right lines. Alessandro Grandi divided his psalms into sections which were more or less complete in themselves; Tarquinio Merula was experimenting with sections bound together with *ostinato* figures. Monteverdi preferred rather conservatively to stick to the long duet and trio sections which Viadana had evolved. The result is that some of these works, while full of fertile ideas, seem to lack an overall sense of climax.

But where Monteverdi sees a real opportunity for large-scale organization, he writes church music that is both expressive of the words and worthily splendid in the Venetian tradition. Perhaps the most splendid of all his church music is to be found in the *Gloria* with trombones and strings which he composed in 1631 for the Mass in thanksgiving for the relief from the plague (included in the *Selva morale e spirituale*). The liturgical text suited him, for it was not unmanageably long and it had contrasting ideas to offset its general mood of rejoicing. The tenor intones with a lively rhythm, and then through a series of duets Monteverdi works up a motif into a tremendous climax (see Ex. 44). 'Peace on earth' ('et in terra pax') suggests a homophonic passage for the full choir, using the lower register of all the voices, just as in the peaceful section of 'Hor che'l ciel e la terra e'l vento tace'. Then there is a series of duets, two-bar phrases for tenors or sopranos being answered or echoed by a pair of violins. The words 'gloriam tuam' ('Thy great glory') suggest the opening motif again, and it is given to each of the voices in turn; but, very skilfully, it is not worked up to the massive climax of the first section and is deliberately broken off for more duet work. 'Qui tollis peccata mundi ('Who takest away the sins of the world') is set in duet and trio textures held together with a *ritornello*. When Monteverdi

Ex. 44

(continued)

comes to 'in gloria Dei Patris' ('in the glory of God the Father'), he naturally brings back the beginning, and this time there is no interruption. The opening climax comes back with the increased force of complete thematic recapitulation after a broken development.

This form comes naturally out of the words. Elsewhere Monteverdi has to impose it on them. In the 'Beatus vir' in which he parodies 'Chiome d'oro', the *ostinato* bass of the madrigal comes to his aid; but even then he makes his opening vocal motif return from time to time to make a rondo, and a rondo which is clearer because the memorable violin figure of the 'Chiome d'oro' *ritornello* usually comes back with it. The variations on the bass take the form of painting the image of the verse. 'Gloria' provides a sequential, lively, melismatic figure, 'irascetur' ('shall be grieved') a semiquaver motif, and so on. In this way, Monteverdi finds a happy solution of maintaining unity while providing variety. There are other pieces where he tends to overdo the formal aspect, notably an extraordinary setting of the psalm 'Laetatus sum' for six voices, two violins, two trombones and bassoon (in the *Messa . . . et salmi*), where a four-note *ostinato* is repeated more or less exactly until the doxology, giving the effect of a seventeenth-century equivalent of Ravel's *Bolero*.

He solved the problem in the third setting of 'Laudate Dominum omnes gentes' which he included in the *Selva morale e spirituale*. Here he wrote a duet for sopranos with a choir joining in from time to time to give the appearance of a rondo. In the duet section, the phrases have to develop – and very attractive they are:

Ex. 45

(Praise ye the Lord . . .)

The great climax comes when the sopranos' phrases are given to the full choir and extended with repetitions; thereafter Monteverdi is content to leave the doxology to the sopranos alone. Another solution was his setting of 'Confitebor tibi Domine' in the French style (the third 'Confitebor' in the *Selva morale e spirituale*), borrowing material from 'Dolcissimo uscignolo' and 'Chi vol haver felice e lieto il core' from the eighth book of madrigals, and using the same basic treatment, that is, making the soprano soloist sing each section which is then expanded with a full harmonization of it by the

141

choir.[15] Just as the original madrigals 'Dolcissimo uscignolo' and 'Chi vol haver felice' have great charm, so has the psalm, though it seemingly lacks powers in the innocence of its harmony and the regularity of its phrase structure. And then, as the word 'Gloria' comes, Monteverdi lets out an impassioned and triumphant cry from the soprano:

Ex. 46

This, if proof is still needed, must convince us of the sincere and deep conviction which made Monteverdi turn to the priesthood towards the end of his life.

[15]On the problematic term 'canto [cantare, etc.] alla francese', see the overview in John Whenham, 'The Later Madrigals and Madrigal Books', in Arnold and Fortune (eds.), *The New Monteverdi Companion*, pp. 216–47, at pp. 230–5.

8

Reputation and influence

'The greatest fame which a man may have on earth.' With these words Follino coaxed Monteverdi back to Mantua to compose *Arianna* (see page 17). Was the promise fulfilled? The question is of some importance to a biographer, and the search for an answer has a twofold value. The reputation that a composer had in his lifetime reveals the manner of man which he appeared to be to his contemporaries. The reputation that his name has acquired in the years since his death throws light on our attitude towards him. To study both these things can therefore help us to avoid the more obvious errors of appraisal and prevent our reading into his life and work merely what we would like to find there. At the same time, it must be admitted that the evidence which we possess is insufficient to give us anything like a complete picture of the growth of Monteverdi's fame. Nor can it tell us how deeply his art affected other composers, for many things which today seem exclusively Monteverdian were in fact the common language of his day. We can, however, deduce certain attitudes, certain preferences for and antipathies to his music which are revealing and significant.

Monteverdi came into prominence comparatively slowly. This is quite clear from the lack of reprints of his early music. The popular anthologies to which composers were invited to contribute by editors and publishers contain little of his music in his early years. While he was living at Cremona this was understandable enough. For his first years at Mantua it is significant. Living among Wert, Pallavicino and Gastoldi he must have had every opportunity to be brought in touch with the Venetian publishers. Apparently this was of no avail. After his third book of madrigals, fewer than half a dozen pieces of his music appeared in his first decade there. The only reason for this lack of quick success can be that he was not considered a composer of light-weight or occasional music. He was essentially a serious composer who made few concessions to his audience. This is not contradicted by his sudden leap into fame after the production of *Orfeo*. His music then seemed to take on a new lease of life. A large number of editions of his madrigal books, a large number of contributions to the anthologies, display his widening audience – a large number, that is, until we look at the work of somebody like Marenzio, whose work appeared in anthology after anthology for over twenty years, and whose madrigal books rarely went through fewer than five or six reprints. But Marenzio was publishing at a time when the music-printing industry was expanding rather than severely contracting, as now.

Monteverdi's sudden success appears to be due to the enthusiasm of connoisseurs. It lasted about six or seven years, during which the fourth and fifth books of madrigals found a special favour. Adriano Banchieri at this time could write in his *Conclusioni del suono dell' organo* (1609):

> I must not omit the name of the most sweet composer of music in the modern style, Claudio Monteverdi, head of music to the Most Serene Signor Don Vincenzo Gonzaga, Duke of Mantua (universally well known to the professional musician is his work), since his expression of the emotions, full of art, is truly worthy of complete commendation.[1]

How rapidly things had changed. A few years earlier the same Bolognese writer and composer had acknowledged the receipt of Artusi's vicious attack on Monteverdi in these terms:

> I have examined it all, and I say that the book is worthy of eternal praise, rebutting the crudity of certain destroyers of the good rules of Zarlino, Franchino, Guido and other intelligent writers, among whom, however, are not included the modern followers of the admirable Roman school, and in particular in the church style Signor Giovanni Pietro Pallestina [*sic*], and in the chamber style Signor Luca Marenzio.[2]

This tide of popularity carried Monteverdi to Venice. After his arrival there the reprints of his old madrigal books gradually died away, and the new ones were never accompanied by the same demand from the public. The reason for this was surely that Monteverdi never bothered to follow the fashions. The song-books of his assistants, Alessandro Grandi and Giovanni Rovetta, were selling well. Monteverdi, on the other hand, made no concession to public taste until his second book of *Scherzi musicali* was published. By this time the Roman writer Vincenzo Giustiniani could bewail the decline of conventional madrigal singing: 'In the present course of

---

[1] In Fabbri, *Monteverdi*, p. 153.
[2] Adriano Banchieri to Giovanni Maria Artusi, undated, in Adriano Banchieri, *Lettere armoniche* (Bologna, 1628), p. 94.

our age music is not much in use, not being practised in Rome by gentlemen, nor do they sing with several voices to the book as in past years'.[3] It is no wonder that Monteverdi's madrigal books, written for his Mantuan virtuosos, gradually faded into the past.

Oddly enough, in spite of this state of affairs in Italy, foreigners began to take to his music. The vogue for madrigals flowered in both Germany and England just late enough to give his works a new lease of life. The Germans had been interested in his work for some years, and the Nuremberg collector Paul Kauffmann and the organist to the King of Denmark Melchior Borchgrevinck (a pupil of Giovanni Gabrieli) had both found opportunities to print Monteverdi's madrigals while he was still at Mantua. Then Pierre Phalèse, the enterprising publisher living in Antwerp, took them up, and from about 1615 found a market for the third, fourth and fifth books. He had no audience for the sixth book until 1639, and seems to have had no interest in the *continuo* madrigals.

England was slightly behind the times — when choosing Italian madrigals to copy or print it usually relied on the taste of Phalèse. Some Italophiles admittedly knew of Monteverdi's work. The younger Francis Tregian, copying his immense collection of vocal and instrumental music to while away time in the Fleet Prison about 1615, put a number of Monteverdi's madrigals into score, including virtually all of Book IV (why he missed out the first number, 'Ah dolente partita', remains a mystery), but he clearly had an abnormal source of supply in Italy.[4] Another lover of things Italian was Henry Peacham, who published his book *The Compleat Gentleman* in 1622 and included a chapter on the art of music. After singling out Marenzio, Vecchi and Croce for high praise, he went on:

[3] Carol MacClintock (trans.), *Hercole Bottrigari, 'Il Desiderio . . .'; Vincenzo Giustiniani, 'Discorso sopra la musica'*, 'Musicological Studies and Documents', ix (American Institute of Musicology, 1962), p. 76. Giustiniani was writing c.1628, and compare Domenico Mazzocchi's comment in the preface to his *Madrigali a cinque voci, et altri varii concerti* (Rome, 1638): 'the most ingenious field of study in Music is that of madrigals; but today few are composed, and fewer are sung, given that to their misfortune they seem more or less banished from the Academies.'

[4] Tregian's vocal anthology is in London, British Library, Egerton 3665, continued in New York, Public Library at Lincoln Center (Library and Museum of the Performing Arts), Drexel 4302 (the 'Sambrooke' MS). Versions of Monteverdi's madrigals also survive in London, British Library, Add. MS 31440, perhaps copied by Walter Porter (see page 203), see Pamela J. Willetts, 'A Neglected Source of Monody and Madrigal', *Music & Letters*, xliii (1962), 329–39. See also Charles W. Hughes, 'Porter, Pupil of Monteverdi', *The Musical Quarterly*, xx (1934), 278–88.

There are many other authors very excellent, as [Giovanni] Boschetto and Claudio de Monteverdi, equal to any before named, Giovanni Ferretti, Stephano Felis, Giulio Rinaldi, Philippe de Monte, Andrea Gabrieli, Cipriano de Rore, Pallavicino, Geminiano [Capilupi], with others yet living . . .[5]

Monteverdi is in similar company in another context. One of the earliest biographers of Milton tells us that when Milton was returning home after a journey in Italy he arrived at Venice, whence

. . . when he had spent a Month's time in viewing of that Stately City, and Shipp'd up a Parcel of curious and rare Books which he had pick'd up in his Travels; particularly a Chest or two of choice Musick-books of the best Masters flourishing about that time in *Italy*, namely, *Luca Marenzio, Monte Verde, Horatio Vecchi, Cifa* [Cifra], the Prince of *Venosa*, and several others,[6]

he returned to France and from there to England.

These were all men who had some special interest in Italian music; but there is no sign that Monteverdi was as popular as Marenzio or Croce with ordinary madrigal singers. If the two books of *Musica transalpina* (1588, 1597) came too early for his music, it is still significant that the manuscript part-books which have come down to us from the late sixteenth and early seventeenth centuries rarely include it either. This perhaps was due quite simply to the fact that the poetry which he set in his madrigals could hardly be translated with the exactness which would make the madrigals coherent and acceptable. Even so, such a theory must remain unproven since we find some of the most literary madrigals of Books III and IV in still stranger surroundings. There are a number of manuscripts of viol music which contain these, among fantasies and dances of such composers as Lupo, Ferrabosco and Wilbye.[7] The anthologists who selected them had good taste and chose the best. What they made of them without the words is a matter for conjecture.

In Italy, meanwhile, it seems clear that it was the professional musicians and composers who were most appreciative of his work. One of the most distinguished composers of monodies, Claudio

[5]In Strunk, *Source Readings in Music History*, p. 336.

[6]Edward Phillips, *The Life of Mr. John Milton* (1694), in Helen Darbishire, *The Early Lives of Milton* (London, 1932), p. 59.

[7]For example, London, British Library, Add. MSS 29427, 37402–6; Oxford, Christ Church, MSS 2, 21, 44; Dublin, Marsh's Library, MSS Z3, 4, 7–12. Full details of these and other manuscript sources are in Stattkus, *Claudio Monteverdi: Verzeichnis der erhaltenen Werke*.

Saracini, dedicated to Monteverdi the first solo madrigal of his *Le seconde musiche* (Venice, 1620). Whether or not he was an actual pupil of Monteverdi, the two composers were certainly musical kinsmen. Saracini was one of the composers who developed the passionate *arioso* and the striking harmonic clashes in Monteverdi's manner. Both composers were prone to academic arguments about the importance of monody in 'moving the affections'. More superficially influenced, perhaps, was Alessandro Grandi. He arrived in Venice a little too late to have his style completely founded on the master, and soon acquired an interest in the modern ariettas which were the favourites of the Venetians. In his church music, on the other hand, the change of style after his arrival to be Monteverdi's assistant was too marked for it to be purely a coincidence. From being a writer of conventional, though often beautiful, *concertato* motets he became one of the principal composers of the solo motet, written in the recitative-arioso style which Monteverdi had introduced in the solo music of the 1610 *Vespers*. Refrain techniques and the use of a rhythmic motif distinguished Grandi's work also and lead to the same sort of emotional richness. He even took up the *stile concitato*, and one of his psalm settings, 'Dixit Dominus' (published in 1629), is full of the repeated-note string passages which he must have learned from the *Combattimento di Tancredi et Clorinda* (see Ex. 47 on the following page).

Much the same can be said of Francesco Cavalli, who certainly borrowed various ideas from Monteverdi. The 'lament' appears in his operas to form a climax as in *Arianna*; and his solo motets have the same complete secularity which we have seen in Monteverdi's music. Even so, the detail of the Monteverdian style is left well behind in his work, which has none of the old-fashioned declamatory recitative or the virulent harmony of his great master.

At least two pupils came from abroad. One of them was an Englishman, Walter Porter, who, in publishing his *Mottets of two voyces . . . with the continued bass* (London, 1657), proudly pointed out that these were in the Italian style and were the result of his studies in Italy. In a manuscript note found in a copy of this book in Christ Church, Oxford, he tells us that his teacher was Monteverdi himself. What had Porter learned? Undoubtedly the technique of writing *continuo* madrigals and some of the tricks of the trade. In his book of *Madrigales and Ayres, of two, three, foure and five voyces, with the continued base* (London, 1632) he displays the ability to write declamatory melodic lines, the expressive use of dissonance and chromaticism, and the various ornaments which were the stock-in-trade of Italian composers. Further than this it is

Ex. 47

(he shall wound . . .)

difficult, if not impossible, to find specifically Monteverdian traits. It is true that he occasionally uses that favourite downward leap of a sixth, but instead of expressing the meaning of some passionate poetic phrase, it is nearly always pictorial (to express the idea of 'falling', for example) in an older English tradition. And he is maladroit in his application of ornaments. The sobbing trill is just as likely to occur on the words 'and' or 'of' as on 'love' or 'grief'. The only closer connection with Monteverdi that we may notice is that his madrigals and airs are for the most part old-fashioned, at least for 1632, and follow the forms to be found in Monteverdi's seventh book. But in fact, Porter could have learned everything from even a minor Italian composer.

The other foreigner, Heinrich Schütz, is much more important. By the time of his visit to Monteverdi in Venice in 1628 he was a man of considerable attainments and over forty years old. It was not his first period of study in Italy, for he had come to Venice to work with Giovanni Gabrieli twenty years before. His style was by this time a unique mixture of Italian and German, completely personal in its adaptation of the techniques of Venetian church music to German usage. All the more remarkable, then, was his receptiveness in face of the work of Monteverdi. Whether he was a formal pupil of the Italian is not known and is unimportant; what is certain is that he studied Monteverdi's work with the greatest care. He did more than pick up a few tricks of style – though we can find Monteverdi's downward sixth, chromatic changes and astringent harmonies in Schütz's work too. He studied the very basis of Monteverdi's 'academic philosophy' as we can see from a book by his own pupil, Christoph Bernhard, whose *Tractatus compositionis augmentatus* goes into the theory of the affections in some detail and with some insight. Most especially, since it was Monteverdi's latest invention, the *stile concitato* affected Schütz's attitude. It is no coincidence that a recently discovered German manuscript of the period (probably the earliest German copy of a Monteverdi work) is a score of part of the *Combattimento di Tancredi et Clorinda*, complete with a translation.[8] Schütz may not have made this copy himself, but it must have been his interest that gave it its *raison d'être*. In his own music there are passages in this manner, and his motet 'Es steh Gott auf', in the second part of his *Symphoniae sacrae* (1647), is largely an adaptation of two of Monteverdi's *continuo* madrigals, 'Armato il cor d'adamantina fede' and 'Zefiro torna, e di soavi accenti'. Quite apart from details of the new recitative and *arioso* melody which are to be found all over the *concertato* motets which he published after this journey, we find a change of attitude in his religious music which is very Monteverdian. Such works as 'Fili mi Absalon' and 'Saul, Saul, was verfolgst du mich?' are full of dramatic force and remind us of the description of Monteverdi's music for the memorial requiem of Cosimo II of Tuscany. Although we have lost Monteverdi's music for this occasion, Schütz's style helps us to fill in the gap.

In a way this influence on German music and especially on

---

[8]Now in Tokyo, Bibliotheca Musashino Academia Musicae. For a facsimile, see Wolfgang Osthoff, 'Monteverdis *Combattimento* in deutscher Sprache und Heinrich Schütz', in *Festschrift Helmuth Osthoff* (Tutzing, 1961), pp. 195–227.

German theory was to be more important than the direct influence of Monteverdi's music on his immediate successors. He left no school of composers behind him. Cavalli, Antonio Cesti and the rest learned a great deal from the variety of forms in *Il ritorno d'Ulisse in patria* and *L'incoronazione di Poppea*: they did not directly imitate them. Monteverdi was by this time a little too old-fashioned for forward-looking composers. As Alfred Einstein suggests, he had too many 'scruples',[9] that is, he was always a serious-minded composer with his roots in the old academic theories. His influence had passed into the life of music gradually over the years, by giving the ultimate power to technical means which for the most part had been discovered by other people. Hence in an age which had little historical sense his progress in the art was taken for granted and soon forgotten. When he died, however, he was revered as a great master. Caberloti's memoir shows us that.[10] So does Sansovino's guidebook to Venice, which, describing the Cappella dei Lombardi in S. Maria Gloriosa dei Frari, says that 'in the Chapel and tomb of the Milanesi is buried Claudio Monteverdi, *maestro di cappella* of St Mark's, a great theorist of vocal and instrumental music, famous for his valour and for his compositions, of which a great many are in print.'[11]

It was to the learned men, the writers of treatises, that Monteverdi's reputation was entrusted. Naturally their interests were in his theoretical writings, small in extent though they were. Even in his lifetime one writer, Giovanni Battista Doni, was discussing his work from the academic point of view. And Monteverdi had one especially valuable thing to offer. Precisely because he was unable to understand the Greek writers clearly, precisely because he was primarily a practical musician, he had tried to realize what the Platonic theorists meant in terms of musical practice. His promised treatise on the Second Practice was to be a very practical book dealing with methods of representation, with details of harmony and rhythm. To reinforce this, his *stile concitato* was an attempt to apply theory to musical idiom in the most lucid way possible. This was worth more than all the vague references to Platonic theory, all the acoustics and arguments about temperament that had filled the Renaissance treatises. It was a line which had a great deal to offer any composer.

[9]Einstein, *The Italian Madrigal*, II, p. 867.

[10]Relevant extracts from Matteo Caberloti's *Laconismo delle alte qualità di Claudio Monteverde*, printed in Giovan Battista Marinoni (ed.), *Fiori poetici raccolti nel funerale del molto illustre e molto reverendo signor Claudio Monteverde* (Venice, 1644), are in Fabbri, *Monteverdi*, pp. 344–6.

[11]Francesco Sansovino, *Venetia, città nobilissima* (rev. Venice, 1663), p. 195, in Fabbri, *Monteverdi*, p. 345.

First Doni, then Schütz's pupil Christoph Bernhard, then a number of minor German writers began to speak of 'moving the affections' in terms of specific musical figures. By the eighteenth century this had flowered into a veritable philosophy of music, and Johann Sebastian Bach's contemporaries such as Johann Adolph Scheibe and Johann Mattheson developed a guide to musical invention based on the various emotions of the verbal texts, which, while certainly more complicated than anything envisaged by Monteverdi, none the less followed up his line of thought.

In this way Monteverdi's work passed into the main stream of musical tradition; and, as so often happens when a composer's ideas are developed rather than imitated by his followers, his music in itself had little interest for the musician and the public. By the early eighteenth century only an historian would have heard of it – and music historians were very few. When Padre Martini was gathering together his library at Bologna, he took care to collect all of Monteverdi's works that he could find, and he read the Artusi-Monteverdi polemic with some attention. Naturally his attention turned to the madrigals which had been criticized for their dissonance, and especially 'Cruda Amarilli, che col nome ancora' (in the fifth book). Although interested more in the style of Palestrina and the orthodox church composers of the sixteenth century, he was no dry-as-dust theorist. He saw Monteverdi's point quite clearly even though he thought it better for the young contrapuntist not to imitate him:

> The young composer must reflect that the author [Monteverdi] does not use dissonances prohibited by the rules, except in cases where the expression of the words demands it, and then only in madrigals. And since by common agreement, as consonances are agreeable to the hearing, so dissonances are displeasing, thus it is that these must not be used out of order, but either in suspensions or in passing notes, so that they do not become horrible and displeasing. They are used in madrigals because, being sung only by the parts of which they are composed, and without the accompaniment of any instrument, it was easier for them to be sung perfectly in tune by a few singers than in church music, in which a crowd of singers sings, which singers, as experience teaches us, are not all capable of a just and perfect intonation.[12]

[12]Giovanni Battista Martini, *Esemplare o sia saggio fondamentale pratico di contrappunto sopra il canto fermo*, II (Bologna, 1774), pp. 193–4, in Fabbri, *Monteverdi*, pp. 366–7 n. 32. Other extracts from Martini's analyses are in *ibid.*, p. 365 n. 11.

This is true enough, and Martini knew that Monteverdi could write orthodox counterpoint when he chose because he had scored part of the *Missa 'In illo tempore'*. But what is interesting is that he printed for the modern reader quotations from two extreme madrigals, full of the more progressive harmonies. This was equally true of Charles Burney in his *History of Music*. Burney had examined Monteverdi's music in Martini's library and naturally came to look at the novel passages (as they seemed to him). The legend of Monteverdi the revolutionary was now well established:

> Monteverde was the first who used double discords, such as the $\frac{9}{4}$, $\frac{9}{7}$ and $\frac{7}{2}$, as well as the flat fifth, and the seventh unprepared; and as he was possessed of more genius and science than the Prince of Venosa, his innovations were not merely praised, and then avoided, but abused, and adopted by other composers.[13]

Neither Burney nor Martini had, we may suspect, transcribed much of Monteverdi's music – the Burney transcripts now in the British Library show a more complete coverage of many other madrigalists. Yet their authority was sufficient for this picture to persist into the nineteenth century, and Monteverdi's apparently revolutionary discoveries were made more prominent still by the appearance of music from the 1610 *Vespers* in Carl von Winterfeld's study of the music of Giovanni Gabrieli, published in 1834. A few personal documents which came to light about the same time did nothing to change this state of affairs. Verdi, thinking out a curriculum for the young composer to follow, recommended a thorough study of counterpoint, but took care to exclude Monteverdi on the grounds that his part-writing was bad.

As late as 1880 it was possible for a conscientious man such as W. S. Rockstro to write of Monteverdi in the first edition of Grove's *A Dictionary of Music and Musicians*:

> Well would it have been for Polyphonic Art, and for his own reputation, also, had he recognized [that his true vocation was dramatic music] sooner. Had he given his attention to Dramatic Music, from the first, the Mass and the madrigal might, perhaps, have still been preserved in the purity bequeathed to them by Palestrina and Luca Marenzio. As it was, the utter demolition of the older School was effected, before the newer one was built upon its ruins: and Monte-

[13]Charles Burney, *A General History of Music from the Earliest Ages to the Present Period* (London, 1776–89), III, p. 235; ed. Frank Mercer, 2 vols. (London, 1935; repr. New York, 1957), II, p. 191.

verde was as surely the destroyer of the first, as he was the founder of the second.

Rockstro certainly knew more than most people about Monteverdi, and had examined the score of *Orfeo* with care and admiration; but he relied on the same old sources – Artusi, Martini and Burney – for his knowledge of the madrigals. As by this time the music of the sixteenth century meant in fact the music of the Roman school, it is not to be wondered at that even scholars could accept this picture of Monteverdi heaving up the very roots of counterpoint and founding the new music single-handed.

Fortunately rescue was at hand. The Swiss historian Jacob Burckhardt, John Addington Symonds and a number of other believers in history as a study of culture rather than of politics were at work in the 1860s and 1870s. Painting and literature were their first subjects. Music followed a little later, being more difficult of access. Inspired by this new attitude a number of musicians and historians began researches into the music of the sixteenth and seventeenth centuries. Stefano Davari, in charge of the Gonzaga archives at Mantua, was the first to show an interest in Monteverdi. Working on the various papers over many years, he found the huge series of letters which form the principal material for a biographer, together with most of the minor documents which still exist there. Emil Vogel, a more professional music historian, made a wider search and wrote the first biography of any value, after examining documents at Cremona and Venice, as well as looking at and transcribing a great deal of the music.

By this time the music itself was coming back into view. Alongside the new histories and music journals, which the German revival of old music started with such great enthusiasm, were the new editions. *Orfeo* came out in 1881 in an edition by Robert Eitner, and from then until the beginning of the First World War the madrigals and operas were gradually made public again. By the 1920s Monteverdi's music was reasonably well known to scholars, and a number of these made the attempt to revive the various works. *Orfeo* and *L'incoronazione di Poppea* were given a number of performances, and some years later the 1610 *Vespers* became almost a popular work in the edition of Hans Redlich. The resurgence of Italian nationalism between the wars bore one of its few pleasant fruits in a collected edition, and a number of excellent monographs have appeared in French, English, German, and Italian.

All this is very reminiscent of the Bach revival of the last century, and although there has been no formal 'Monteverdi Association' as there was a Bachgesellschaft, there are now 'Monteverdi Choirs' and other organizations which have done a great deal to further our knowledge of his music. The operas are now almost repertory fare in many theatres, though the lesson that Monteverdi's music does not need an elaborate orchestration in a modern style has yet to be completely learned there. The *Vespers* now draws vast popular audiences at the Promenade Concerts in London, and it is no longer considered eccentric to find its music worthy of a place beside the Mass in B minor. The first edition of this book ended with a plea to consider Monteverdi not as the creator of modern music but simply as a genius. This is no longer necessary. There are surely few music lovers who cannot detect and feel his expression of human suffering and jöÿ, in music as timeless as that of any of the greatest composers.

9

Afterword

The quatercentenary of Monteverdi's birth in 1967 prompted renewed interest in the study and performance of his music. Several conferences were held uniting an international body of Monteverdi scholars, including the 'Convegno Internazionale di Studi Monteverdiani' (Siena, 28–30 April 1967) – the proceedings appeared in the *Rivista Italiana di Musicologia*, ii/2 (1967) – and 'Claudio Monteverdi e il suo tempo' (Cremona, Mantua and Venice, 3–7 May 1968; again, Raffaello Monterosso's edition of the proceedings was published). Plans for a new complete edition of Monteverdi's music (now some half-way complete) to replace Malipiero's were also set in train. The celebrations also prompted a number of other major projects, including Denis Arnold and Nigel Fortune's *The Monteverdi Companion* (1968), with its important collection of essays on aspects of Monteverdi's secular, sacred and theatrical music (a revised edition with significant new material appeared in 1985). Domenico de' Paoli's edition of the letters, dedications and prefaces (1973) brought together almost the complete corpus of this fascinating material – perhaps the richest of its kind for a composer of the period – and Denis Stevens's translation (1980) of the letters (prepared from new transcriptions) further opened up Monteverdi's world to English-speaking audiences. The letters and other archival documents provided the basis for Paolo Fabbri's near-definitive biography (1985; it will shortly appear in English translation), while broader accounts of Monteverdi in his various contexts have been provided by Silke Leopold (1982; again a translation will soon appear) and by Gary Tomlinson (1987). Now we approach the 350th anniversary of Monteverdi's death (1993), which will very likely offer no less impetus to new generations of scholars and performers fascinated by the music of Monteverdi and his contemporaries. Meanwhile, an overview of developments since 1967 may help us see where we have been, and where we might go.

For a student learning the musicological trade in the 1970s, perhaps the most striking trend was the enthusiastic adoption, at least in some circles, of archival research as the nuts and bolts of serious musicological enquiry, adopting methods long standard in other historical disciplines but still a matter of debate in a subject that could not, indeed cannot, decide whether it is dealing with historical artefacts or transcendental art-works. Of course, previous generations of Monteverdi scholars had already done distinguished service in the archives: the most obvious example is the seminal research (published in the 1880s) of Stefano Davari in the Archivio di Stato in Mantua. But now the search was for a clearer understanding of the institutional networks and patronage systems within which the composer and his contemporaries worked, and of how these networks and systems may have influenced their output. Denis Arnold himself was adventurous in his use of archives – exceptionally so since such approaches rarely found much sympathy in his day among English students of Italian music – and he was followed by a number of scholars who developed increasingly refined methods for dealing with archival sources. Two studies in particular had a direct bearing on a new understanding of the contexts for Monteverdi's work: Anthony Newcomb's *The Madrigal in Ferrara, 1579–1597* of 1979, and Iain Fenlon's *Music and Patronage in Sixteenth-Century Mantua* of 1980 (both stem from doctoral theses completed in 1970 and 1977 respectively). Newcomb's study of Duke Alfonso II d'Este's patronage of music, particularly via his virtuoso vocal and instrumental group known as the *concerto di donne*, and its status as a role-model for the Gonzagas in Mantua and the Medici in Florence (both of whom established *concerti* on the Ferrarese example) offers important light on the soprano-dominated textures so characteristic of Wert's and Monteverdi's madrigal books of the 1590s. Moreover, Newcomb's discussion of changing trends in the Ferrarese madrigal of the last decade of the century, under the influence both of new literary tendencies and of the music of Gesualdo, provides a context for the experiments in text-setting and dissonance treatment that led to the Monteverdi–Artusi controversy (which itself seems to have occurred within a Ferrarese ambit, perhaps linked to the little-known Accademia degli Intrepidi, to the members of which Monteverdi dedicated his fourth book of madrigals of 1603).

Fenlon's study of Mantua focusses largely on the period before Monteverdi's rise to importance in the city, examining the frottola as it developed in the court of Marquis Francesco Gonzaga and Isabella d'Este, the musical and ecclesiastical reforms of Cardinal Ercole Gonzaga, and the carefully calculated piety of Duke Guglielmo Gonzaga, whose foundation of the Church of S. Barbara in Mantua in the 1560s powerfully projected the image required of a Counter-Reformation prince. Duke Guglielmo, himself a composer, was anxious to secure a musical *cappella* worthy of such symbolic articulation – the recruitment of the Fleming Giaches de Wert in 1565 is just one obvious example – and it was largely due to Guglielmo that Monteverdi found himself among such distinguished musicians when he arrived in Mantua. But the interests of Guglielmo's son and heir, Vincenzo (reigned 1587–1612), lay more in secular spheres. Vincenzo spent much of his youth in Ferrara, and he brought to Mantua a love of secular music and theatrical entertainments that clearly influenced the young Monteverdi. He had also married a Florentine, Eleonora de' Medici, which, as Fenlon rightly notes, marked a new orientation in Mantuan cultural politics. This orientation – further encouraged by the close connections between Prince, later Cardinal and Duke, Ferdinando Gonzaga and Florence (he studied at the University in Pisa and was a chief patron of the Florentine musical academy founded by Marco da Gagliano in 1608, the Accademia degli Elevati) – makes itself clearly apparent in the new focus of Mantuan theatrical endeavour from the 1590s onwards, embracing the planned (and eventually realized) production of Guarini's *Il pastor fido*, Monteverdi's first opera, *Orfeo*, and the festivities for the wedding of Vincenzo's son, Prince Francesco Gonzaga, to Margherita of Savoy in 1608.

Although music in sixteenth-century Mantua is now well documented, the same cannot be said for the seventeenth century. Surprisingly, there is as yet no thorough archival study of music in Mantua during Monteverdi's tenure as *maestro di cappella* to Duke Vincenzo. Similarly, although some of Monteverdi's Mantuan contemporaries have received complete editions (notably Wert and Pallavicino), others no less important for the composer (such as Giovanni Giacomo Gastoldi and Salamone Rossi) still await the attention of publishers and performers. Given that quotation and allusion were integral to the madrigal, at least when it was designed to appeal to sophisticated connoisseurs, the lack of editions of the music of Monteverdi's contemporaries (one might also include Alfonso Fontanelli and Tomaso Pecci) and thus of the repertory through which cross-references could be made, is a serious weakness.[1]

Other Monteverdi scholars have chosen to focus on different aspects of the composer and his art. Nino Pirrotta's contribution to the tercentenary celebrations was a long essay on Monteverdi's 'poetic choices' which first appeared in the *Nuova Rivista Musicale Italiana* in 1968 (it has now been translated into English). Pirrotta

[1]Useful background information is provided in Joel Newman, *The Madrigals of Salamon de' Rossi* (PhD diss., Colombia University, 1962), and Anthony Newcomb, 'Alfonso Fontanelli and the Ancestry of the Seconda Pratica Madrigal', in Robert L. Marshall (ed.), *Studies in Renaissance and Baroque Music in Honor of Arthur Mendel* (Kassel, 1974), pp. 47–68. On cross-

revised and expanded the attributions of verse set by Monteverdi in his madrigal books, explored Monteverdi's different approaches to text-setting throughout his career, and analysed his choice of poets – from the Tasso and Guarini texts favoured in Mantua to the verses by Giambattista Marino and his followers seemingly preferred in Venice – in relation to his own development as a composer. The issue was further explored in the work of Paolo Fabbri, with a detailed study of Monteverdi's first book of madrigals, and it provided a basis for Gary Tomlinson's persuasive survey of text-setting issues in his *Monteverdi and the End of the Renaissance* (1987). Tomlinson's is the best account to date of rhetorical structures within the poetry set by Monteverdi and of how these structures are transferred to his music. His analyses of the third and fourth books of madrigals are particularly impressive, and he is also eloquent on Monteverdi's association with the Florentine poet Ottavio Rinuccini (for example, in the *Lamento d'Arianna*), whose verse, Tomlinson argues, provided Monteverdi with precisely the rhetorical and structural requirements for the impassioned musical speech that underlay his notion of a *seconda prattica*.

As his title suggests, Tomlinson also concentrates on broader perspectives. Monteverdi has long been seen as a composer straddling the divide between the Renaissance and Baroque periods: Tomlinson sharpens the focus by exploring the composer's debt to Renaissance Humanism and charting the shifts (some might say, decline) in Monteverdi's secular output as Humanism itself was rendered increasingly sterile by Counter-Reformation and emerging Baroque sensibilities, if not by the various political, social and economic crises of the early seventeenth century. Monteverdi is one of several innovators at the turn of the century who came into conflict with the increasingly repressive orthodoxy of the establishment (in his case, the theorist Giovanni Maria Artusi): there are striking parallels with Giovanni Battista Guarini's clash with the academies over the propriety of *Il pastor fido*, and Galileo Galilei's battle with the Church over his new cosmography. Moreover, in this context Monteverdi is not a 'creator of modern music' – to borrow the title of Leo Schrade's study of the composer (1950) – but instead is the last of the great Humanist composers, and one who fell increasingly out of step with stylistic, cultural and philosophical developments during his long life.

references, see Glenn E. Watkins and Thomasin La May, '"Imitatio" and "Emulatio": Changing Concepts of Originality in the Madrigals of Gesualdo and Monteverdi in the 1590s', in Finscher (ed.), *Claudio Monteverdi*, pp. 453–87.

Tomlinson offers a possible explanation for the unease which a number of scholars seem to feel about Monteverdi's Venetian secular music. In part, this unease may be a result of ignorance. Despite Nigel Fortune's work on solo song 1600–1635, and John Whenham's on duets and dialogues in the age of Monteverdi, we still know little about the broad contexts of secular music in Italy during Monteverdi's Venetian period. Such contexts could well alter our perception of his music: for example, Margaret Mabbett's recent work on the madrigal at the time suggests a number of models for Monteverdi's own endeavours, and in particular her identification of various stylistic and technical features of Monteverdi's eighth book shared with composers associated with the Habsburg court in Vienna (Book VIII is dedicated to the Emperor Ferdinand III) offers the potential for a striking reassessment of the volume.[2] Nevertheless, the problem remains. After the richness of the Mantuan madrigals, many interpreters seem unhappy with Monteverdi's turning to more overtly popular styles and genres (for example, in the seventh book) and to the perhaps rather arid mimetic gestures of the madrigals in Book VIII (embodied most obviously in the 'warlike' *stile concitato*). Similarly, Monteverdi's attempt to retain expressive and structural devices from his earlier period in these new styles and genres (for example, Denis Arnold notes the way in which his Venetian duets retain and reinterpret techniques from the polyphonic madrigals) can be viewed as a sign of his discomfort with contemporary musical developments.

Whether one should interpret this discomfort as a failure of the times is, of course, a matter for debate. Another possibility is that Monteverdi's evident stylistic ambivalence is a result of unresolved (and perhaps unresolvable) tensions within the music even of his Mantuan period. The Artusi–Monteverdi controversy merits reexamination in this light. The controversy itself fits clearly into a series of 'pamphlet wars' that had animated musical debate between 'ancients' versus 'moderns' and/or innovation versus tradition in the sixteenth century: witness the controversies between Nicola Vicentino and Vicente Lusitano in the 1550s, and Vincenzo Galilei and Gioseffo Zarlino in the 1580s.[3] Both Vicentino and Galilei sought in

[2] Margaret Mabbett, *The Italian Madrigal, 1620–1655* (PhD diss., King's College (London), 1989).

[3] The broader issues are covered in Claude V. Palisca, *Humanism in Italian Renaissance Musical Thought* (New Haven & London, 1985), while Palisca's 'The Artusi-Monteverdi Controversy' in Arnold and Fortune (eds.), *The New Monteverdi Companion*, pp. 127–58, remains the best introduction to Monteverdi's debate. Note, too, Palisca's 'Vincenzo Galilei's Counterpoint Treatise: A Code for the *Seconda Pratica*', *Journal of the American Musicological Society*, ix (1956), 81–96.

their various ways to build new styles on the precedents of classical antiquity, their aim being to correct the evident defects of contemporary polyphony of the Josquin to Palestrina succession (for example, in setting and expressing texts effectively). Monteverdi fits precisely into this context. But he and his defender, the annoyingly anonymous 'L'Ottuso', redefine the debate in subtle ways. First, Monteverdi's tracing of the *seconda prattica* from Rore onwards suggests a clear sense of the historical tradition within which he was working, and this historicization anchors his arguments in such a way as to make them seem more than the aberrations of a hot-headed iconoclast. Second and perhaps more important still, although Monteverdi opposes the traditional views of music espoused by Artusi he does not make the mistake of denying their right to exist: indeed, he legitimizes them within his own epistemological framework. Distinguishing between a *prima prattica* and a *seconda prattica* is a cunning move: Artusi is not wrong to believe what he does, but he is wrong to apply the standards of one system to the music of another.

One subtext, as it were, of the Artusi–Monteverdi controversy is the development of a critical vocabulary to explore and explain issues of compositional aesthetics. The poetics of musical composition was not an issue covered by traditional music theory, but it became a burning need in the Humanist climate of the Renaissance (and also in the context of a newly developing 'print culture' for music). Monteverdi remained exercised by the problem: witness his attempts to produce a treatise eventually titled *Melodia, overo Seconda pratica musicale*, which is first mentioned in 1605 and remains a possibility even in his letters of the 1630s (see page 43). (Here 'Melodia' is to be interpreted in the Classical sense of the art of composition, embracing all musical parameters: Plato's harmony, rhythm and words.) Monteverdi seems never to have written the treatise, probably (or so we assume) because he was no scholar. But he may also have put it aside because he realized the fundamental impossibility of the task: a thorough poetics of music remains an ideal unfulfilled even today.

There is perhaps yet another reason why Monteverdi never completed his project: did he come to realize that his notion of the *seconda prattica* was essentially untenable? For all his fine and no doubt deeply felt statements on the primacy of the text in the relationship between word and music, no serious composer could afford to follow through the logical implications of such a view. 'Music . . . must never cease to be music', as Mozart succinctly put it.[4] Moreover, even if the Mantuan madrigals do embody some

[4]Mozart to his father, Vienna, 26 September 1781, given in E. Anderson (ed.), *The Letters of Mozart and His Family* (3/London, 1985), p. 769.

notion of word as mistress of music (that itself is a matter for debate), Monteverdi's Venetian settings do not. The changing function of triple-time aria is symptomatic both of the problem and of its solution. In the early songbooks, arias were lightweight counterparts to the serious madrigals which generally provided the emotional focus of a collection. By the 1620s, however, such arias had developed the maturity to bear the weight of profoundly moving emotional impulses. 'O sia tranquillo il mare, o pien d'orgoglio', discussed by Arnold on page 93, is emblematic of this shift: the first two-thirds of the sonnet is presented in appropriate madrigalian/recitative style, but this only prepares for the outpouring of the triple-time aria (at 'Ma tu non torni, o Filli', 'But you do not return, o Phyllis'), which devotes no less than 50 or so bars of sensuous music to only half a line of verse. The argument is sealed, as it were, by the *Lamento della ninfa* in Book VIII: here the nymph's love-sick suffering is elaborated over a ground-bass that supports a triple-time melody in the best Venetian manner.[5] This is no concession to popular taste; nor is it a sign of cultural weakness and decline. Instead, it is an intensely powerful and moving statement. It is also a triumphant vindication of the power of music over words. This piece has little if anything in common with the *seconda prattica*, at least as it was defined in 1605–7. Perhaps the time has come to explore the notion of a *terza prattica* in Monteverdi's later output.

The problems apparently experienced by recent scholars in interpreting Monteverdi's Venetian secular music may reflect broader historiographical trends – mid seventeenth-century Italy has not always proved a popular subject for historical research – and also perhaps prejudices invoked by the generally protestant ethic of recent historical discourse. The same issues perhaps affect studies of Monteverdi's church music, which with only a few exceptions have not yet attained the depth and sensitivity of work on the secular music. In 1967, the 'unity' of the 1610 *Vespers* was still very much a matter of debate, even if Stephen Bonta's article of that year began to offer solutions to the problem. The introit, five psalm-settings, hymn and Magnificat are clearly appropriate for a Marian Vespers – they were published as such in Denis Stevens's 1961 edition – but the *Sonata sopra 'Sancta Maria, ora pro nobis'* and the motets between the psalms have no place within an established Marian liturgy, however Marian they may be in intent. Thus their function in the volume is unclear, and they appear to be intended more as make-

[5]See Ellen Rosand, 'The Descending Tetrachord: An Emblem of Lament', *The Musical Quarterly*, lxv (1979), 346–59.

weights than as part of a coherent plan. Bonta, however, argued that the liturgical sequence of vesper psalms, each preceded and succeeded by its antiphon, allowed the possibility of using non-liturgical motets as antiphon substitutes (for example, after the psalm): the practice is well documented in northern Italy in contemporary writings. In this light, Monteverdi's motets can be seen to have a place in a Vespers service (similar arguments allow the interpolation of 'Sancta Maria, ora pro nobis'),[6] and so the 1610 *Vespers* could indeed be planned as a single entity. Bonta's thesis has been confirmed by the recent work of James Moore on Vespers liturgies in Venice: Monteverdi's collection sits squarely in this context. However, there remains the question of the place and occasion (if any) for which Monteverdi specifically wrote the collection: Iain Fenlon suggests that the 1610 *Vespers* were written for performance during the 1608 wedding festivities in Mantua, while Graham Dixon postulates an original version of the *Vespers* devoted to Santa Barbara (the patron saint of Mantua) that was then modified in favour of the Blessed Virgin when it came to publishing the set for more general consumption.[7] As for the style of the music, this has been admirably elucidated by Jeffrey Kurtzman, although there is more still to be done on Monteverdi's typical interleaving of old and new elements, and also of improvised and notated ones (a mixture that may well become a defining feature of the emerging Baroque style).

The problems of the 1610 *Vespers* suggest that liturgical practice was not as conformant in this period as is often assumed, despite the standardizations imposed by the Council of Trent (1545–63) and its offshoots. The issue becomes particularly acute in the two volumes of Monteverdi's sacred music published in Venice (the *Selva morale e spirituale* of 1640–1, and the *Messa . . . et salmi* of 1650). Both have been regarded as rather miscellaneous collections of pieces produced at various times during Monteverdi's tenure as *maestro di cappella* of St Mark's. It is possible – as Monteverdi and/or his publisher doubtless intended – to use these collections as a storehouse of items to be selected for particular liturgical celebrations: Denis Stevens's construction of a Christmas Vespers and Frits Noske's of Vespers for the feast of St John the Baptist are two examples.[8] But again our understanding of Monteverdi's church music has suffered through scant awareness of his contemporaries. Jerome Roche's 1968

[6]The *Sonata* is most recently discussed in Blazey, 'A Liturgical Role for Monteverdi's *Sonata sopra Sancta Maria*'.

[7]See Fenlon, 'The Monteverdi Vespers'; Dixon, 'Monteverdi's Vespers of 1610'.

[8]Stevens, 'Monteverdi's Other Vespers' (an edition was published by Novello in 1979); Noske, 'An Unknown Work by Monteverdi'.

dissertation on north Italian liturgical music in the early seventeenth century (a revised version was published in 1984) did much to rescue Alessandro Grandi, Giovanni Antonio Rigatti and Giovanni Rovetta for posterity. But not until James Moore's pioneering work on church music in Venice did we have any real notion of how Monteverdi's music fits into broader liturgical and ceremonial contexts. Moore identifies particular liturgies unique to St Mark's that were staunchly preserved as powerful political symbols of Venetian independence in the face of pressures for ecclesiastical conformity coming from Rome: Monteverdi's evident choice of texts makes much more sense in this institutional light. Similarly, Moore's work (1984) on the ceremonies staged when Venice was beset by plague in 1630 and 1631 (including laying the foundation-stone of the Church of S. Maria della Salute as a votive offering on the liberation of the city from the pestilence) allows us to locate a large part of the contents of the *Selva morale e spirituale* (including the spiritual madrigals, the Mass with interpolated Gloria and Credo, and some of the motets) as relating to this difficult period.

A clearer sense of contexts also helps clarify a number of difficult issues in Monteverdi's operas. 1967 saw the appearance of Denis Stevens's edition of *Orfeo* which, despite its lack of scholarly apparatus and some errors, allowed easy access to this rich work. The theatrical and stylistic traditions into which *Orfeo* was born were elucidated by Nino Pirrotta's splendid *Li due Orfei* of 1969 (translated in 1982 as *Music and Theatre from Poliziano to Monteverdi*), while Howard Mayer Brown's work on Jacopo Peri (including his edition of *Euridice*) clarified Monteverdi's most immediate precedent. Pirrotta also concerned himself with the question of staging and the problems of the two alternative finales (one, closer to the myth with the death of Orpheus, in the 1607 libretto, and the other, with Orpheus' 'rescue' by Apollo, in the 1609 score). These issues are further explored in John Whenham's Cambridge Opera Handbook on the opera (1986), where in addition Iain Fenlon presents important new documentation on the first performance, and Nigel Fortune a survey of performances and editions of the opera that itself acts as a magisterial study of the reception of Monteverdi through the ages. But questions about *Orfeo* remain. For example, its reception in the early seventeenth century is still open to scrutiny (evidence of regular performances in Salzburg from 1614 is intriguing);[9] and the important analytical

[9]See the reference in Warren Kirkendale, 'Zur Biographie des ersten Orfeo, Francesco Rasi', in Finscher (ed.), *Claudio Monteverdi*, pp. 297–335, at p. 327 n. 115.

issues raised by the opera (for example, its use of 'tonal' structures) have scarcely been broached (this is symptomatic of the weakness of current analytical approaches to all of Monteverdi's music).[10]

Monteverdi's Venetian operas remain problematic. Early doubts about the authenticity of *Il ritorno d'Ulisse in patria* seem to be have been assuaged, although we still need a rigorous study of the opera and its sources building on Wolfgang's Osthoff's pioneering work. But *L'incoronazione di Poppea*, whose authenticity was rarely questioned, has now become something of a *cause célèbre*. Raymond Leppard's notable (and notorious) revival at Glyndebourne in 1962 alerted many to the glories of mid seventeenth-century Venetian opera. But Leppard soon became the bogyman of the 'authenticity' movement – largely for his too rich orchestrations and for taking other liberties with the score – and several distinguished early-music groups have since sought alternatives to his 'realization', with varying degrees of success. Meanwhile, Monteverdi's apologists have struggled to account for the questionable taste of Busenello's libretto,[11] and musicologists have jumped on their various band-wagons. Not only have most scholars got the title wrong (*La corona-tione di Poppea*, later *Il Nerone, overo L'incoronatione di Poppea*), and likewise the date of the first performance (Carnival 1642–3, probably early 1643). But also, a fair amount of the opera that survives is probably not even by Monteverdi.

The problem lies in the sources for the opera (a survey is provided by Alessandra Chiarelli). We have two manuscripts of the music, one in the Biblioteca Nazionale Marciana, Venice (copied in part by Francesco Cavalli's wife, with performance indications by Cavalli himself), and the other in the Conservatorio di Musica S. Pietro a Majella, Naples (which may relate to a Neapolitan performance by the opera troupe known as the Febiarmonici in 1651). For the text, there is a *scenario* (synopsis) printed in 1643, a libretto issued for the 1651 Naples performance, an edition included in Busenello's 'complete works' (*Delle hore ociose*, Venice, 1656), and various manuscript copies of uncertain date and provenance. Aside from the *scenario*, probably none of this material relates directly to the first performance. The opening sinfonia of the opera in the Venice manuscript is very close to the first sinfonia of Cavalli's *Doriclea* (1645), and the text of the final duet between Nero and Poppaea appears in the libretto of Benedetto Ferrari's *Il pastor regio* (Venice,

---

[10]An important first step is made in Chew, 'The Perfections of Modern Music'.
[11]The best attempt is Rosand, 'Seneca and the Interpretation of *L'Incorona-zione di Poppea*'.

1640) as revived in Bologna in 1641 (the music is lost). Elsewhere in the final scenes, we find music known to have been used in one version of Francesco Sacrati's *La finta pazza* (first performed Venice, 1641). Other music in the opera (including at least some of Otho's part) may also be by another hand. Whatever the status of the original *Poppea*, the versions that survive seem to reflect the contribution of one or more other composers. Cavalli, Ferrari and Sacrati are all contenders: Sacrati's claim (as Alan Curtis argues) is particularly strong.

Whether that matters or not depends on one's point of view. In a sense, to search for one composer of *Poppea* is to miss the point of a genre where the composer or composers were only one element in the production process, and possibly lower down the scale than, say, the librettist or stage-designer. Thus the notion of a single-composer masterpiece, one so ridden with nineteenth-century prejudices, is essentially alien to the modes of production characteristic of 'public' opera, or for that matter of music in general, in the seventeenth century.[12] But this is not to devalue Monteverdi's achievement during his long life. Indeed, as many of his contemporaries realized, he was clearly the most significant Italian musician of his time. The more we broach music in the seventeenth century, the more apparent his legacy becomes: Arnold rightly explores his influence on Italian and northern composers of the next generation, and to Cavalli in Italy and Schütz in Germany one could add Lully in France and Purcell in England.[13] He remains a fascinating musician whose works epitomize in many varied ways the musical and cultural issues of his age. There is much still to be done: Monteverdi will long continue to be a composer rich in potential for everyone fascinated by music in late Renaissance and early Baroque Italy.

[12]The issues are raised in Lorenzo Bianconi and Thomas Walker, 'Production, Consumption and Political Function of Seventeenth-Century Opera', *Early Music History*, iv (1984), 209–96. Bianconi's *Music in the Seventeenth Century* provides the best survey of opera in the early seventeenth century, and indeed the best introduction to the period.

[13]See Franklin B. Zimmerman, 'Purcell and Monteverdi', *The Musical Times*, xcix (1958), 368–9.

Appendix A

Calendar

Year	Age	Life	Contemporary musicians and events
1567		Claudio Zuan [Giovanni] Antonio Monteverdi born (baptized May 15) at Cremona, son of barber-surgeon Baldassare M. (born 1542) and Maddalena Zignani (married early 1566).	Vaet dies, Jan. 8; Campion born, Feb.; Giacobbi born, Aug.; (?) Rosseter born. Anerio (F.) c. 7; Artusi c. 37; Bull c. 5; Byrd 24; Caccini 16; Cavalieri c. 17; Corteccia 65; Croce c. 10; Dowland 4; Du Caurroy 18; Eccard 14; Ferrabosco (i) 24; Fontanelli 10; Gabrieli (A.) c. 34; Gabrieli (G.) c. 11; Gesualdo c. 6; Guerrero 39; Handl 17; Hassler 5; Ingegneri c. 20; Lassus 35; Le Jeune c. 39; Luzzaschi c. 22; Marenzio c. 14; Mauduit 10; Merulo 34; Monte 46; Morley c. 10; Nanino (G. M.) c. 24; Palestrina c. 42; Pallavicino 16; Peri 6; Philips c. 7; Porta (C.) c. 39; Rovigo c. 26; Ruffo c. 59; Soriano c. 19; Striggio (i) c. 37; Sweelinck 5; Tallis c. 62; Tye c. 62; Vecchi (Orazio) 17; Viadana c. 7; Victoria 19; Walter (J.) 71; Wert 32; White (R.) c. 29; Zarlino 50. Palestrina's *Missa Papae Marcelli* published.
1568	1		Banchieri born, Sept. 3; Arcadelt (c. 63) dies.
1569	2		Giambattista Marino (poet) born, Oct. 18.

1570	3		Walter (J.) (74) dies, March 25; Rossi (S.) born, Aug. 19; (?) Pilkington born.
1571	4	Maria Domitilla M. (sister) born (baptized May 16).	(?) Praetorius (M.) born, Feb. 15; Corteccia (68) dies, June 7. Venice defeats the Turks at the battle of Lepanto, Oct. 7.
1572	5		Certon dies, Feb. 23; Goudimel (*c*. 58) dies, Aug.; Tomkins (T.) born; (?) Tye (*c*. 67) dies.
1573	6	Giulio Cesare M. (brother) born (baptized Jan. 31).	Alessandro Striggio jr. born. Tasso's *Aminta* performed in Ferrara.
1574	7		Rasi born, May 14; White (R.) (*c*. 36) dies, Nov.; Wilbye born.
1575	8		
1576	9	M.'s mother dies; father remarries Giovanna Gadio in this or next year.	(?) Weelkes born, Oct.; (?) Pecci (T.) born. Titian dies, Aug. 27.
1577	10		Peter Paul Rubens born, June 28.
1578	11		Agazzari born, Dec. 2.
1579	12	Clara Massimilia M. (step-sister) born (baptized Jan. 8). Margherita Gonzaga marries Duke Alfonso II d'Este.	
1580	13		Farrant dies, Nov. 30. Andrea Palladio dies, August.
1581	14	Luca M. (step-brother) born (baptized Feb. 7). Vincenzo Gonzaga marries Margherita Farnese.	
1582	15	*Sacrae cantiunculae* published Aug.; M. styles himself pupil of Marc'Antonio Ingegneri.	Da Gagliano (M.) born, May 1; (?) d'India born.
1583	16	Filippo M. (step-brother) born (baptized Jan.). *Madrigali spirituali* published July. M.'s father marries	Frescobaldi born, Sept.; (?) Agostini (P.) born; Gibbons born.

		Francesca Como some time after 1583.	
1584	17	*Canzonette a tre voci* published Oct. Vincenzo Gonzaga marries Eleonora de' Medici.	
1585	18		Gabrieli (A.) (*c.* 52) dies, Aug. 30; Schütz born, Oct.; Tallis (*c.* 80) dies, Nov. 23. *Edipo Tiranno* performed at the opening of the Teatro Olimpico, Vicenza, with music by Andrea Gabrieli.
1586	19	Prince Francesco Gonzaga born.	Schein born, Jan. 20; (?) Grandi born.
1587	20	1st book of madrigals published Jan. Dedication to Count Marco Verità suggests that M. seeks post in Verona. Duke Guglielmo Gonzaga dies Sept.; succeeded by his son, Vincenzo. Prince Ferdinando Gonzaga born.	Ruffo (*c.* 79) dies, Feb. 9; Scheidt born, Nov. Grand Duke Francesco I de' Medici dies, Oct. 19; succeeded by his brother, Ferdinando.
1588	21		Ferrabosco (i) (45) dies, Aug. 12. The English fleet routs the Spanish Armada.
1589	22	M. visits Milan seeking employment and plays the *viola* for, among others, Giacomo Ricardi (dedicatee of 2nd book of madrigals).	Grand Duke Ferdinando de' Medici marries Christine of Lorraine: festivities include *La pellegrina*, with magnificent *intermedi*.
1590	23	2nd book of madrigals published Jan. (the last volume in which M. calls himself pupil of Ingegneri). Francesco Rovigo returns to Mantua as organist at S. Barbara. M. moves to Mantua in this year or shortly thereafter as string-player to Duke Vincenzo Gonzaga.	Zarlino (73) dies, Feb. 4. Giovanni Battista Guarini's *Il pastor fido* first published.

1591	24		Handl (41) dies, July 18; Galilei (V.) dies.
1592	25	3rd book of madrigals published June. Lodovico Grossi da Viadana appointed *maestro di cappella* of S. Pietro Martire, Mantua; Giovanni Giacomo Gastoldi appointed *maestro di cappella* of S. Barbara, Mantua, replacing Wert.	Striggio (i) (*c.* 52) dies, Feb. 29; Ingegneri (*c.* 45) dies, July 1; Mazzocchi (D.) born, Nov.; Jenkins born.
1593	26		
1594	27	Francesco Campagnolo, later a distinguished virtuoso tenor, becomes M.'s pupil. 4 canzonettas by M. included in Antonio Morsolino's *Il primo libro delle canzonette a tre voci*.	Palestrina (*c.* 68) dies, Feb, 2; Lassus (62) dies, June 14; (?) Merula born.
1595	28	M. accompanies Duke Vincenzo Gonzaga on military campaign in Hungary, June–Nov.; visits Trent, Innsbruck, Linz, Prague, Vienna, Venice.	(?) Rovetta born. Torquato Tasso dies in Rome, 25 April.
1596	29	Benedetto Pallavicino appointed Duke Vincenzo's *maestro di cappella* as successor to Wert. M. begins association with Ferrarese circles.	Lawes (H.) born, Jan. 5; Wert (61) dies, May 6.
1597	30	6 madrigals by M. included in Paul Kauffman's *Fiori del giardino*.	Mazzocchi (V.) born, July; Rovigo (*c.* 56) dies, Oct. 7; (?) Rossi (L.) born. Duke Alfonso II d'Este dies Oct. 27; Ferrara secedes to Papal States. Orazio Vecchi's *L'Amfiparnaso* published.
1598	31	Paolo Virchi appointed organist at S. Barbara as successor to Rovigo. Guarini's *Il pastor fido* performed Mantua, Nov. According to Artusi, madrigals by M. performed in house of Antonio Goretti,	Crüger born, April 9. *Dafne* by Ottavio Rinuccini and Jacopo Peri performed in Florence, Carnival. Philip II of Spain dies, Sept. 13.

		Ferrara, Nov. 16, initiating the Artusi–Monteverdi controversy. Princess Eleonora Gonzaga born.	
1599	32	M. marries Mantuan singer Claudia Cattaneo, daughter of court string-player, Giacomo Cattaneo, May 20. He accompanies Duke Vincenzo Gonzaga on a health-cure in Spa, Flanders, June–Oct.; visits Trent, Innsbruck, Basel, Nancy, Liège, Antwerp, Brussels.	Marenzio (*c.* 46) dies, Aug. 22; Guerrero (71) dies, Nov. 8. Gabriello Chiabrera's: *Le maniere dei versi toscani* published.
1600	33	Henri IV of France marries Maria de' Medici, Florence, Oct. Duke Vincenzo Gonzaga attends ceremony (retinue includes Alessandro Striggio and ?M.).	Le Jeune (*c.* 72) dies, Sept. Emilio de' Cavalieri's *Rappresentatione di anima, et di corpo* performed Rome, Feb. *Euridice* by Ottavio Rinuccini and Jacopo Peri performed Florence, Oct. 6 (published Feb. 1601). *L'Artusi, overo Delle imperfettioni della moderna musica* published Nov.
1601	34	Duke Vincenzo Gonzaga on military campaign in Hungary, July–Dec. Francesco Baldassare M. (son) born (baptized Aug. 27). M. petitions for and gains post of *maestro di cappella* to Duke Vincenzo in succession to Pallavicino, Nov.	Porta (C.) (*c.* 73) dies, May 19; Pallavicino (50) dies, Nov. 26.
1602	35	Gabriello Chiabrera visits Mantua. M. granted Mantuan citizenship, April 10. Moves to new house nearer ducal palace in parish of S. Pietro. Rubens comes to Mantua.	Cavalli born, Feb. 14; Cavalieri (*c.* 52) dies, March 11; Lawes (W.) born, April; Morley (*c.* 45) dies, Oct. Giulio Caccini's *Le nuove musiche* published July. Lodovico Grossi da Viadana's *Cento concerti ecclesiastici* published.

1603	36	Leonora Camilla M. (daughter) born (baptized Feb. 20). 4th book of madrigals published March. *Seconda parte dell'Artusi overo Delle imperfettioni della moderna musica* published March, including an exchange of correspondence with 'L'Ottuso Academico' (the latter defending M. and the moderns) begun in 1599. Caterina Martinelli arrives in Mantua to study with M. by early Sept.	Monte (82) dies, July 4.
1604	37	Massimiliano Giacomo M. (son) born (baptized May 10).	Albert born, July 8; Merulo (71) dies, May 5.
1605	38	?*Gli amori di Diana ed Endimione* (*ballo*) performed Mantua, Carnival. 5th book of madrigals published July, with preface defending M. against Artusi and two poems praising M. by Cherubino Ferrari. 4 madrigals by M. included in Melchior Borchgrevinck's *Giardino novo bellissimo di varii fiori musicali scieltissimi: il primo libro de madrigali a cinque voci*; 1 canzonetta by M. included in Amante Franzoni's *I nuovi fioretti musicali a tre voci*. The poet Tommaso Stigliani dedicates a madrigal, 'O sirene de' fiumi, adorni cigni', to M. in his *Rime* (Venice, 1605).	Vecchi (Orazio) (54) dies, Feb. 19; Carissimi born, April; Benevoli born, April 19. Venice placed under the Interdict by newly elected Pope Paul V (Camillo Borghese).
1606	39	2 madrigals by M. included in Melchior Borchgrevinck's *Giardino novo bellissimo di varii fiori musicali scieltissimi: il secondo*	Pecci (T.) (*c.* 30) dies.

171

libro de madrigali a cinque
voci.

1607   40   *Orfeo* performed Mantua, Feb. 24, Mar. 1. M. visits Cremona, July, and is admitted to the Accademia degli Animosi, Aug. 10. M. sends one of two sonnet-settings (later included in 6th book?) to Duke Vincenzo Gonzaga in Genoa via Annibale Iberti, July 28. *Scherzi musicali* published by Giulio Cesare M., July, with a *Dichiaratione* elaborating the preface to M's 5th book of madrigals. M. visits Milan, late Aug., and shows *Orfeo* to his friend, Cherubino Ferrari. Spiritual *contrafacta* of M.'s madrigals published by Aquilino Coppini in Milan, Sept. Claudia Cattaneo dies in Cremona, Sept. 10. M. summoned to Mantua by Federico Follino, Sept. 24; returns soon thereafter and begins work on *Arianna* for forthcoming wedding festivities of Prince Francesco Gonzaga and Margherita of Savoy. Ottavio Rinuccini arrives on visit to Mantua, Oct. 23. Prince Ferdinando Gonzaga nominated Cardinal, Dec. 24.

Nanino (G. M.) (*c.* 64) dies, March 11; Luzzaschi (*c.* 62) dies. Sept. 10.

1608   43   Antonio Braccino da Todi (? = Artusi) publishes his *Discorso secondo musicale . . . per la dichiaratione della lettera posta ne' Scherzi musicali del sig. Claudio Monteverde* (the first discourse responding

to the preface to the 5th
book is now lost). Man-
tuan wedding is postponed;
Dafne by Ottavio Rinuc-
cini and Marco da Gagliano
performed Mantua, Car-
nival. Caterina Martinelli
dies March 7. Francesco
Gonzaga marries Mar-
gherita of Savoy, May. *Arianna* performed Mantua,
May 28; Guarini's *L'idropica* (with prologue by
M.), June 2; *Ballo delle
ingrate*, June 4. Aquilino
Coppini's second book of
contrafacta of madrigals
by M. and others pub-
lished Aug. M., exhausted
by work on the festivities,
stays in Cremona,
July–Dec.; sends a musical
setting to Cardinal Ferdinando Gonzaga, Nov. 26.
Antonio Taroni, then Stefano Nascimbeni, takes
charge of music at S. Barbara, Mantua, during Gas-
oldi's final illness. M.
seeks permission to resign
from Mantuan service,
Dec. 2. 2 madrigals by M.
included in Giaches de
Wert's posthumous *Il duodecimo libro de madrigali.*

1609	42	M. awarded pension of 100 scudi *per annum* by Duke Vincenzo Gonzaga, Jan. 19, and salary increase to 300 scudi *per annum* a week later; securing the pension will trouble M. until his death. Aquilino Coppini's third book of *contrafacta* of madrigals by M. published May. *Orfeo* published Aug.; a	Gastoldi dies, Jan. 4; Croce (*c.* 52) dies, May 15; Du Caurroy (60) dies, Aug. 7. Giulio Cesare Martinengo succeeds Giovanni Croce as *maestro di cappella* at St Mark's, Venice, Ascension Day.

		bound copy is presented to its dedicatee, Prince Francesco Gonzaga. M. in Cremona Aug.–?Oct. and reports on musicians for Mantuan court; attends meeting of Accademia degli Animosi, Sept. 27.	
1610	43	Prince Francesco Gonzaga, in Turin, requests score of *Orfeo* from Mantua, Jan. Adriana Basile, virtuoso singer, arrives in Mantua from Rome, early summer. M. prepares *Sestina* and polyphonic arrangement of the *Lamento d'Arianna* (both included in the 6th book of madrigals), July. *Missa . . . ac vespere* published Sept. M. visits Rome, staying in Florence *en route*, to present volume to its dedicatee, Pope Paul V, and to secure a scholarship at the Roman Seminary for his son, Francesco. M. in Cremona, Dec. 2 spiritual canzonettas and 3 *contrafacta* by/of M. copied into manuscript by Michele Pario of Parma.	
1611	44	M. sends an eight-part 'Dixit Dominus' and other music to Prince Francesco Gonzaga, March 26. Ottavio Bargnani dedicates an instrumental piece to M. in his *Secondo libro delle canzoni da suonare* (Milan, 1611).[1] Eleonora de' Medici, Duchess of Mantua, dies Dec. 8. Psalms by M. performed	Victoria (63) dies, Aug. 20; Eccard (58) dies; (?) Hammerschmidt born.

[1]For other instrumental works dedicated to Monteverdi, see Fabbri, *Monteverdi*, p. 118 (and n. 148).

by Gemignano Capilupi
in Modena Cathedral,
Christmas.

1612	45	Duke Vincenzo Gonzaga dies Feb. 18; succeeded by his son, Francesco. M. and his brother dismissed from court service, 30 July (Santi Orlandi becomes *maestro di cappella*); M. goes to Cremona. He visits Milan, Sept. Marc'Antonio Negri appointed vice-*maestro di cappella* at St Mark's, Venice, Dec. 22. Duke Francesco Gonzaga dies Dec. 22; Cardinal Ferdinando Gonzaga becomes regent. M.'s *Missa 'In illo tempore'* included in Pierre Phalèse's *Missae senis et octonis vocibus*.	Hassler (49) dies, June 8, Gabrieli (G.) (*c.* 56) dies, Aug.
1613	46	M. auditions for post of *maestro di cappella* of St Mark's, Venice, to succeed Martinengo, Aug.; appointed Aug. 19 at an annual salary of 300 ducats. M. takes up the position in early Oct. (he is attacked by highwaymen on the journey to Venice) and reorganizes the *cappella* and restocks its music library. Prince Francesco de' Medici asks Cardinal Ferdinando Gonzaga for a score of *Arianna*, Dec.	Martinengo dies, July 10; Artusi (*c.* 73) dies, Aug. 18; Gesualdo (*c.* 52) dies, Sept. 8. Gesualdo's collected madrigals published in score.
1614	47	*Orfeo* performed in Salzburg. 6th book of madrigals published (by Aug.); M. sends copy and other music in manuscript to Angelo Grillo.	Anerio (F.) (*c.* 54) dies, Sept. 26–7; Tunder born.
1615	48	Pierre Phalèse, Antwerp printer, initiates a series of editions of M.'s madrigals. M. summoned to Mantua	Rigatti born.

by Cardinal Ferdinando
Gonzaga to compose a
favola in musica for his
proposed marriage to
Camilla Fàa, but no trip is
made. M. awarded 50
ducats for services at St
Mark's during Holy week
and Easter; Francesco M.
awarded 10 ducats for
same. 1 motet by M. included in Giovanni Battista
Bonometti's *Parnassus
musicus Ferdinandaeus*; 1
psalm-setting by M. included in Georg Gruber's *Reliquiae sacrorum concen-
tuum.*

1616	49	Cardinal Ferdinando Gon-	Froberger born, May.
		zaga crowned Duke of	

Mantua; *Tirsi e Clori*
(*ballo*) performed Mantua,
Jan. M.'s annual salary at
St Mark's increased to 400
ducats, Aug. 24. M. writes
a Mass for St Mark's,
Christmas Eve. 1 madrigal
by M. included in Pierre
Phalèse's *Il Helicone.*

1617	50	M. begins composing *Le*

nozze di Tetide, Jan. (for
forthcoming Mantuan
wedding festivities),
having considered the libretto in Dec. 1616, but it
remains unfinished. M. invited by Ottavio Rinuccini
to visit Florence. Duke
Ferdinando Gonzaga mar-
ries Caterina de' Medici,
Florence, Feb. 7. G. B.
Andreini's *La Maddalena*
(with prologue by M.) performed as part of the wedding celebrations,
Mantua, March. Baldas-
sare M. dies Nov. 10.

1618	51	M. receives libretto of *An-dromeda* from Mantua, Spring; works sporadically on project during this and next year. M. prepares a Mass and motets for the Feast of the Holy Cross, Venice, May 3,[2] and a cantata for Ascension Day. 1 motet by M. included in Giovanni Battista Ala's *Primo libro delli concerti ecclesiastici*.	Caccini (67) dies, Dec. Thirty Years' War begins.
1619	52	M. moves his son Francesco from the University of Padua to Bologna because Francesco is spending too much time in musical circles; he visits Bologna in Jan. M. travels to Mantua, July, and starts work on a *ballo* for Mantua, *Apollo*, by Oct.[3] 7th book of madrigals published Dec. Dedication to Caterina de' Medici, Duchess of Mantua, is rewarded by a necklace. Giovanni Battista Grillo appointed 1st organist at St Mark's, Dec. 30. M. acts as agent for Paolo Giordano Orsini, Duke of Bracciano, in having Alessandro Vincenti print Francesco Petratti's *Il primo libro d'arie* (pub. Jan. 1620).	Orlandi dies, July.
1620	53	Lament from *Apollo* performed in house of Giovanni Matteo Bembo, Venice, Jan. *Andromeda* performed Mantua, Car-	Campion (53) dies, Feb.

[2]Possibly including 'Adoramus te Christe' and 'Christe adoramus te' included in Giulio Cesare Bianchi's *Libro primo de motetti* (Venice, 1620), see Stevens, *The Letters of Claudio Monteverdi*, p. 138.

[3]Stevens argues that the *ballo* and *Apollo* are two separate works, see *The Letters of Claudio Monteverdi*, pp. 143, 145.

nival; *Apollo (ballo)* performed Mantua, late Feb.
(plus repeat performance
in July). Rumours spread
in Venice of M. returning
to Mantua after death of
Santi Orlandi, but he
finally refuses repeated
offers on March 13 (Fran-
cesco Dognazzi is appointed *maestro di cappella* of
Gonzaga court). M. notes
his regular service in the
private oratory of Marc'
Antonio Cornaro, Primi-
cerius of St Mark's, March.
Arianna planned for performance in Mantua for
Caterina de' Medici's
birthday (May 2) but
abandoned. M. visits Bol-
ogna on account of his
son's plans to drop his
legal studies and enter a
monastery; attends meet-
ing of Adriano Banchieri's
Accademia dei Floridi,
June 13.[4] M. visits
Mantua, Sept., and pro-
vides music for the feast of
S. Carlo Borromeo for the
Milanese community in S.
Maria Gloriosa dei Frari,
Venice, Nov. 4. Alessan-
dro Grandi appointed
vice-*maestro di cappella* of
St Mark's, Nov. 17. Bartolomeo Magni initiates
series of reprints of M.'s
madrigal-books (–1622).
4 motets by M. included in
Giulio Cesare Bianchi's
(M.'s pupil) *Libro primo de*

[4]Stevens suggests that Monteverdi's 'En gratulemur hodie', a hymn for the
Feast of St Anthony of Padua (13 June) later published in Gasparo Casati's
Racolta di motetti (Venice, 1651), was intended for this occasion, see *The Letters
of Claudio Monteverdi*, p. 212.

motetti; 1 litany by M.
included in Bianchi's *Libro
secondo de motetti*; 2
motets by M. included in
Lorenzo Calvi's *Symbolae
diversorum musicorum*; 1
aria by M. included in Giovanni Battista Camarella's
Madrigali et arie. Claudio
Saracini dedicates a
solo-voice madrigal,
'Udite, lagrimosi', to M. in
his *Le seconde musiche*
(Venice, 1620).

1621 54 M. provides music for an
entertainment in Mantua,
Carnival, and for the re-
quiem mass of Grand
Duke Cosimo II (died Feb.
28) for the Florentine community in Venice, Church
of SS. Giovanni e Paolo,
May 25. His son Francesco
takes part in performance.
M. seeks to have his son
Massimiliano admitted to
medical studies in Bol-
ogna.

Praetorius (M.) (*c*. 50)
dies, Feb. 15; Sweelinck
(59) dies, Oct. 16; Rasi
(47) dies, Dec.; Soriano (*c*.
73) dies.

1622 55 Eleonora Gonzaga marries
Emperor Ferdinand II;
Ercole Marigliani's *Le tre
costanti* (with at least two
of six *intermedi* by M.)
performed Mantua, Jan.
18. M. acts as agent for
Lorenzo Giustiniani to
bring to Venice the Man-
tuan theatrical troupe
headed by Giovanni Bat-
tista Andreini, Oct. M. is ill
in winter, 1622–3. 1 motet
by M. included in Johann
Donfrid's *Promptuarii
musici . . . pars prima*.

Fontanelli (65) dies, Feb.
11.

1623 56 Duke (and later Duchess)
of Mantua visits Venice,
April–June. Carlo Fillago

Reincken born, April 27;
Rosseter (*c*. 56) dies, May
5; Byrd (80) dies, July 4;

appointed first organist at St Mark's, May 1. Francesco M. appointed singer at St Mark's, July. M. organizes music for the Scuola di San Rocco, Aug. *Lamento d'Arianna* (solo-voice version) published in Venice, and in Fei and Ruuli's *Il maggio fiorito* (Orvieto). 1 *contrafactum* of M. included in Pietro Lappi's *Concerti sacri . . . libro secondo*; 2 madrigals by M. included in *Madrigali del signor cavaliero Anselmi . . . posti in musica* (dedication dated Dec. 23).

Cesti born, Aug.; Weelkes (*c.* 47) dies, Nov. 30. Maffeo Barbarini elected Pope Urban VIII.

1624 57 *Combattimento di Tancredi et Clorinda* performed Palazzo Mocenigo, Venice, Carnival. M. sends compositions to Cesare d'Este, Duke of Modena, March, June. M. involved in extended litigation with Ippolito de Belli over the estate of his father-in-law, Giacomo Cattaneo (died April 24); visits Mantua, July. Giovanni Pietro Berti appointed 2nd organist of St Mark's, Sept. 16. 3 arias by M. (and 1 by Francesco M.) included in Carlo Milanuzzi's *Quarto scherzo delle ariose vaghezze*; 3 motets by M. included in Lorenzo Calvi's *Seconda raccolta de sacri canti*. M. made an honorary member of the Accademia dei Filomusi (successor to the Accademia dei Floridi) in Bologna in 1624 or 1625.

1625	58	M. prepares Mass (March 9) and other music for visit to Venice of Prince Ladislas of Poland. Nicholas Lanier visits Venice, July. M. develops interest in alchemy. 1 motet by M. included in Francesco Sammaruco's *Sacri affetti*; 4 motets by M. included in Leonardo Simonetti's *Ghirlanda sacra . . . libro primo*.	Gibbons (42) dies, June 5. Marino dies, March 25.
1626	59	M. is associated with Accademia dei Filomusi, Bologna. Massimiliano M. graduates in medicine from Bologna, March; M. seeks post for him in Mantua. M. writes madrigal for an official banquet in Venice, June 15. Duke Ferdinando Gonzaga dies Oct. 29; succeeded by his brother, Vincenzo II (crowned 16 May 1627). *Armida abbandonata* (dramatic cantata) composed towards end of year. 1 litany by M. included in Lorenzo Calvi's *Rosarium litaniarum Beatae V. Mariae*.	Dowland (62) dies, Jan.; Legrenzi born, Aug. *La catena d'Adone* by Ottavio Tronsarelli and Domenico Mazzocchi performed Rome.
1627	60	M. receives Mantuan approaches for a new opera and offers Ottavio Rinuccini's *Narciso* and Giulio Strozzi's *La finta pazza Licori*, May. He works on the latter, June–July, but (?) it is left incomplete. M. prepares chamber music for English ambassador to Venice, Sir Isaac Wake, and his visitor, Elector Georg Wilhelm, and music for the feast of Our Lady of Mount Carmel, July 17;	Viadana (*c.* 67) dies, May 2; Mauduit (69) dies, Aug. 21.

and music for a banquet in Chioggia, Sept. 22. M. approached by Marquis Enzo Bentivoglio to provide music for forthcoming wedding of Odoardo Farnese, Duke of Parma, and Margherita de' Medici, Aug.; work continues for rest of year. Massimiliano M. arrested by Inquisition for reading a prohibited book, Mantua, Sept.; M. later sells a necklace (received for the 7th book of madrigals?) for his son's bail. M. seeks a canonry in Cremona, Sept. M. visits Parma, via Modena, in Oct.–Dec.; Procurators of St Mark's order his return, Nov. 27. Alessandro Grandi appointed *maestro di cappella* at S. Maria Maggiore, Bergamo; Giovanni Rovetta appointed vice-*maestro di cappella* of St Mark's, Nov. 22. Duke Vincenzo II Gonzaga dies Dec. 25; succeeded by Duke Carlo Gonzaga of Nevers. M.'s edition of Jacques Arcadelt's *Madrigali a 4* is published in Rome. 1 motet by M. included in Johann Donfrid's *Promptuarii musici . . . pars tertia*; 1 psalm-setting by M. included in Giovanni Maria Sabino's *Psalmi de vespere.*

| 1628 | 61 | M. works on music for the Farnese wedding; visits Parma again Jan.–March. *Ballo delle ingrate* performed Vienna. *Gli Argo-* | Bull (*c*. 65) dies, March 13; Philips (*c*. 68) dies. |

nauti (*mascherata*) per-
formed Parma, March. M.
sets (?as duets) *I cinque
fratelli*, five sonnets by
Giulio Strozzi in honour of
Grand Duke Ferdinando II
and Prince Giovanni Carlo
de' Medici, for banquet in
the Arsenale, Venice, April
8. Massimiliano M. still
under threat from Inquisition, July. M. organizes
music for the Scuola di San
Rocco, Aug. Heinrich
Schütz visits Venice, Nov.
(–Oct. 1629). Duke Odo-
ardo Farnese and Margher-
ita de' Medici marry in
Florence, Oct. (festivities
include Marco da Gagli-
ano's *La Flora*). M. is in
Parma for the festivities
there (Procurators of St
Mark's order his return,
Dec. 13): Tasso's *Aminta*
(with six *intermedi* by M.)
performed Parma, Dec. 13;
Mercurio e Marte (tournament) performed Dec. 21.

1629	62	3 motets by M. included in Lorenzo Calvi's *Quarta raccolta de sacri canti*.	Agostini (P.) (*c.* 46) dies, Oct. 3; d'India (*c.* 47) dies.
1630	63	M. writes music for nuns at S. Lorenzo, Venice, and a canzonetta for (?)Marquis Enzo Bentivoglio (sent 9 March).[5] *Proserpina rapita* performed for the wedding of Lorenzo Giustiniani and Giustiniana Moccnigo,	Schein (44) dies, Nov. 19; Grandi (*c.* 44) dies; (?) Rossi (S.) dies.

[5]The letter which contained the canzonetta is given in Fabbri, *Monteverdi*, pp. 281–2; it is not in De' Paoli's and Stevens's editions of the letters. Internal evidence here weakens Stevens's arguments in favour of identifying the recipient of Monteverdi's letter of 23 February 1630 (which also refers to the canzonet) as Don Ascanio Pio di Savoia.

Palazzo Mocenigo, Venice, April. Imperial troops (carrying plague) threaten Mantua; Alessandro Striggio heads delegation seeking help from Venice, unwittingly bringing plague to the city. Striggio dies June 15–16. Mantua sacked by Imperial troops, July 18–21. Plague infests northern Italy, reaching its peak in Venice in Autumn: some 46,000 Venetians die by Autumn 1631.

1631	64	Venice plans new church interceding for relief from plague: foundation stone of S. Maria della Salute laid April 1, with music provided by M. Mass to celebrate end of plague held Nov. 21, with music again by M. (including the *Gloria*).	
1632	65	*Scherzi musicali* published June: M. is styled 're-verendo', suggesting that he has taken holy orders. M. visits Mantua, spring-summer; return delayed by illness through August.	Lully born, Nov. 28. Stefano Landi's *Il Sant' Alessio* performed Rome, Feb. 21.
1633	66	M. still contemplates a treatise on the 'second practice' (first promised in 1605) in letters to the theorist Giovanni Battista Doni (Oct. 22, and 2 Feb. 1634). 1 motet by M. included in Heirs of Pierre Phalèse's *Luscinia sacra*.	Peri (71) dies, Aug. 12.
1634	67	M. writes a Mass for St Mark's, Christmas Eve. 2 arias by M. included in Alessandro Vincenti's *Arie de diversi*.	Banchieri (66) dies.

1635	68	M. directs music at S. Maria Gloriosa dei Frari for the feast of S. Carlo Borromeo, 3–4 Nov.	D'Anglebert born.
1636	69	Francesco M. sings in Felice Sances's *Ermiona*, Padua. 'Volgendo il ciel per l'immortal sentiero – Movete al mio bel suon le piante snelle' (*ballo*) performed for the coronation of Emperor Ferdinand III, Vienna, Dec. ?30.	
1637	70	Francesco Manelli's *Andromeda* performed at Teatro S. Cassiano, 6 March, marking the arrival of 'public' opera in Venice. M. involved in dispute with Domenico Aldegati, singer at St Mark's, June. Duke Carlo Gonzaga dies Sept. 21; Maria Gonzaga acts as regent for Carlo II. M. provides music for Giulio Strozzi's Accademia degli Unisoni, Venice. 1 motet by M. included in *Fasciculus secundus geistlicher wolklingender Concerten mit 2. vnd 3. stimmen.*	(?) Buxtehude born.
1638	71	Bellerofonte Castaldi praises M. in a poem written in Naples, May. 8th book of madrigals published Sept.	Pilkington (*c.* 68) dies; Wilbye (64) dies.
1639	72	Francesco Cavalli appointed 2nd organist of St Mark's, Jan. 23.	Marco Marazzoli and Virgilio Mazzocchi's *Chi soffre speri* performed Rome, Feb 27.
1640	73	*Arianna* performed Teatro S. Moisè, Venice, Carnival. *Il ritorno d'Ulisse in patria* performed Teatro S. Cassiano, Venice, Carnival, and later in year in Bologna.	(?) Agazzari (61) dies, April 10.

1641	74	*Vittoria d'Amore (ballo)* performed Piacenza, Feb. 7. *Il ritorno d'Ulisse in patria* revived in Venice, Carnival. *Le nozze d'Enea con Lavinia* performed Teatro SS Giovanni e Paolo, Venice, Carnival. *Selva morale e spirituale* published May. 1 *contrafactum* of M. included in Ambrosius Profe's *Erster Theil geistlicher Concerten und Harmonien*; 1 *contrafactum* of M. included in Profe's *Ander Theil geistlicher Concerten und Harmonien.*	
1642	75	1 psalm-setting, 1 motet and 2 *contrafacta* by/of M. included in Ambrosius Profe's *Dritter Theil geistlicher Concerten und Harmonien.*	Bononcini (G.M.) born, Sept. Luigi Rossi's *Il palazzo incantato* performed Rome, Feb. 22.
1643	76	*L'incoronazione di Poppea* performed Teatro SS Giovanni e Paolo, Venice, Carnival. M. visits Lombardy and Mantua, spring-summer, with a view to guaranteeing finally his pension. M. dies of fever Nov. 29, after nine days' illness: buried in S. Maria Gloriosa dei Frari. A further commission for an entertainment for Piacenza for Carnival 1644 arrives shortly after M.'s death. (?) M. was also to have provided a sequel to *Il ritorno d'Ulisse in patria*, *Ulisse errante* (eventually set by Francesco Sacrati).	Da Gagliano (M.) (60) dies, Feb. 25; Frescobaldi (59) dies, March 1. Albert 39; Benevoli 38; Bononcini (G.M.) 1; Buxtehude *c.* 6; Carissimi 38; Cavalli 41; Cesti 20; Crüger 45; D'Angelbert 8; Froberger 27; Hammerschmidt 32; Jenkins 51; Lawes (H.) 47; Lawes (W.) 41; Legrenzi 17; Lully 11; Mazzocchi (D.) 51; Mazzocchi (V.) 46; Merula *c.* 49; Reincken 20; Rigatti (28); Rossi (L.) *c.* 46; Rovetta *c.* 48; Scheidt 56; Schütz 58; Tomkins 71; Tunder 29. Louis XIV becomes King of France.
1644		Giovanni Rovetta appointed *maestro di cappella* at St Mark's,	

	Feb 21. Memorial volume for M., *Fiori poetici*, published, including eulogy by Matteo Caberloti.
1645	1 motet by M. included in *Motetti a voce sola de diversi eccelentissimi autori*.
1649	6 *contrafacta* of M. included in Ambrosius Profe's *Corollarium geistlicher Collectaneorum*.
1650	Alessandro Vincenti publishes M's *Messa . . . et salmi*, Dec.
1651	*Poppea* performed by the Febiarmonici in Naples. Alessandro Vincenti publishes M.'s 9th book of madrigals, June. 1 motet by M. included in Philipp Friedrich Böddecker's *Sacra partitura*; 1 psalm-setting and 1 motet by M. included in Gasparo Casati's *Racolta di motetti*.
1659	1 psalm-setting by M. included in Johann Havemann's *Erster Theil geistlicher Concerten*.
1661	Massimiliano M. dies Cremona, Oct. 14.

Appendix B

Catalogue of works

This list owes much both to Paolo Fabbri's *Monteverdi* and to Manfred Stattkus's *Claudio Monteverdi: Verzeichnis der erhaltenen Werke*, from which the *SV* (*Stattkus-Verzeichnis*) numbers are derived. A 'k' in the *SV* number indicates a contrafactum (thus *SV* 96k is a contrafactum of *SV* 96), an 'a' an alternative version, and an 'm' an arrangement. Locations in the Malipiero edition of Monteverdi's complete works are indicated by '*M*' followed by a roman numeral denoting the volume. Printed volumes indicated by date and superscript number (e.g., 1597^{13}) refer to the listing in RISM B/I/1: *Recueils imprimés, XVIe—XVIIe siècles*, ed. F. Lesure (Munich 1960). Manuscripts are listed selectively, in general only when they include material not contained in contemporary prints. Libraries are cited by the following RISM *sigla*:

A–Wn	Vienna, Österreichische Nationalbibliothek
D–Kl	Kassel, Murhardsche Bibliothek der Stadt und Landesbibliothek
D–Lr	Lüneberg, Ratsbücherei
DDR–Dlb	Dresden, Sächsische Landesbibliothek
GB–Lbl	London, British Library
GB–Och	Oxford, Christ Church
I–Bc	Bologna, Civico Museo Bibliografico Musicale
I–BRq	Brescia, Biblioteca Civica Queriniana
I–Fn	Florence, Biblioteca Nazionale Centrale
I–MOe	Modena, Biblioteca Estense
I–Nc	Naples, Conservatorio di Musica S. Pietro a Majella
I–Nf	Naples, Biblioteca Oratoriana dei Filippini
I–Rvat	Rome, Biblioteca Apostolica Vaticana
I–Vc	Venice, Conservatorio di Musica Benedetto Marcello
I–Vnm	Venice, Biblioteca Nazionale Marciana
J–Tma	Tokyo, Bibliotheca Musashino Academia Musicae
PL–WRu	Wroclaw, Biblioteka Uniwersytecka

Scorings (Tr = Treble; S = Soprano; Ms = Mezzo soprano; A = Alto; T = Tenor; Bar = Baritone; B = Bass) follow the cleffing in the source (Tr = G2; S = C1; Ms = C2; A = C3; T = C4; Bar = F3; B = F4): these do not necessarily accord with specific voice-types (thus a part in the C3 clef could be sung by a (high) tenor, and one in tne C4 clef by a (high) baritone). Other abbreviations employed here include: arr., arrangement/arranged; bc, basso continuo; bsn, bassoon; cf, contrafactum(-a); ct, cornett; fif, fifara; fl, flute (recorder); inst., instrument(s); pub., published; rev. revived/revised; tbn, trombone; vla, *viola*;[a] vln, violin; 2p, *secunda pars/seconda parte* (3p, etc.). Voices/instruments given in parentheses are optional and/or alternatives.

The styling of text incipits (in Italian, normally the first full line of verse unless this consists of just a single word) generally follows Stattkus, with some added punctuation and accents, etc. Matter in parentheses gives rubrics included in the source in cases where such rubrics give significant additional information: the styling follows Stattkus. Where there are two or more such rubrics (e.g. in different partbooks), the most informative entry or entries have been selected. Matter in square brackets is editorial, by and large giving details of poets, scorings and cross-references to/ between contrafacta. Lost and /or unidentified works are excluded except in the list of dramatic works.

SV

DRAMATIC WORKS

Gli amori di Diana ed Endimione [ballo, Mantua (Palazzo Ducale), ?Carnival 1605: lost]

245   *De la bellezza le dovute lodi* [ballo, ?Ferdinando Gonzaga, Mantua,?: pub. in *Scherzi musicali* (1607)]

318   *Orfeo* [*favola in musica*, Alessandro Striggio jr., Mantua (Palazzo Ducale), 24 February 1607]. Pub. as L'ORFEO / FAVOLA IN MVSICA / DA CLAVDIO MONTE-VERDE / RAPPRESENTATA IN MANTOVA / l'Anno 1607. & nouamente data in luce. / AL SERENISSIMO SIGNOR / D. FRANCESCO GONZAGA / Prencipe di Mantoua, & di Monferato, &c. (Venice, Ricciardo Amadino, 1609; 1615). Monteverdi's dedication to Prince Francesco Gonzaga is dated Venice, 22 August 1609 [M XI].

291   *Arianna* [*tragedia in musica*, Ottavio Rinuccini, Mantua (Palazzo Ducale), 28 May 1608, rev. Venice (Teatro S. Moisè), Carnival 1640: lament pub. 1623 (=SV 22; M XI)]

Ha cento lustri con etereo giro [prologue for G.B. Guarini, *L'idropica*, Mantua (Palazzo Ducale), 2 June 1608: lost]

167   *Ballo delle ingrate* [Rinuccini, Mantua (Palazzo Ducale), 4 June 1608, rev. Vienna, 1628: pub. in *Madrigali guerrieri, et amorosi* (1638); M VIII]

---

[a]Monteverdi's term 'viola' embraces a range of bowed string instruments of the *viola da braccio* family (not all of which are played 'da braccio', i.e. on the arm) in treble, alto/tenor, bass and double-bass registers. The register of the instrument in question is not distinguished in the present list.

145   *Tirsi e Clori* [*ballo*, ?Striggio, Mantua (Palazzo Ducale), January 1616: pub. in *Concerto: settimo libro de madrigali* (1619); *M* VII]

Le nozze di Tetide (*favola marittima*, Scipione Agnelli, for Mantua, begun January 1617, but unfinished: lost]

333   Su le penne de' venti il ciel varcando [prologue for G.B. Andreini's *La Maddalena*, Mantua (Palazzo Ducale), March 1617: pub. in *Musiche* ... *per La Maddalena* (Venice, Bartolomeo Magni, 1617³); *M* XI]

Andromeda [opera, Ercole Marigliani, Mantua (Palazzó Ducale), Carnival 1620: lost]ᵇ

Apollo [*ballo*, Striggio, Mantua (Palazzo Ducale), February 1620: lost]

La contesa di Amore e Cupido, etc. [six *intermedi* (at least two by Monteverdi) for Marigliani, *Le tre costanti*, Mantua (Palazzo Ducale), 18 January 1622: lost]

153   *Combattimento di Tancredi et Clorinda* [dramatic cantata, Torquato Tasso, Venice (Palazzo Mocenigo), Carnival 1624: pub. in *Madrigali guerrieri, et amorosi* (1638); *M* VIII]

Armida abbandonata [dramatic cantata, after Tasso, composed late 1626: lost]

La finta pazza Licori [opera, Giulio Strozzi, composed ?mid–1627 but ?unfinished: lost]

Gli Argonauti [*mascherata*, Claudio Achillini, Parma, March 1628: lost]

Teti e Flora, etc. [six *intermedi* for Tasso, *Aminta*, Achillini and Ascanio Pio di Savoia, Parma, 13 Dec. 1628: lost]

Mercurio e Marte [tournament, Achillini, Parma, 21 Dec. 1628: lost]

323   *Proserpina rapita* [opera, Strozzi, Venice (Palazzo Mocenigo), April 1630: one canzonetta (*SV* 173) pub. in *Madrigali e canzonette* ... *libro nono* (1651); *M* IX]

154   Volgendo il ciel per l'immortal sentiero – Movete al mio bel suon le piante snelle [*ballo*, Rinuccini, Vienna, ?30 Dec. 1636: pub. in *Madrigali guerrieri, et amorosi* (1638); *M* VIII]

325   *Il ritorno d'Ulisse in patria* [opera, Giacomo Badoaro, Venice (Teatro S. Cassiano), Carnival 1640: in *A–Wn* MS 18763; *M* XII]

Vittoria d'Amore [*ballo*, Bernardo Morando, Piacenza, 7 Feb. 1641: lost]

Le nozze d'Enea con Lavinia [Venice (Teatro SS. Giovanni e Paolo), Carnival 1641: lost]

ᵇSee Albi Rosenthal, 'Monteverdi's "Andromeda": A Lost Libretto Found', *Music & Letters*, lxvi (1985), 1–8; Iain Fenlon, 'Mantua, Monteverdi and the History of "Andromeda"', in Finscher (ed.), *Claudio Monteverdi*, pp. 163–73.

308   *L'incoronazione di Poppea* [opera, Giovanni Francesco
Busenello, Venice (Teatro SS. Giovanni e Paolo), Carnival
1642–3: in *I–Nc* MS Rari 6.4.1, *I–Vnm* MS 9963 (It.
IV.439); *M* XIII]

SECULAR WORKS

CANZONETTE / A TRE VOCI: / DI CLAVDIO
MONTEVERDE / Cremonese, Discepolo del Sig. Marc'
Antonio / Ingegnieri, nouamente poste in luce. / LIBRO
PRIMO. (Venice, Giacomo Vincenti & Ricciardo Amadino,
1584) [*M* X]

     Dedication: Monteverdi to Pietro Ambrosini, Cremona, 31
October 1584

1	1 Qual si può dir maggiore [TrTrA]
2	2 Canzonette d'amore [TrTrA]
3	3 La fiera vista e'l velenoso sguardo [TrSA]
4	4 Raggi, dov'è il mio bene? [TrTrA]
5	5 Vita de l'alma mia, cara mia vita [TrSA]
6	6 Il mio martir tengo celat'al cuore [TrTrA]
7	7 Son questi i crespi crini e questo il viso [TrTrA]
8	8 Io mi vivea com'aquila mirando [Giovanni Battista Guarini: TrTrA]
9	9 Su, su, che'l giorno è fore [TrTrA]
10	10 Quando sperai del mio servir mercede [TrSA]
11	11 Come farò, cuor mio, quando mi parto [TrTrA]
12	12 Corse a la morte il povero Narciso [TrTrMs]
13	13 Tu ridi sempre mai [SST]
14	14 Chi vuol veder d'inverno un dolc'aprile [TrTrA]
15	15 Già mi credev'un sol esser in cielo [SST]
16	16 Godi pur del bel sen, felice pulce [TrSA]
17	17 Giù lì a quel petto giace un bel giardino [SSMs]
18	18 Sì come crescon alla terra i fiori [SSA]
19	19 Io son fenice, e voi sete la fiamma [TrTrMs]
20	20 Chi vuol veder un bosco folto e spesso [TrTrMs]
21	21 Hor care canzonette [TrTrA]

MADRIGALI A CINQVE VOCI / DI CLAVDIO
MONTEVERDE CREMONESE / DISCEPOLO DEL SIG.
MARC'ANTONIO INGIGNERI / Nouamente Com-
posti, & dati in luce. / LIBRO PRIMO. (Venice, Angelo
Gardano, 1587) [*M* I]

     Dedication: Monteverdi to Count Marco Verità,
Cremona, 27 January 1587

     Reprinted: Venice, Alessandro Raverii, 1607; Bartolo-
meo Magni, 1621

23   1 Ch'ami la vita mia nel tuo bel nome [TrSMsAT]

24   2 Se per havervi, ohimè, donato il core [TrTrMsABar]
25   3 A che tormi il ben mio [TrTrMsABar]
26   4 Amor, per tua mercè vattene a quella [Giovanni Maria Bonardo: TrTrMsAT]
27   5 Baci soavi e cari [Giovanni Battista Guarini: TrSMsABar]
28   6 Se pur non mi consenti [Luigi Groto: TrTrMsAT]
29   7 Filli cara et amata [Alberto Parma: SATTB]
30   8 Poichè del mio dolore [TrSMsABar]
31   9 Fumia la pastorella [Antonio Allegretti: TrTrMsABar]
         (2p) Almo divino raggio
         (3p) All'hora i pastor tutti
32   10 Se nel partir da voi, vita mia, sento [Bonardo: TrTrMsA Bar]
33   11 Tra mille fiamme e tra mille catene [TrSMsAT]
34   12 Usciam, Ninfe, homai fuor di questi boschi [TrTrMsAT]
35   13 Questa ordì il laccio, questa [Giovanni Battista Strozzi (i): SSATB]
36   14 La vaga pastorella [TrTrMsAT]
37   15 Amor, s'il tuo ferire [TrMsAABar]
38   16 Donna, s'io miro voi ghiaccio divengo [TrTrMsABar]
39   17a Ardo sì, ma non t'amo [Guarini: TrTrMsAT]
     17b Ardi o gela a tua voglia (Risposta) [Torquato Tasso: TrTrMsAT]
     17c Arsi et alsi a mia voglia (Contrarisposta) [Tasso: TrTrMsAT]

IL SECONDO LIBRO / DE MADRIGALI A CINQVE VOCI / DI CLAVDIO MONTEVERDE CREMONESE / Discepolo del Signor Ingegneri. / Nouamente posti in luce. (Venice, Angelo Gardano, 1590) [M II]
    Dedication: Monteverdi to Giacomo Ricardi, President of the Senate and Council of Milan, Cremona, 1 January 1590
    Reprinted: ?Venice, Gardano, 1593; Alessandro Raverii, 1607; Bartolomeo Magni, 1621

40   1 Non si levava ancor l'alba novella [Torquato Tasso: SSATB]
         (2p) E dicea l'una sospirand'all'hora
41   2 Bevea Fillide mia [Girolamo Casoni: SSATB]
42   3 Dolcissimi legami [Tasso: SSATB]
43   4 Non giacinti o narcisi (Casoni: SSATB]
44   5 Intorno a due vermiglie e vaghe labbra [SSATB]
45   6 Non sono in queste rive [Tasso: SSATB]
46   7 Tutte le bocche belle [Filippo Alberti: TrTrMsABar]
47   8 Donna, nel mio ritorno il mio pensiero [Tasso: TrMsAA Bar]
48   9 Quell'ombra esser vorrei [Casoni: TrMsAABar]
49   10 S'andasse Amor a caccia [Tasso:SSATB]

50	11	Mentre io miravo fiso [Tasso: SSATB]
51	12	Ecco mormorar l'onde [Tasso: SSATB]
52	13	Dolcemente dormiva la mia Clori [Tasso: TrTrMsABar]
53	14	Se tu mi lassi, perfida, tuo danno [Tasso: SSATB]
54	15	La bocca onde l'asprissime parole [Enzo Bentivoglio: SSATB]
55	16	Crudel, perchè mi fuggi [Giovanni Battista Guarini: SSATB]
56	17	Questo specchio ti dono [Casoni: SMsATB]
57	18	Non mi è grave il morire [Bartolomeo Gottifredi: SSATB]
58	19	Ti spontò l'ali, Amor, la donna mia [Alberti: TrTrMsABar]
59	20	Cantai un tempo, e se fu dolc'il canto [Pietro Bembo: TrMsAABar]

Nos. 1, 13 also in *Fiori del giardino di diversi eccellentissimi autori à quattro, cinque, sei, sette, otto, & nove voci* (Nuremberg, Paul Kauffmann, 1597[13]).

DI CLAVDIO / MONTEVERDE / IL TERZO LIBRO DE MADRIGALI / A CINQVE VOCI. / Nouamente composto & datto in luce. (Venice, Ricciardo Amadino, 1592) [M III]

Dedication: Monteverdi to Duke Vincenzo Gonzaga, Mantua, 27 June 1592

Reprinted: Venice, Amadino, 1594, 1598, 1600, 1604, 1607, 1611; Antwerp, Pierre Phalèse, 1615; Venice, Bartolomeo Magni, 1621

60	1	La giovinetta pianta [SSMsAB; cf in Coppini 1608]
61	2	O come è gran martire [Giovanni Battista Guarini: TrTrSABar; cf in Coppini 1608]
62	3	Sovra tenere herbette e bianchi fiori [TrTrMsAT]
63	4	O dolce anima mia, dunque è pur vero [Guarini: TrTrMsABar]
64	5	Stracciami pur il core [Guarini: SSATB]
65	6	O rossignuol, ch'in queste verdi fronde [Pietro Bembo: SSMsAB]
66	7	Se per estremo ardore [Guarini: SAATB]
67	8	Vattene pur, crudel, con quella pace [Torquato Tasso: TrTrMsABar]
		(2p) Là tra'l sangu'e le morti egro giacente
		(3p) Poi ch'ella in se tornò, deserto e muto
68	9	O primavera, gioventù dell'anno [Guarini: SSATB; cf in Coppini 1608]
69	10	Perfidissimo volto [Guarini: SSATB]
70	11	Ch'io non t'ami, cor mio [Guarini: SSATB]
71	12	Occhi un tempo mia vita [Guarini: TrTrMsABar]
72	13	Vivrò fra i miei tormenti e le mie cure [Tasso: TrSMsABar]
		(2p) Ma dove, o lasso me, dove restaro
		(3p) Io pur verrò là dove sete, e voi

73   14 Lumi, miei cari lumi [Guarini: SSSAB]

74   15 'Rimanti in pace', a la dolente e bella [Livio Celiano
     (=Angelo Grillo): SSATB]
     (2p) Ond'ei di morte la sua faccia impressa

Nos. 1, 3, 5 also in *Fiori del giardino di diversi eccellentissimi
autori à quattro, cinque, sei, sette, otto, & nove voci* (Nuremberg, Paul Kauffmann, 1597[13]); no. 14 also in *Il Helicone:
madrigali de diversi eccellentissimi musici a cinque voci* (Antwerp, Pierre Phalèse, 1616[10]).

IL QVARTO LIBRO / DE MADRIGALI / A CINQVE
VOCI, / DI CLAVDIO MONTEVERDE / Maestro
della Musica del Sereniss. Sig. / Duca di Mantoua. /
Nuouamente composto, dato in luce. (Venice, Ricciardo
Amadino, 1603) [*M* IV]

 Dedication: Monteverdi to the Accademia degli Intrepidi
(Ferrara), Mantua, 1 March 1603

 Reprinted: Venice, Amadino, 1605, 1607, 1611, 1615;
Antwerp, Pierre Phalèse, 1615; Venice, Bartolomeo Magni,
1622; Antwerp, Heirs of Pierre Phalèse, 1644

75   1 Ah dolente partita [Giovanni Battista Guarini: TrTrMsA
     Bar; cf in Coppini 1608]

76   2 Cor mio, mentre vi miro [Guarini: SMsATB; cf in Coppini
     1609]

77   3 Cor mio, non mori? E mori [SMsATB; cf in Coppini 1609]

78   4 Sfogava con le stelle [Ottavio Rinuccini: SSATB; cf in
     Coppini 1609]

79   5 Volgea l'anima mia soavemente [Guarini: SSATB; cf in
     Coppini 1609]

80   6 Anima mia, perdona [Guarini: SSATB; cf in Coppini 1609]
     (2p) Che se tu se' il cor mio

81   7 Luci serene e chiare [Ridolfo Arlotti: SSATB; cf in Coppini
     1609]

82   8 La piaga c'ho nel core [Aurelio Gatti: SMsATB; cf in
     Coppini 1609]

83   9 Voi pur da me partite, anima dura [Guarini: SSATB; cf in
     Coppini 1609]

84   10 A un giro sol de' bell'occhi lucenti [Guarini: SSATB; cf in
     Coppini 1609]

85   11 Ohimè, se tanto amate [Guarini: SMsATB]

86   12 Io mi son giovinetta [SSATB; cf in Coppini 1609]

87   13 Quel augellin che canta [Guarini: SSATB; cf in Coppini
     1609]

88   14 Non più guerra, pietate [Guarini: SSATB]

89   15 Sì ch'io vorrei morire [Maurizio Moro: SMsATB; cf in
     Coppini 1609]

90   16 Anima dolorosa che vivendo [SSATB; cf in Coppini 1609]

91	17	Anima del cor mio [SMsATB; cf in Coppini 1609]
92	18	Longe da te, cor mio [SMsTTB; cf in Coppini 1609]
93	19	Piagn'e sospira, e quand'i caldi raggi [Torquato Tasso: SSATB; cf in Coppini 1609]

No 1 first pub. in *Fiori del giardino di diversi eccellentissimi autori à quattro, cinque, sei, sette, otto, & nove voci* (Nuremburg, Paul Kauffmann, 1597[13]); nos. 1, 12–14 also in Melchior Borchgrevinck (ed.), *Giardino novo bellissimo di varii fiori musicali scieltissimi: il primo libro de madrigali a cinque voci* (Copenhagen, Henrik Waltkirch, 1605[7]; 1606); no. 2 also in Borchgrevinck (ed.), *Giardino novo bellissimo di varii fiori musicali scieltissimi: il secondo libro de madrigali a cinque voci* (Copenhagen, Henrik Waltkirch, 1606[5]).

IL QVINTO LIBRO / DE MADRIGALI / A CINQVE VOCI. / DI CLAVDIO MONTEVERDE / Maestro della Musica del Serenissimo / Sig. Duca di Mantoa. / Col Basso continuo per il Clauicembano Chittarone od altro / simile istromento, fatto particolarmente per li sei vl- / timi, & per li altri a beneplacito. / Nouamente composti, & dati in luce. (Venice, Ricciardo Amadino, 1605) [*M* V]

Dedication: Monteverdi to Duke Vincenzo Gonzaga, Mantua, 30 July 1605

Reprinted: Venice, Amadino, 1606, 1608, 1610, 1611, 1613, 1615; Antwerp, Pierre Phalèse, 1615; Venice, Bartolomeo Magni, 1620; Antwerp, Heirs of Pierre Phalèse, 1643

94	1	Cruda Amarilli, che col nome ancora [Giovanni Battista Guarini: TrSAABar, bc; cf in Coppini 1607; arr. in *GB–Lbl* Add. MS 31440, *GB–Och* MS 878/880]
95	2	O Mirtillo, Mirtillo anima mia [Guarini: SSATB, bc; cf in Coppini 1608]
96	3	Era l'anima mia [Guarini: SSATB, bc; cf in Coppini 1607]
97	4	Ecco, Silvio, colei che in odio hai tanto [Guarini: TrTrMsABar, bc; cf in Coppini 1607, Coppini 1609; arr. in *GB–Lbl* Add. MS 31440]
		(2p) Ma se con la pietà non è in te spenta
		(3p) Dorinda, ah dirò mia se mia non sei
		(4p) Ecco piegando le genocchie a terra
		(5p) Ferir quel petto, Silvio?
98	5	Ch'io t'ami, e t'ami più de la mia vita [Guarini: SSATB, bc; cf in Coppini 1607, Coppini 1608; arr. in *GB–Lbl* Add. MS 31440]
		(2p) Deh bella e cara e sì soave un tempo
		(3p) Ma tu, più che mai dura
99	6	Che dar più vi poss'io? [SSATB, bc]
100	7	M'è più dolce il penar per Amarilli [Guarini: SSATB, bc; cf in Coppini 1608]

101	8	Ahi come a un vago sol cortese giro [Guarini: SSTTB, bc; cf in Coppini 1607; arr. in *GB–Och* MS 878/880]
102	9	Troppo ben può questo tiranno Amore [Guarini: SMsATB, bc; cf in Coppini 1607]
103	10	Amor, se giusto sei [SSATB, bc; cf in Coppini 1609]
104	11	'T'amo mia vita', la mia cara vita [Guarini: SSATB, bc; cf in Coppini 1607; arr. in *GB–Och* MS 878/880]
105	12	E così poco a poco [Guarini: SSATTB, bc]
106	13	Questi vaghi concenti [SSATB, SATB, 9 inst., bc]

Bc is optional for Nos. 1–7. No. 1 also in Melchior Borchgrevinck (ed.), *Giardino novo bellissimo di varii fiori musicali scieltissimi: il secondo libro de madrigali a cinque voci* (Copenhagen, Henrik Waltkirch, 1606[5]).

SCHERZI / MVSICALI / A TRE VOCI, / DI CLAVDIO MONTEVERDE, / RACCOLTI DA GIVLIO CESARE / Monteuerde suo fratello, & nouamente / posti in luce. / Con la Dichiaratione di vna Lettera, che si ritroua stampata / nel Quinto libro de suoi Madregali. / DEDICATI / AL SERENISSIMO S. DON FRANCESCO GONZAGA / Prencipe di Mantoua, & di Monferrato. / CON PRIVILEGGIO. (Venice, Ricciardo Amadino, 1607) [M X]

Dedication: Giulio Cesare Monteverdi to Prince Francesco Gonzaga, Venice, 21 July 1607

Reprinted: Venice, Amadino, 1609, 1615; Bartolomeo Magni, 1628

All pieces are for TrTr(or SS/TrS)B, 2 vln, bc.

230	1	I bei legami [Gabriello Chiabrera]
231	2	Amarilli onde m'assale [Chiabrera]
232	3	Fugge il verno dei dolori [?Chiabrera]
233	4	Quando l'alba in oriente [Chiabrera]
234	5	Non così tosto io miro [Chiabrera]
235	6	Damigella tutta bella [Chiabrera; cf in *I–BRq* MS L.IV.99]
236	7	La pastorella mia spietata e rigida [Jacopo Sannazaro]
237	8	O rosetta, che rossetta [Chiabrera; cf in *I–BRq* MS L.IV.99]
238	9	Amorosa pupilletta [Ansaldo Cebà]
239	10	Vaghi rai di cigli ardenti [Chiabrera]
240	11	La violetta che'n su l'herbetta [Chiabrera]
241	12	Giovinetta ritrosetta [Cebà]
242	13	Dolci miei sospiri [Chiabrera]
243	14	Clori amorosa [?Chiabrera]
244	15	Lidia, spina del mio core [Cebà; cf in *I–BRq* MS L.IV.99]
245	18	Entrata – De la bellezza le dovute lodi (*Balletto*) [?Ferdinando Gonzaga]

Nos. 16 ('Deh chi tace il bel pensiero' [Cebà]), 17 ('Dispiegate guance amate' [Cebà]) by Giulio Cesare Monteverdi; no. 18 unattributed.

IL SESTO LIBRO / DE MADRIGALI / A CINQVE VOCI, / con vno Dialogo a Sette, / Con il suo Basso continuo per poterli con- / certare nel Clauacembano, & altri / Stromenti. / DI CLAVDIO MONTEVERDE / Maestro di Cappella della Sereniss. Sig. / di Venetia In S. Marco. / Nuouamente composti, & dati in luce. / CON PRIVILEGIO (Venice, Ricciardo Amadino, 1614) [*M VI*]

Reprinted: Venice, Amadino, 1615; Bartolomeo Magni, 1620; Antwerp, Heirs of Pierre Phalèse, 1639

107　　1 Lasciatemi morire (*Lamento d'Arianna*) [Ottavio Rinuccini: SSATB, bc]

(2p) O Teseo, o Teseo mio

(3p) Dove, dove è la fede

(4p) Ahi che non pur risponde

108　　2 Zefiro torna e'l bel tempo rimena [Francesco Petrarca: SSATB, bc]

109　　3 Una donna fra l'altre honesta e bella ('concertato nel clauicimbalo') [SSATB, bc; cf in Coppini 1609, *DDR–Dlh* MS Mus Pi 8]

110　　4 A dio, Florida bella, il cor piagato ('concertato nel clauacembano') [Giambattista Marino: SSATB, bc]

111　　5 Incenerite spoglie, avara tomba (*Sestina: Lagrime d'amante al sepolcro dell'amata*) [Scipione Agnelli: SSATB, bc]

(2p) Ditelo, o fiumi, e voi ch'udiste Glauco

(3p) Darà la notte il sol lume alla terra

(4p) Ma te raccoglie, o ninfa, in grembo il cielo

(5p) O chiome d'or, neve gentil del seno

(6p) Dunque, amate reliquie, un mar di pianto

112　　6 Ohimè il bel viso, ohimè il soave sguardo [Petrarca: SSATB, bc]

113　　7 Qui rise, o Tirsi, e qui ver me rivolse ('concertato nel clauacimbano') [Marino: SSTTB, bc]

114　　8 Misero Alceo, dal caro albergo fore ('concertato nel clauacimbano') [Marino: SSATB, bc]

115　　9 'Batto', qui pianse Ergasto, 'ecco la riva' ('concertato nel clauacembano' [Marino: SSATB, bc]

116　　10 Presso a un fiume tranquillo ('Dialogo a 7. Concertato') [Marino: SSSATTB, bc]

No. 3 first pub. as cf in Coppini 1609.

CONCERTO. / SETTIMO LIBRO / DE MADRIGALI / A 1.2.3.4. & Sei voci, con altri / generi de Canti, / DI / CLAVDIO MONTEVERDE / MAESTRO DI CAPELLA / Della Serenissima Republica / Nouamente Dato in Luce. / DEDICATO / ALLA SERENISSIMA MADAMA / CATERI-NA MEDICI / Gonzaga Duchessa di Mantoua di Monferato &c. (Venice, Bartolomeo Magni, 1619) [*M VII*]

Dedication: Monteverdi to Caterina de' Medici, Duchess of

Mantua, Venice, 13 December 1619
Reprinted: Venice, Bartolomeo Magni, 1622, 1623, 1628, 1641

117   1 Sinfonia – Tempro la cetra, e per cantar gli honori – Sinfonia (Giambattista Marino: T, 5 inst., bc)
118   2 Non è di gentil core (?Francesco degli Atti: SS, bc)
119   3 A quest'olmo, a quest'ombre et a quest'onde ('Concerto A Sei Voci. Et Istromenti') [Marino: TrTrMsAABar, 2 vln, 2 fl (or fif), bc]
120   4 O come sei gentile [Giovanni Battista Guarini: SS, bc]
121   5 Io son pur vezzosetta pastorella ['Incolto Accademico Immaturo': SS, bc)
122   6 O viva fiamma, o miei sospiri ardenti [G. Alfonso Gesualdo: SS, bc]
123   7 Vorrei baciarti, o Filli [Marino: AA, bc]
124   8 Dice la mia bellissima Licori [Guarini: TB, bc]
125   9 Ah che non si conviene [TT, bc]
126   10 Non vedrò mai le stelle [TT, bc]
127   11 Ecco vicine, o bella tigre, l'hore [Claudio Achillini: TT, bc]
128   12 Perchè fuggi tra' salci, ritrosetta [Marino: TT, bc]
129   13 Tornate, o cari baci [Marino: TT bc]
130   14 Soave libertate [Gabriello Chiabrera: TT, bc]
131   15 Se'l vostro cor, madonna [Guarini: TB, bc]
132   16 Interrotte speranze, eterna fede [Guarini: TT, bc]
133   17 Augellin che la voce al canto spieghi [TTB, bc]
134   18 Vaga su spina ascosa [Chiabrera: TTB, bc; cf in Lappi 1623, Profe 1641[2]]
135   19 Eccomi pronta ai baci [Marino: TTB, bc]
136   20 Parlo, misero, o taccio? [Guarini: SSB, bc; cf in Profe 1649, *PL–Wru*]
137   21 Tu dormi, ah crudo core [SATB, bc; cf in Profe 1649]
138   22 Al lume delle stelle [Torquato Tasso: SSTB, bc; cf in Profe 1649]
139   23 Con che soavità, labbra adorate [Guarini: S, 9 inst. (including bc)]
140   24 Ohimè, dov'è il mio ben, dov'è il mio core? ('Romanesca') [Bernardo Tasso: SS, bc]
       (2p) Dunque ha potuto sol desio d'honore
       (3p) Dunque ha potuto in me più che'l mio amore
       (4p) Ahi sciocco mondo e cieco, ahi cruda sorte
141   25 Se i languidi miei sguardi ('Let[t]era Amorosa à Voce Sola in genere rapresentatiuo e si canta senza batuta') [Achillini: S, bc]
142   26 Se pur destina e vole ('Partenza Amorosa a Vna Voce in genere rapresentatiuo e si canta senza battuda') [?Ottavio Rinuccini: T, bc]
143   27 Chiome d'oro ('Canzonetta a due voci Concertata con duoi Violini Chitarone o Spinetta') [SS, 2 vln, bc; cf in *D–Kl* 2° MS Mus. 58j]

144	28 Amor, che deggio far? ('Canzonetta A 4. Concertata come di sopra') [SSTB, 2 vln, bc]
145	29 *Tirsi e Clori* ('Ballo concert[ato] con Voci et istrumenti à 5.') [?Alessandro Striggio: SSATB, 5 inst., bc]

LAMENTO / D'ARIANNA / DEL SIGNOR / CLAVDIO MONTEVERDE / MAESTRO DI CAPELLA / Della Serenissima Republica. / Et con due Lettere Amorose in genere Rapresentativo. / CON PRIVILEGIO. (Venice, Bartolomeo Magni, 1623)

22	1 Lasciatemi morire (*Lamento d'Arianna*) [Ottavio Rinuccini: S, bc; *M* XI]
141	2 Se i languidi miei sguardi [Claudio Achillini: S, bc]
142	3 Se pur destina e vole [Rinuccini: T, bc]

No. 1 from *Arianna* (1608): Monteverdi's five-part arrangement (*SV* 107) is in *Il sesto libro de madrigali* (1614); solo-voice version also pub. in *Il maggio fiorito: arie, sonetti, e madrigali, à 1.2.3. de diuersi autori* (Orvieto, Michel'Angelo Fei & Rinaldo Ruuli, 1623[8]), and survives in *GB–Lbl* Add. MS 30491 (copied by Luigi Rossi), *I–Fn* B.R. 238 (Magl. XIX.114), *I–MOe* MS Mus. G.239, *I–Vc* Fondo Fausto Torrefranca MS 28600 (copied by Francesco Maria Fucci);[c] cf (*SV* 288) in *Selva morale e spirituale* (1640–1). Nos. 2, 3 first pub. in *Concerto: settimo libro de madrigali* (1619).

SCHERZI / MVSICALI / Cioè Arie, & Madrigali in stil recitatiuo, / con vna Ciaccona A 1. & 2. voci. / Del M: to Ill.re & M. to R.do Sig.r Claudio Monteuerde. / Maestro di Capella della Sereniss. Repub. / Di Venetia. / Raccolti da Bartholomeo Magni / & Nouamente stampati. / CON PRIVILEGIO (Venice, Bartolomeo Magni, 1632) [*M* X (Nos. 7, 8 in *M* IX)]

Dedication: Bartolomeo Magni to Pietro Capello, Mayor and Captain of Capo d'Istria, Venice, 20 June 1632

246	1 Maledetto sia l'aspetto [S, bc]
247	2 Quel sguardo sdegnosetto [S, bc]
	(2p) Armatevi pupille
	(3p) Begl'occhi a l'armi
248	3 Eri già tutta mia [S, bc]
249	4 Ecco di dolci raggi il sol armato [T, bc]
250	5 Et è pur dunque vero [S, 1 inst., bc]
	6 Io ch'armato sin hor d'un duro gelo [= final stanza of no. 4; cf in Profe 1642]
251	7 Zefiro torna, e di soavi accenti [Ottavio Rinuccini: TT, bc]
150	8 Armato il cor d'adamantina fede [?Rinuccini: TT, bc; cf in Profe 1642]

No. 4 first pub. in Giovanni Battista Camarella, *Madrigali et*

[c]See Irving Godt, 'A Monteverdi Source Reappears: The "Grilanda" of F. M. Fucci', *Music & Letters*, lx (1979), 428–39.

arie (Venice, Alessandro Vincenti, 1620); nos. 7, 8 also in *Madrigali e canzonette . . . libro nono* (1651); no. 8 also in *Madrigali guerrieri, et amorosi* (1638). Nos. 7, 8 were reworked in Schütz's 'Es steh Gott auf' (*SWV* 356).

MADRIGALI / GVERRIERI, ET AMOROSI / Con alcuni opuscoli in genere rappresentatiuo, che saranno / per breui Episodij frà i canti senza gesto. / LIBRO OTTAVO / DI CLAVDIO MONTEVERDE / Maestro di Capella della Serenissima Republica di Venetia. / DEDICATI / Alla Sacra Cesarea Maestà / DELL' IMPERATOR / FERDINANDO III. / CON PRIVILEGIO. (Venice, Alessandro Vincenti, 1638) [*M* VIII/1–2 (nos. 4, 5, 13, 14 in *M* IX)]

Dedication: Monteverdi to Emperor Ferdinand III, Venice, 1 September 1638

Canti guerrieri

No. 5 first pub. in *Scherzi musicali* (1632). A seventeenth-century German version of no. 8 by Dietrich von dem Werden survives in *J–Tma*.

MADRIGALI / E CANZONETTE / A DVE, E TRE, VOCI, / DEL SIGNOR / CLAVDIO MONTEVERDE / Gia Maestro di Cappella della Serenissima Republica / di Venetia. / DEDICATE / All'Illustrissimo Signor mio Patron Colendissimo / IL SIG.R GEROLAMO / OROLOGIO. / LIBRO NONO. / CON PRIVILEGIO. (Venice, Alessandro Vincenti, 1651) [M IX]

Dedication: Alessandro Vincenti to Gerolamo Orologio, Venice, 27 June 1651

176	14 Sì, sì, ch'io v'amo [TTB, bc]
177	15 Su, su, su, pastorelli vezzosi [TTB, bc; different setting from *SV* 166]
178	16 O mio bene, o mia vita [TTB, bc]

No. 2 first pub. in *Scherzi musicali* (1632); nos. 3–6 first pub. in *Madrigali guerrieri, et amorosi* (1638).

COLLECTIONS

Antonio Morsolino, *Il primo libro delle canzonette a tre voci* . . . *con alcune altre de diuersi eccellenti musici* (Venice, Ricciardo Amadino, 1594[15]) [M XVII]

309	2 Io ardo sì, ma'l foco è di tal sorte [TrSBar]
314	6 Occhi miei, se mirar più non debb'io [TrTrBar]
324	10 Quante son stelle in ciel e in mar arene [Scipione Cerreto: SSB]
331	14 Se non mi date aita [TrSBar]

All four have cf in *I–Bc* MS Q.27.

Amante Franzoni, *I nuovi fioretti musicali a tre voci* . . . *co'l suo basso generale per il clauicimbalo, chitarrone, & altri simili stromenti* (Venice, Ricciardo Amadino, 1605[12]; 1607[17]) [M XVII]

332	14 Prima vedrò ch'in questi prati nascano [SSB, bc; cf in *I–Bc* MS Q.27]

Giaches de Wert, *Il duodecimo libro de madrigali* . . . *a 4. a 5. a 6. & 7. con alcuni altri de diuersi eccellentissimi autori* (Venice, Angelo Gardano & Brothers, 1608)
Only the bass partbook survives

319	2 Pensier aspro e crudele
329	3 Sdegno la fiamm'estinse [Orsina Cavaletta]

Carlo Milanuzzi, *Quarto scherzo delle ariose vaghezze commode da cantarsi à voce sola nel clauicembalo chitarrone, arpa doppia, & altro simile stromento con le littere dell'alfabetto con l'intauolatura, e con la scala di musica per la chitarra alla spagnola* (repr. Venice, Alessandro Vincenti, 1624) [M IX]

316	25 Ohimè ch'io cado, ohimè ch'inciampo ancora [S, bc]
310	26 La mia turca che d'amor [S, bc]
	27 Prendi l'arco invitto Amor [=final stanza of no. 26]
332	28 Sì dolce è 'l tormento [S, bc]

Madrigali del signor cavaliero Anselmi nobile di Treviso posti in musica da diuersi eccellentissimi spiriti a 2.3.4.5. voci. Con il basso continuo (Venice, Bartolomeo Magni, 1624[11]) [M IX]

315	1 O come vaghi, o come [Giovanni Battista Anselmi: TT, bc]
334	16 Taci, Armelin, deh taci [Anselmi: AA(=T)B, bc]

Alessandro Vincenti (ed.), *Arie de diversi* . . . *commode da cantarsi nel clauicembalo, chitarrone, & altro simile stromento, con le lettere dell'alfabetto per la chitarra spagnola* (Venice, Alessandro Vincenti, 1634[7]) [*M* XVII]

320   1 Perchè, se m'odiavi [S, bc]
321   2 Più lieto il guardo [S, bc]

Pietro Millioni and Lodovico Monte, *Vero e facil modo d'imparare a sonare, et accordare da se medesimo la chitarra spagnola* (repr. Rome/Macerata, Heirs of Salvioni & Agostino Grisei, 1637; many reprints)
A1   18 Ballo [guitar][d]

MANUSCRIPTS

GB–Lbl Add. MS 30491 [Luigi Rossi (*c*. 1597–1653), *c*. 1620]
22a   Lasciatemi morire (*Lamento d'Arianna*) [S, bc]
A2   Voglio, voglio morir, voglio morire (*Lamento di Olimpia*) [S, bc][e]
S V A2 also in *GB–Lbl* Add. MS 31440.

GB–Lbl Add. MS 31440 [?Walter Porter (d.1659), before 1659]
Contains items from *Il quarto libro de madrigali* (1603; *S V* 75–7, 81, 83, 85, 89), *Il quinto libro de madrigali* (1605; *S V* 96, 98, 101, 102, 104), *Concerto: settimo libro de madrigali* (1619; *S V* 120–28, 130, 132), *Madrigali del signor cavaliero Anselmi* (1624; *S V* 334), plus:
A2   Voglio, voglio morir, voglio morire (*Lamento di Olimpia*) [S, bc]
97m   Ecco, Silvio, colei che in odio hai tanto [TrTr, bc]
98m   Ch'io t'ami, e t'ami più de la mia vita [SS, bc]
94m   Cruda Amarilli, che col nome ancora
For *S V* A2, see *GB–Lbl* Add. MS 30491; *S V* 97m, 98m arr. from *Il quinto libro de madrigali* (1605); *S V* 94m (also from *Il quinto libro*) is bass part of (?3-part) arr. in *GB–Och* MS 878/ 880.

GB–Och MS 878/880 [part by George Jeffreys (*c*. 1610–1685), mid 17th century]
Canto 2 and bc partbooks
104m   'T'amo mia vita', la mia cara vita
101m   Ahi come a un vago sol cortese giro
94m   Cruda Amarilli, che col nome ancora
All arr. (a3?) from *Il quinto libro de madrigali* (1605).

I–MOe MS α.K.6.31 (It. 1384) [Anon. (but belonging to Monaldo Brancaleone), *c*. 1600: *M* XVII]

---

[d]In Fabbri, 'Inediti monteverdiani'.
[e]In Monteverdi, *12 composizioni vocali profane e sacre*, ed. Osthoff, pp. 10–17. The attribution to Monteverdi is questioned in Danckwardt, 'Das Lamento d'Olimpia "Voglio voglio morir"'.

290	16	Ahi che sì parti il mio bel sol adorno ('Villanella') [TrTrT]

I–MOe MS Mus. G.239 [Anon., after 1632]

22	1	Lasciatemi morire (*Lamento d'Arianna*) [S, bc]
241m	4	Giovinetta ritrosetta [S, bc]

No. 4 arr. from *Scherzi musicali* (1607).

I–Nf MS 473.2 (IV–2–23b) [Cristoforo Caresana, c.1700]

337	Voglio di vita uscir, voglio che cadano [S, bc]ᶠ

SACRED AND SPIRITUAL WORKS

SACRAE CANTIVNCULAE / TRIBVS VOCIBVS / CLAVDINI MONTISVIRIDI CREMONENSIS / EGREGII INGENERII DISCIPVLI / LIBER PRIMVS / nuper editus. (Venice, Angelo Gardano, 1582) [*M* XIV/1]
   Dedication: Monteverdi to Don Stefano Canini Valcarenghi, Cremona, 1 August 1582

207	1	Lapidabant Stephanum [SAT]
208	2	Veni sponsa Christi [SAT]
209	3	Ego sum pastor bonus [SAT]
210	4	Surge propera amica mea [SAT]
211	5	Ubi duo vel tres congregati fuerint [SST]
212	6	Quam pulchra es et quam decora amica mea [SST]
213	7	Ave Maria gratia plena [SST]
214	8	Domine pater et Deus [SAT]
215	9	Tu es pastor ovium [SAT]
		(2p) Tu es Petrus
216	10	O magnum pietatis opus [TrMsA]
		(2p) Eli clamans spiritum patri
217	11	O crux benedicta [TrMsA]
218	12	Hodie Christus natus est [TrMsA]
219	13	O Domine Jesu Christe adoro te [TrMsA]
		(2p) O Domine Jesu Christe adoro te
220	14	Pater venit hora clarifica filium tuum [TrMsA]
221	15	In tua patientia possedisti animam tuam [TrMsA]
222	16	Angelus ad pastores ait [TrSA]
223	17	Salve crux pretiosa [SAT]
224	18	Quia vidisti me Thoma credidisti [SAT]
225	19	Lauda Syon salvatorem [SST]
226	20	O bone Iesu illumina oculos meos [SAT]
227	21	Surgens Iesus Dominus noster [TrMsA]
228	22	Qui vult venire post me abneget se [SAT]
229	23	Iusti tulerant spolia impiorum [SAT]

ᶠIn Monteverdi, *12 composizioni vocali profane e sacre*, ed. Osthoff, pp. 18–23.

MADRIGALI / SPIRITVALI / A QVATTRO VOCI, / Posti in Musica da Claudio Monteuerde Cremone- / se, Discepolo del Signor Marc'Antonio / Ingegnieri. / Nouamente posti in luce. (Brescia, Vincenzo Sabbio ('Ad instanza di Pietro Bozzola, Libraro in Cremona'), 1583) [*M* XVII]

Dedication: Monteverdi to Alessandro Fraganesco, Cremona, 31 July 1583

Only the bass partbook survives. All pieces for ?SATB.

179	1	Sacrosanta di Dio verace imago
180	2	L'aura del ciel sempre feconda spiri
		(2p) Poi chè benigno il novo cant'attende
181	3	Aventurosa notte in cui risplende
		(2p) Serpe crudel, se i tuoi primier'inganni
182	4	D'empi martiri e un mar d'orrori varca
		(2p) Ond'in ogni pensier ed opra santo
183	5	Mentre la stell'appar nell'oriente
		(2p) Tal contra Dio de la superbia il corno
184	6	Le rose lascia, gli amaranti e gigli
		(2p) Ai piedi havendo i capei d'oro sparsi
185	7	L'empio vestia di porpora e di bisso
		(2p) Ma quel mendico Lazaro, che involto
186	8	L'human discorso quanto poc'importe
		(2p) L'eterno Dio quel cor pudico scelse
187	9	Dal sacro petto esce veloce dardo
		(2p) Scioglier m'addita, se tal'hor mi cinge
188	10	Afflitto e scalz'ove la sacra sponda
		(2p) Ecco, dicea, ecco l'Agnel di Dio
189	11	De i miei giovenil anni era l'amore
		(2p) Tutt'esser vidi le speranze vane

SANCTISSIMAE / VIRGINI / MISSA SENIS VOCIBVS, / AD ECCLESIARVM CHOROS / Ac Vespere pluribus decantandae / CVM NONNVLLIS SACRIS CONCENTIBVS, / ad Sacella siue Principum Cubicula accommodata. / OPERA / A CLAVDIO MONTEVERDE / nuper effecta / AC BEATISS. PAVLO V. PONT. MAX. CONSECRATA. (Venice, Ricciardo Amadino, 1610) [*M* XIV/ 1–2]

Dedication: Monteverdi to Pope Paul V, Venice, 1 September 1610

205	1	*Missa a 6 voci da capella 'In illo tempore'* [TrTrMsAABar, bc]
		Kyrie
		[Gloria . . .] Et in terra pax
		[Credo . . .] Patrem omnipotentem
		Sanctus
		Benedictus

Agnus Dei I
Agnus Dei II [TrTrMsAABarBar, bc]

2 *Vespro della Beata Vergine*
[Deus in adjutorium] Domine ad adiuvandum me festina
    [SSATTB, 2 vln, 5 vla, 2 ct, 3 tbn, bc]
Dixit Dominus ('Li Ritornelli si ponno sonare et anco
    tralasciar secondo il volere') [SSATTB, 6 inst., bc]
Nigra sum sed formosa [T, bc]
Laudate pueri Dominum ('a 8 voci sole nel organo')
    [SSAATTBB, bc]
Pulchra es amica mea [SS, bc]
Laetatus sum [SSATTB, bc]
Duo seraphim clamabant [TTT, bc]
Nisi Dominus [SATTB, SATTB, bc]
Audi coelum [T, SSATTB, bc]
Lauda Jerusalem [TrTrMsMsABarBar, bc]
Sonata sopra 'Sancta Maria, ora pro nobis' [S, 2 vln, vla,
    2 ct, 3 tbn (or 2 tbn, vla), bc]
Ave maris stella [SATB, SATB, 5 inst., bc]
Magnificat I [TrTrMsAABarBar, 2 vln vla, 2 fl, 2 fif, 3 ct,
    2 tbn, bc][g]
    Magnificat [SSATTBB, 2 vln, vla, 3 ct, bc]
    Et exultavit [ATT, bc]
    Quia respexit [T, 2 vln, vla, 2 fl, 2 fif, 3 ct, 2 tbn, bc]
    Quia fecit mihi magna [ABB, 2 vln, bc]
    Et misericordia eius ('a 6 voci sole in dialogo')
        [SSATBB, bc]
    Fecit potentiam [A, 2 vln, vla, bc]
    Deposuit potentes de sede [T, 2 vln, 2 ct, bc]
    Esurientes implevit bonis [SS, 3 ct, vla, bc]
    Suscepit Israel puerum suum [SST, bc]
    Sicut locutus est [A, 2 vln, vla, 2 ct, 1 tbn, bc]
    Gloria patri et filio [STT, bc]
    Sicut erat in principio ('Tutti gli instrumenti et voci, et
        va cantato et sonato forte. A Organo pieno'
        [SSATTBB, 2 vln, vla, 3 ct, bc]
Magnificat II [TrTrMsAABar, bc][h]
    Magnificat [SSATTB, bc]
    Anima mea [SS, bc]
    Et exultavit [ATT, bc]
    Quia respexit [T, bc]
    Quia fecit mihi magna [SSATTB, bc]
    Et misericordia eius [SST, bc]
    Fecit potentiam [SSA, bc]

[g]For the purpose of the scorings indicated below, the vocal parts are assumed
to be for SSATTBB.

[h]For the purpose of the scorings indicated below, the vocal parts are assumed
to be for SSATTB.

Deposuit potentes de sede [SST, bc]
Esurientes implevit bonis [AT, bc]
Suscepit Israel puerum suum [SS, bc]
Sicut locutus est [SSATB, bc]
Gloria patri et filio [SSATTB, bc]
Sicut erat in principio [SSATTB, bc]

No. 1 (minus bc) also in *Missae senis et octonis vocibus ex celeberrimis auctoribus Horatio Vecchio aliisque collectae* (Antwerp, Pierre Phalèse, 1612[1]), and in MS in *I–Rvat* Cappella Sistina 107 (dated 1683); no. 2:1–2 also in Georg Gruber (ed.), *Reliquiae sacrorum concentuum Giovan Gabrielis, Iohan-Leonis Hasleri, utriusq; praestantissimi musici: . . . motectae, VI. VII. VIII. IX. X. XII. XIII. XIV. XVI. XVIII. XIX. vocum* (Nuremburg, Paul Kauffmann, 1615[2]).

SELVA / MORALE E SPIRITVALE / DI CLAVDIO MONTEVERDE / Maestro Di Capella della Serenissima / Republica DI Venetia / DEDICATA / ALLA SACRA CESAREA MAESTA DELL'IMPERATRICE / ELEONORA / GONZAGA / Con Licenza de Superiori & Priuilegio. (Venice, Bartolomeo Magni, 1640 [some partbooks dated 1641]) [*M* XV/1–3]

Dedication: Monteverdi to Empress Eleonora Gonzaga, Venice, 1 May 1641

252 1 O ciechi, il tanto affaticar che giova? ('Madrigale morale A 5. voci & due violini') [Francesco Petrarca: SSATB, 2 vln, bc]

253 2 Voi ch'ascoltate in rime sparse il suono ('Madrigale morale A 5. voci & due violini') [Francesco Petrarca: STTTB, 2 vln, bc; cf in Profe 1642]

254 3 È questa vita un lampo [Angelo Grillo: SSATB, bc]

255 4 Spuntava il dì quando la rosa sovra ('Canzonetta morale A 3. voci') [ATB, bc]
     (2p) La più dolce ruggiada
     (3p) La vagheggiano gli alberi
     (4p) Per valletta o per campagna
     (5p) Ahi quel sole che dianzi in su l'aurora

256 5 Chi vol che m'innamori ('Canzonetta morale A 3. con due violini') [ATB, 2 vln, bc]

257 6 *Messa a 4 da capella* [TrMsABar, bc]
     Kyrie
     [Gloria . . .] Et in terra pax
     [Credo . . .] Patrem omnipotentem
     Sanctus
     Benedictus
     Agnus Dei

274	23 Laudate Dominum omnes gentes III [in G] ('Laudate dominum Terzo A 8. voci') [SSAATTBB, bc]
275	24 Credidi propter quod locutus sum ('Credidi del Quarto Tuono à 8.'; 'Credidi à 8. voci da Capella') [SATB, ΛTTB, bc]
276	25 [Memento Domine David] et omnis mansuetudinis ('A 8. Quarti Toni'; 'Memento à 8. voci da Capella') [SATB, ATTB, bc]
277	26 Sanctorum meritis I [in C] ('Primo Himnvs Comune plurimorum Martirum'; 'Sanctorum meritis Primo à voce sola & due violini sopra alla qual aria si potranno cantare anco altri Hinni pero che sijno dello stesso Metro') [S, 2 vln, bc]
278	27 Sanctorum meritis II [in d] ('Comune Plurimorum Martirum Sopra ad vna medesima aria'; 'Sanctorum meritis secondo à voce sola concertato con due violini sopra a la qual aria si puo cantare anco altri Hinni delo stesso Metro') [T, 2 vln, bc]
	27a Deus tuorum militum I ('Comune vnius Martiris Sopra ad vna medesima aria') [T, 2 vln, bc]
	27b Iste confessor I ('Comune Confessorum Sopra ad vna medesima aria') [T, 2 vln, bc]
279	28 Iste confessor II [in G] ('Himnvs Comune Confessorum'; 'Iste Confessor a voce sola [sic] & due violini sopra alla qual Aria si puo cantare parimente Vt queant laxis di S. Gio. Batt. & simili') [SS, 2 vln, bc]
	28a Ut queant laxis ('Himnvs Sancti Ioannis. Sopra lo stesso metro') [SS, 2 vln, bc]
280	29 Deus tuorum militum II [in C] ('Himnus vnius Martiris'; 'Hinno con doi violini'; 'Sopra la stessa aria si potranno cantare ancora Iesu corona Virginum, Christe Redemptor omnium, & altri del medesimo Metro') [TTB, 2 vln, bc]
281	30 Magnificat I [in d] ('Magnificat Primo à 8. voci & due violini, & quattro viole ouero quatro Tronboni quali in acidente si ponno lasciare') [SATB, ST+2 vla(=AB?), 2 vln, (4 vla or tbn), bc]
282	31 Magnificat II [in g] ('Primo Tuono A 4. voci da Capella') [TrMsAT, bc]
283	32 Salve Regina I [in C; begins 'Audi coelum'] ('Voce sola. Salue in ecco concertata con doi violini') [TT, 2 vln, bc]
284	33 Salve Regina II [in d] ('Salue Regina à 2. voci due Tenori o due soprani') [TT(SS), bc; cf in D–Lr MS Mus. Ant. Pract. K.N.206]
285	34 Salve [o] Regina III [in d] ('Salue Regina à 3. voci. Alto Basso & Tenore o Soprano') [ATB(SAB), bc; cf in D–Lr MS Mus. Ant. Pract. K.N.206]

286   35 Jubilet tota civitas ('Motetto à voce Sola in Dialogo.') [S, bc]
287   36 Laudate Dominum in sanctis eius ('Voce sola Soprano ò Tenore') [S(T), bc]
288   37 Iam moriar mi fili ('Pianto della Madona à voce sola Sopra il Lamento d'Arianna') [S, bc; cf of *Lamento d'Arianna* (*SV* 22)]

Nos. 8–10 are alternative sections for the *Credo* in no. 6; nos. 27, 27a, 27b have the same music, and likewise nos. 28, 28a. No. 15 also in Johann Havemann (ed.), *Erster Theil geistlicher Concerten mit 1.2.3.4.5.6. und 7. Stimmen theils mit theils ohne Instrumenten nebenst ihrem gewöhnlichen Basso Continuo, und absonderlichem Basso pro Violono* (Berlin, Daniel Reichel, 1659³); no. 34 first pub. in Lorenzo Calvi (ed.), *Quarta raccolta de sacri canti a una, due, tre, et quattro voci con il basso per l'organo. De diuersi eccellentissimi autori* (Venice, Alessandro Vincenti, 1629⁵) and in another print that cannot be identified; nos. 36, 37 (plus cf of no. 2) in Ambrosius Profe (ed.), *Dritter Theil geistlicher Concerten und Harmonien, a 1.2.3.4.5. etc. voc. cum & sine violinis* (Leipzig, Henning Kölern, 1642⁴).

MESSA / A QVATTRO VOCI, / ET/ SALMI / A Vna, Due, Tre, Quattro, Cinque, Sei, Sette, & Otto Voci, / Concertati, e Parte da Cappella, & con le Letanie della B.V. / DEL SIGNOR / CLAVDIO MONTEVERDE / Gia Maestro di Cappella della Serenissima / Republica di Venetia. / DEDICATA / AL R.MO P. D. ODOARDO / BARANARDI / Abbate di Sante Maria delle Carceri della Congregatione / Camaldolense. (Venice, Alessandro Vincenti, 1650) [*M* XVI/1–2]

Dedication: Alessandro Vincenti to Odoardo Baranardi, Abbot of S. Maria delle Carceri (Padua), Venice, 11 December 1649)

190   1 *Messa a 4 da capella* [TrMsAT, bc]
        Kyrie
        [Gloria . . .] Et in terra pax
        [Credo . . .] Patrem omnipotentem
        Sanctus
        Benedictus
        Agnus Dei
191   2 Dixit Dominus I [in G: SATB, SATB, bc]
192   3 Dixit Dominus II [in d] ('A 8. voci, Alla Breue') [SATB, ATTB, bc]
193   4 Confitebor tibi Domine I [in C] ('A Voce Sola, con Viole.'; 'A Voce Sola con Violini') [S, 2 vln (2 vla), bc]
194   5 Confitebor tibi Domine II [in C: ST, 2 vln, bc]
195   6 Beatus vir [SSSATTB], 2 vln, bc]

196	7	Laudate pueri Dominum ('A 5. Alla quarta Bassa. Da Capella.') [TrMsAABar, bc]
197	8	Laudate Dominum omnes gentes [B, bc]
198	9	Laetatus sum I [in G: SSTTBB, 2 vln, 2 tbn, bsn, bc]
199	10	Laetatus sum II [in G: SATTB, bc]
200	11	Nisi Dominus I [in G: STB, 2 vln, bc]
201	12	Nisi Dominus II [in G: SSATTB, bc]
202	13	Lauda Jerusalem I [in g: ATB, bc]
203	14	Lauda Jerusalem II [in G: SATTB, bc]
204	15	*Letanie della Beata Vergine* [SSATTB, bc]

No 8 (ornamented) also in Gasparo Casati, *Racolta di motetti a 1.2.3. voci di Gasparo Casati et de diuersi altri eccelentissimi autori* (Venice, Francesco Magni, 1651[2]); no. 15 first pub. in Giulio Cesare Bianchi, *Libro secondo de motetti, in lode della gloriosissima Vergine Maria nostra signora, a' vna, due, tre, quattro, e cinque voci, & vna messa, a' quattro, con il basso generale . . . con le Letanie à sei voci del Sig. Claudio Monteuerde* (Venice, Alessandro Vincenti, 1620[4]), and in Lorenzo Calvi (ed.), *Rosarium litaniarum Beatae V. Mariae ternis, quaternis, quinis, senis, septenis, et octonis vocibus concinandarum. Una cum basso ad organum* (Venice, Alessandro Vincenti, 1626[3]).

COLLECTIONS

Aquilino Coppini (ed.), *Musica tolta da i madrigali di Claudio Monteverde, e d'altri autori, a cinque, et a sei voci, e fatta spirituale . . . con la partitura, e basso continuo . . . per i quattro vltimi canti à sei* (Milan, Agostino Tradate, 1607[20]; Melchiore Tradate, 1611[15])

94k	1	Felle amaro me potavit populus ['Cruda Amarilli, che col nome ancora']
97:1k	3	Qui pependit in cruce deus meus ['Ecco, Silvio, colei che in odio hai tanto', 1p]
97:5k	4	Pulchrae sunt genae tua amica mea ['Ecco, Silvio . . .', 5p]
96k	5	Stabat Virgo Maria mestissimo dolore ['Era l'anima mia']
98:3k	6	Spernit deus cor durum ['Ch'io t'ami, e t'ami più de la mia vita', 3p]
98:2k	8	Sancta Maria quae Christum peperisti ['Ch'io t'ami . . .', 2p]
97:3k	9	Maria quid ploras ad monumentum ['Ecco, Silvio . . .', 3p]
97:4k	10	Te Jesu Christe liberator meus ['Ecco, Silvio . . .', 4p]
102k	17	Ure me Domine amore tuo ['Troppo ben può questo tiranno Amore']
104k	18	Gloria tua manet in aeternum ['"T'amo mia vita", la mia cara vita']

101k   20 Vives in corde meo deus meus ['Ahi come a un vago sol
               cortese giro']

Aquilino Coppini (ed.), *Il secondo libro della musica di Claudio
Monteverde e d'altri autori a cinque voci fatta spirituale . . . con
la partitura* (Milan, Heirs of Agostino Tradate, 1608)

61k   1 O dies infelices ['O come è gran martire']
60k   2 Florea serta laeti contexite ['La giovinetta pianta']
98:1k   3 Te sequar Jesu mea vita ['Ch'io t'ami, e t'ami più de la mia
               vita', 1p]
99k   4 Qui regnas super alta poli ['Che dar più vi poss'io?']
100k   5 Animas eruit e domo ['M'è più dolce il penar per Amarilli']
95k   6 O mi fili mea vita Jesu ['O Mirtillo, Mirtillo anima mia']
68k   7 Praecipitantur e torrente nives ['O primavera, gioventù
               dell'anno']
75k   8 O infelix recessus ['Ah dolente partita']

Aquilino Coppini (ed.), *Il terzo libro della musica di Claudio
Monteverde a cinque voci fatta spirituale . . . con la partitura*
(Milan, Alessandro & Heirs of Agostino Tradate, 1609)

109k1   1 Una es o Maria ['Una donna fra l'altre honesta e bella']
103k   2 Amem te domine spes mea ['Amor, se giusto sei']
97:2k   3 Qui pietate tua ['Ecco, Silvio, colei che in odio hai tanto',
               2p]
76k   4 Jesu dum te contemplor ['Cor mio, mentre vi miro']
77k   5 Jesu tu obis ['Cor mio, non mori? E mori']
81k   6 Luce serena lucent animae ['Luci serene e chiare']
82k   7 Plagas tuas adoro Christe ['La piaga c'ho nel core']
83k   8 Tu vis a me abire ['Voi pur da me partite, anima dura']
84k   9 Cantemus laeti quae deus effecit ['A un giro sol de'
               bell'occhi lucenti']
93k   10 Plorat amare ['Piagn'e sospira, e quand'i caldi raggi']
91k   11 Anima quam dilexi ['Anima del cor mio']
92k   12 Longe a te mi Jesu ['Longe da te, cor mio']
89k   13 O Jesu mea vita ['Sì ch'io vorrei morire']
90k   14 Anima miseranda quae offendis deum tuum ['Anima dolor-
               osa che vivendo']
78k   15 O stellae coruscantes ['Sfogava con le stelle']
79k   16 Ardebat igne puro ['Volgea l'anima mia soavemente']
80k   17 Domine deus meus peccavi ['Anima mia, perdona']
            18 (2p) O gloriose martyr
86k   19 Rutilante in nocte exultant ['Io mi son giovinetta']
87k   20 Qui laudes tuas cantat ['Quel augellin che canta']

Giovanni Battista Bonometti (ed.), *Parnassus musicus Ferdinandaeus in quo musici nobilissimi, quà suauitate, quà arte
prorsus admirabili, & diuina ludunt: 1.2.3.4.5. vocum* (Venice,
Giacomo Vincenti, 1615[13]) [M XVI/2]

292 25 Cantate Domino canticum novum ('2 Canti o Tenori') [SS(TT), bc]

Giovanni Battista Ala, *Primo libro delli concerti ecclesiastici a vna, due, tre, e quattro voci. Con la partitura per l'organo* (Milan, Filippo Lomazzo, 1618) [M XVI/2]

328 7 Sancta Maria succurre miseris [SS, bc]

Also in Johann Donfrid (ed.), *Promptuarii musici, concentus ecclesiasticos CCLXXXVI. selectissimos, II. III. & IV. vocum. Cum basso continuo & generali, organo applicato, . . . pars tertia: quae est de festis mobilibus et propriis sanctorum celebritatibus per totum annum* (Strasbourg, Paul Ledertz, 1627[1]), and in *Luscinia sacra: sive cantiones unius. II. III. IV. vocum cum basso continuo* (Antwerp, Heirs of Pierre Phalèse, 1633).

Giulio Cesare Bianchi, *Libro primo de motetti in lode d'Iddio nostro signore a vna, due, tre, quattro, cinque, e à otto voci con il basso generale . . . con vn altro à cinque, e tre à sei del Sig. Claudio Monteverde* (Venice, Bartolomeo Magni, 1620[3]) [M XVI/2]

294 22 Christe adoramus te [SSATB, bc]
289 23 Adoramus te Christe [SSATTB, bc]
298 24 Domine ne in furore tuo [SSATBB, bc]
293 25 Cantate Domino canticum novum [SSATTB, bc]

Lorenzo Calvi (ed.), *Symbolae diversorum musicorum binis, ternis, quaternis, & quinis vocibus, cantandae. Vna cum basso ad organum* (Venice, Alessandro Vincenti, 1621[4] [bc partbook dated 1620]) [M XVI/2]

305 1 Fuge anima mea mundum [SA, vln, bc]
312 2 O beatae viae ('Doi Canti, ò Tenori') [SS(TT), bc]

Johann Donfrid (ed.), *Promptuarii musici, concentus ecclesiasticos II. III. et IV. vocum cum basso continuo & generali, organo applicato, . . . pars prima: quae concertationes selectiores tempore hyemalisc. ab Adventu Domini usq; ad Paschatis festum, SS. Ecclesia usui inservientes comprehendit* (Strasbourg, Paul Ledertz, 1622[2]) [M XVI/2]

313 47 O bone Jesu, o piissime Jesu [SS, bc]

Also in *Fasciculus secundus geistlicher wolklingender Concerten mit 2. vnd 3. stimmen sampt dem Basso Continuo pro Organis* (Nordhausen, Nicolas Dunckern, 1637[3]).

Pietro Lappi, *Concerti sacri a 1.2.3.4.5.6.7. voci. Libro secondo, con il basso continuo* (Venice, Bartolomeo Magni, 1623)

134.k1 11 Ave Regina mundi ['Vaga su spina ascosa']

Lorenzo Calvi (ed.), *Seconda raccolta de sacri canti a una, due, tre, et quattro voci de diuersi eccellentissimi autori . . . con il basso continuo per sonar nell'organo* (Venice, Alessandro Vincenti, 1624²) [*M* XVI/2]

326   1 Salve [o] Regina [T(S), bc]
301   2 Ego flos campi [A, bc]
335   9 Venite sitientes ad aquas Domini [SS, bc]

Francesco Sammaruco (ed.), *Sacri affetti, con testi da diversi eccelentissimi autori . . . a2 a3. a4. ò aggiunt[o]ui nel fine le letanie della B.V.* (Rome, Luca Antonio Soldi, 1625¹) [*M* XVI/2]

300   1 Ego dormio et cor meum vigilat [SB, bc]

Leonardo Simonetti (ed.), *Ghirlanda sacra scielta da diuersi eccellentissimi compositori de uarij motetti à voce sola. Libro primo opera seconda* (Venice, Bartolomeo Magni, 1625²; 1636²) [*M* XVI/2]

299   1 Ecce sacrum paratum convivium [T, bc]
297   2 Currite populi, psallite timpanis [T, bc]
317   3 O quam pulchra es amica mea [T, bc]
327   4 Salve Regina [T, bc]

No. 1 (ornamented) also in Philipp Friedrich Böddecker, *Sacra partitura: voce sola cum 2. sonat: violin: et fagott: solis* (Strasbourg, Johann Heinrich Mittel, 1651).

Giovanni Maria Sabino, *Psalmi de vespere a quattro voci* (Naples, Ambrosio Magnetta, 1627⁴)

295   11 Confitebor tibi Domine [SATB, bc]ⁱ
Also in *D–Kl* 2° MS Mus. 51v.

Lorenzo Calvi (ed.), *Quarta raccolta de sacri canti a una, due, tre, et quattro voci con il basso per l'organo. De diuersi eccellentissimi autori* (Venice, Alessandro Vincenti, 1629⁵)

303   1 Exulta filia Sion [S, bc; *M* XVII]
285   26 Salve [o] Regina
304   39 Exultent caeli et gaudeant angeli ('Questa Cantada di Exultent celi si puol radoppiare, cioè ricopiarla, & farla sonare da gli Istromenti, & cantare insieme con le voci, acciò faccia vn bel corpo di Musica, il rimanente poi, và cantato nel modo che stà scritto.') [SSATB, bc; *M* XVII]

No. 26 also pub. in *Selva morale e spirituale* (1640–1).

Ambrosius Profe (ed.), *Erster Theil geistlicher Concerten und Harmonien à 1.2.3.4.5.6.7. & c. Vocibus, cum & sine Sinfoniis, & Basso ad Organa* (Breslau, Christoph Jacob, 1641²)

134k2   12 Jesum viri senesque ['Vaga su spina ascosa']

Ambrosius Profe (ed.), *Ander Theil geistlicher Concerten und*

ⁱIn Monteverdi, *12 composizioni vocali profane e sacre*, ed. Osthoff, pp. 45–64. Malipiero's doubts about its authenticity have not been shared by other scholars.

Harmonien, à 1.2.3.4.5.6.7 Voc. cum & sine Violinis, & Basso ad Organa (Leipzig, Henning Kölern, 1641³)

155k   22 Pascha concelebranda ['Altri canti di Marte e di sua schiera']

        23 (2p) Ergo gaude laetare [also texted 'Lauda anima mea']

Ambrosius Profe (ed.), *Dritter Theil geistlicher Concerten und Harmonien, a 1.2.3.4.5. etc. Voc. cum & sine Violinis, & Basso ad Organa* (Leipzig, Henning Kölern, 1642⁴)

287   1 Laudate Dominum

288   2 Iam moriar mi fili (*Pianto della Madonna*)

249:2k   3 Spera in domino ['Io ch'armato sin hor d'un duro gelo' (i.e. final stanza of 'Ecco di dolci raggi il sol armato')]

150k   5 Heus bone vir ['Armato il cor d'adamantina fede']

253k   24 Haec dixit Deus tuus ['Voi ch'ascoltate in rime sparse il suono']

Nos. 1, 2 first pub. in *Selva morale e spirituale* (1640–1).

Motetti a voce sola de diuersi eccelentissimi autori (Venice, Bartolomeo [?Francesco] Magni, 1645³) [M XVII]

336   1 Venite videte martirem [S, bc]

Ambrosius Profe (ed.), *Corollarium geistlicher Collectaneorum, berühmter Authorum* (Leipzig, Timotheus Ritzsch, 1649⁶)

136k1   6 Longe mi Jesu ['Parlo, misero, o taccio?']

137k   10 O Jesu lindere meinen Schmertzen ['Tu dormi, ah crudo core']

138k   11 O rex supreme Deus ['Al lume delle stelle']

147k   14 O du mächtiger Herr ['Hor che'l ciel e la terra e'l vento tace']
         (2p) Dein allein ist ja grosser Gott

156k   15 Resurrexit de sepulchro [also texted 'Veni soror mea': 'Vago augelletto che cantando vai']

152k   16 Alleluja, kommet, jauchzet [also texted 'Freude, kommet, lasset uns gehen': 'Ardo, avvampo, mi struggo, ardo: accorrete']

Gasparo Casati, *Racolta di motetti a 1.2.3. voci di Gasparo Casati et de diuersi altri eccelentissimi autori* (Venice, Francesco Magni, 1651²) [M XVI/2]

197a   1 Laudate Dominum omnes gentes [B, bc]

302   2 En gratulemur hodie [T, 2 vln, bc]

No. 1 is ornamented version of setting in *Messa . . . et salmi* (1650)

MANUSCRIPTS

D–Kl 2° MS Mus. 51v [Anon., 17th century]

| 311 | 1 | Laudate pueri Dominum [SATTTB, bc][j] |
| 295 | 2 | Confitebor tibi Domine |

No. 2 first pub. in Sabino 1627

D–Kl 2° MS Mus. 58j [Anon., 17th century]

| 143k | 2 | Güldne Haare, gliech Aurore ['Chiome d'oro'] |

D–Lr MS Mus. Ant. Pract. K.N.206 [part by Matthias Weckmann (d.1674), Hamburg, 15 June 1647]
Contains items from *Selva morale e spirituale* (1640–1; *SV* 263–74, 287, 288), Calvi 1621 (*SV* 312), Simonetti 1625 (*SV* 299), Calvi 1629 (*SV* 303), Profe 1641[3] (*SV* 155k), plus:

| 285k | 41 | Salve Jesu o pater misericordiae ['Salve Regina III'] |
| 284k | 44 | Salve mi Jesu ['Salve Regina II'] |

DDR–Dlb MS Mus. Pi 8 [Johann Cadner, *c.* 1626–30]

| 109k2 | 2 | Wie ein Rubin in feinem Golde leuchtet ['Una donna fra l'altre honesta e bella'] |

I–Bc MS Q.27 [Anon., early 17th century]

[309k]	Bella fiamma d'amor, dolce Signore ['Io ardo sì, ma'l foco è di tal sorte']
[324k]	Quante son stell'intorn'a l'aureo crine' ['Quante son stelle in ciel e in mar arene']
[314k]	Occhi miei, se mirar più non debb'io ['Occhi miei, se mirar più non debb'io']
[331k]	Se non mi date aita ['Se non mi date aita']
[332k]	Prima vedrò [ch'] in questi prati nascano ['Prima vedrò ch'in questi prati nascano']

I–BRq MS L.IV.99 [Michele Pario, Parma 1610][k]
Canto partbook

306	3	Fuggi, fuggi cor, fuggi a tutte l'hor
244k	5	Dolce spina del mio core ['Lidia, spina del mio core']
235k	28	Su fanciullo per trastullo ['Damigella tutta bella']
[237k]	29	O rosetta, che rossetta ['O rosetta, che rossetta']
330	54	Se d'un angel'il bel viso

I–Nf MS 473.1 (IV–2–23a) [Anon., 17th century]

| 307 | Gloria [SATB, SATB, bc][l] |

PL–WRu [no shelf-mark; Daniel Sartorius, 17th century; lost since 1945]

| 136k2 | O Jesu, o dulcis Jesu ['Parlo, misero, o taccio?'] |

[j]In Monteverdi, *Laudate pueri Dominum (a 6 voci)*, ed. Arnold.
[k]See Jeffrey Kurtzman, 'An Early 17th-Century Manuscript of *Canzonette e madrigaletti spirituali*', *Studi Musicali*, viii (1979), 149–72.
[l]In Monteverdi, *12 composizioni vocali profane e sacre*, ed. Osthoff, pp. 65–105.

Appendix C

Personalia

Achillini, Claudio (1574–1640), jurist, diplomat and poet, Professor of Civil Law at Bologna, Ferrara and (1626–36) Parma. Author of verse in Monteverdi's seventh book of madrigals (1619) and of entertainments (set by Monteverdi) for the wedding of the Duke Odoardo Farnese and Margherita de' Medici (Parma, 1628).

Ala, Giovanni Battista (*c.* 1598–*c.* 1630), composer and organist. Held various posts in Milan; included one work by Monteverdi in his *Primo libro delli concerti ecclesiastici* (1618).

Amadino, Ricciardo (fl. 1572–1621), printer and publisher. In partnership in Venice with Giacomo Vincenti from 1583 to 1586, and independent from 1586 to 1621. Monteverdi's *Canzonette* (1584) were published by Vincenti & Amadino; Amadino alone published all Monteverdi's works from the third book of madrigals (1592) to the sixth (1614) inclusive.

Andreini, Giovanni Battista (1579–1654), actor, dramatist and poet. Possibly educated at the University of Bologna, he joined his parents in a company of actors, the Comici Gelosi, and then became director (by 1604) of the Comici Fedeli, who served the dukes of Mantua and had particular success on various tours in Paris. Author of the *sacra rappresentazione*, *La Maddalena* (1617), for which Monteverdi set the prologue.

Andreini, Virginia (née Ramponi) (1583–?1630), wife of the foregoing, actress and singer, known as 'La Florinda'. She took the title-role in Monteverdi's *Arianna* at short notice and also sang (probably as Venus) in his *Ballo delle ingrate*, both for the wedding of Prince Francesco Gonzaga and Margherita of Savoy in 1608.

Archilei, Vittoria (née Concarini) (b. 1550), singer and lutenist, wife (1578) of the musician Antonio A. A protégée of Emilio de' Cavalieri and Grand Duke Ferdinando I de' Medici, she was in Medici service for many years as a soprano: Cavalieri, Caccini, Peri and d'India all praise her virtuosity. Conflicting evidence places her death in the late 1620s or early 1640s.

Artusi, Giovanni Maria (*c.* 1540–1613), theorist and composer, canon of S. Salvadore, Bologna. A student of Zarlino, he engaged in theoretical debates with Ercole Bottrigari and, more famously, Monteverdi: his dialogue *L'Artusi, overo Delle imperfettioni della moderna musica* (1600; a second part appeared in 1603) criticizes passages from anonymous madrigals published in Monteverdi's fourth (1603) and fifth (1605) books. He continued the polemic under the pseudonym Antonio Braccino da Todi.

217

Badoaro, Giacomo (1602–54), Venetian nobleman, member of the libertine Accademia degli Incogniti, Venice. Librettist of Monteverdi's *Il ritorno d'Ulisse in patria* (1640) and of Sacrati's *L'Ulisse errante* (1644). He may also have provided the text for (?Cavalli's) *Helena rapita da Theseo* (1653), but not, as sometimes claimed, the libretto of Monteverdi's *Le nozze d'Enea con Lavinia* (1641).

Banchieri, Adriano (1568–1634), composer, organist, theorist and writer. Studied with Gioseffo Guami and as a Benedictine monk became closely associated with the monastery of S. Michele in Bosco near Bologna. Founded the Accademia dei Floridi (later Accademia dei Filomusi) in 1614: Monteverdi visited the academy in 1620. His treatises are distinguished by their practical focus and balanced assessment of the moderns.

Basile, Adriana (*c.* 1580–*c.* 1640), singer and instrumentalist, known as 'La bella Adriana'. Having made her reputation in Naples – she married the Calabrian nobleman Muzio Baroni – she was recruited to service at the Gonzaga court (1610), where her virtuoso contralto singing was highly prized. Returned to Naples in 1624, moving to Rome in 1633. Her sister, Margherita, was also a singer in Mantua, and the vocal talents of her daughter Leonora (1611–70) won the admiration of Milton.

Benevoli, Orazio (1605–72), composer. Trained in the choir of S. Luigi dei Francesi, Rome, he held several important posts in Rome, including *maestro di cappella* of S. Luigi dei Francesi from 1638 to 1644. Canvassed to succeed Monteverdi at St Mark's, Venice, but instead moved to Vienna as Kapellmeister to Archduke Leopold Wilhelm. In 1646, he became *maestro* of the Cappella Giulia at St Peter's, Rome. His large-scale polychoral music offers good examples of the Roman 'colossal Baroque' style, although the 53-part *Missa salisburgensis* once thought to be by him is a later work.

Berti, Giovanni Pietro (d. 1638), composer, organist and singer. Tenor at St Mark's, Venice, and second organist from 1624. His two books of *Cantade et arie* (1624, 1627) are fine examples of the new Venetian styles, with elegant triple-time melodies and large-scale formal structures.

Bianchi, Giulio Cesare (1576/7–in or after 1637), composer and musician. A Cremonese, he studied with Monteverdi and in early 1603 was in service at the Gonzaga court; later that year he was employed by the governor of Milan. By 1620 he had returned to Cremona: he included works by Monteverdi in his two books of motets of that year, and in 1637 he was leasing a house owned by the composer.

Böddecker, Philipp Friedrich (1607–83), German composer, organist and bassoonist. Held various posts in northern Europe, including organist at Strasbourg Cathedral (1642) and in Stuttgart (1652). His *Sacra partitura* (1651) contains one piece by Monteverdi with added ornamentation.

Bonometti, Giovanni Battista, singer. Employed at Milan Cathedral from 1608 to 1613, he moved to the court of Archduke Ferdinand at Graz in 1615. Editor of *Parnassus musicus Ferdinandaeus* (1615), including one motet by Monteverdi (whom Bonometti may have met in Milan).

Borchgrevinck, Melchior (?*c*. 1570–1632), Danish composer, organist and instrumentalist. In the service of King Christian IV of Denmark. Studied in Venice with Giovanni Gabrieli in 1599; he returned to Venice in 1601–2. Editor of the first major music publications in Denmark, two anthologies (1605, 1606) of works by popular Italian madrigalists of the day, including Monteverdi.

Busenello, Giovanni Francesco (1598–1659), librettist, lawyer and poet, member of the libertine Accademia degli Incogniti, Venice. Born into a wealthy Venetian family, he studied law at Padua. Librettist of Monteverdi's *L'incoronazione di Poppea* (1643) and of Cavalli's *Gli amori d'Apollo e di Dafne* (1640), *Didone* (1641), *La prosperità infelice di Giulio Cesare dittatore* (1646; possibly never composed) and *Statira, principessa di Persia* (1655 or 1656).

Caccini, Giulio (1551–1618), singer, instrumentalist and composer. Trained in Rome, he was recruited to service in Florence in 1565, remaining at the Medici court until his death. Member of the 'camerata' organized around Giovanni de' Bardi, to whom he dedicated his opera *Euridice* (1600; first performed complete in December 1602). His *Le nuove musiche* (1602) was one of the earliest collections of songs for solo voice and basso continuo.

Calvi, Lorenzo (*fl*. 1609–29), singer. Bass at Pavia Cathedral and editor of four important sacred anthologies (1620, 1624, 1626, 1629) of church music by prominent north Italian composers, including Monteverdi.

Camarella, Giovanni Battista, composer and musician. In service at Venice and a member of the Accademia dei Filoleuteri. His *Madrigali et arie* (1620) has one song by Monteverdi later included in his *Scherzi musicali* (1632).

Casati, Gasparo (*c*. 1610–41), composer. *Maestro di cappella* of Novara Cathedral from 1635 and a popular and prolific composer of church music. One of his collections (1651) includes two works by Monteverdi.

Cavalli, (Pietro) Francesco (1602–76), composer, organist and singer. Son of Giovanni Battista Caletti, he took the name Cavalli from the Venetian governor of his native Crema. Appointed singer at St Mark's, Venice (1616; also organist at SS. Giovanni e Paolo, 1620–30), then organist (1639) and *maestro di cappella* (1668). The most significant opera composer in Venice: his first opera, *Le nozze di Teti e di Peleo*, was performed in 1639, and he wrote nearly 30 works for Venetian theatres. May have edited Monteverdi's *Messa . . . et salmi* (1650), which includes a six-part Magnificat by Cavalli; the Venice manuscript of Monteverdi's *L'incoronazione di Poppea* also opens with a sinfonia very closely related to the first sinfonia of Cavalli's *Doriclea* (1645).

Chiabrera, Gabriello (1552–1638), poet and librettist. A native of Savona, he was closely associated with Florence, receiving a stipend from the Medici Grand Dukes (from 1 November 1600). Also enjoyed the patronage of Carlo Emanuele I of Savoy, the Gonzagas in Mantua and Pope Urban VIII. Most of Monteverdi's *Scherzi musicali* (1607) are set to his verse.

Croce, Giovanni (*c.* 1557–1609), composer, singer and priest. A pupil of Zarlino, he was a choirboy of St Mark's, Venice, and then employed at S. Maria Formosa. Appointed vice-*maestro di cappella* of St Mark's (early 1590s), then *maestro* (1603). His madrigals were often reprinted and imitated in northern Europe.

Crotti, Archangelo, composer. A monk living in Ferrara, he published his *Il primo libro de' concerti ecclesiastici* in 1608: it includes a *Sonata sopra Sancta Maria* significantly anticipating the *Sonata* in Monteverdi's 1610 *Vespers*.

Donfrid, Johannes (1585–1654), German singer, teacher and composer. Employed as a teacher and Kapellmeister at Rottenburg (near Tübingen), his important anthologies of sacred works – including the tripartite *Promptuarii musici* (1622, 1623, 1627) – disseminated Italian church music (some by Monteverdi) in Catholic southern Germany.

Doni, Giovanni Battista (1595–1647), theorist. Born in Florence. After a Humanist education (and later in law), he became associated with the Barberini family in Rome. Appointed secretary of the sacred College of Cardinals (1629), and Professor of Rhetoric at Pisa (1640). Corresponded with Marin Mersenne. His classicizing theoretical works follow traditions established by the Florentines Girolamo Mei and Vincenzo Galilei, and he offers important, if somewhat prejudiced, insights into early opera and the 'new music'.

Ferrari, Benedetto (1603/4–1681), librettist, composer, instrumentalist and impresario. Trained in Rome, he was employed in Parma and perhaps Modena prior to moving to Venice. Together with Francesco Manelli, he inaugurated 'public' opera in Venice with *Andromeda* (1637; Ferrari wrote the libretto) and produced several other operas (some with his music) for Venice and on tour. Later moved to Modena as court *maestro di cappella*. Three books of songs (1633, 1637, 1641) provide an important context for Monteverdi's late secular music. May have written the text (and perhaps the music) for the final duet of Monteverdi's *L'incoronazione di Poppea* as it survives in later sources.

Ferrari, Cherubino, theologian and poet. A Carmelite in Gonzaga service and a staunch admirer of Monteverdi's music, which he praises in his correspondence. Also provided two laudatory poems to preface Monteverdi's fifth book of madrigals (1605).

Fillago, Carlo (*c.* 1586–1644), composer and organist. A pupil of Luzzaschi, he was organist at Treviso Cathedral from 1608 to 1623, then first organist at St Mark's, Venice. Also succeeded Cavalli as organist of SS. Giovanni e Paolo in 1631.

Franzoni, Amante (*fl.* 1605–30), composer. Servite father in Mantuan service before 1605, and *maestro di cappella* of Forlì Cathedral in 1611. Returned to Mantua as *maestro* of S. Barbara in 1612, where he stayed until 1630. His *I nuovi fioretti musicali* (1605) contains one piece by Monteverdi.

Gabrieli, Andrea (*c.* 1533–85), organist and composer. At St Mark's, Venice, as second organist (1565 or 1566) and first organist (1584 or 1585). Perhaps the most significant Venetian composer of his generation.

Gabrieli, Giovanni (d. 1612), nephew of the foregoing, organist and composer. Ambiguous evidence dates his birth at 1553 or 1556. Taught by his uncle, he was in the service of Duke Albrecht V of Bavaria at Munich in the mid to late 1570s. Appointed second organist of St Mark's, Venice, in 1585, and also associated with the Scuola di San Rocco. Edited his uncle's music for publication, and his two volumes of *Symphoniae sacrae* (1597, 1615) offer important examples of the Venetian concerted style.

Gagliano, Marco da (1582–1643), composer. A pupil of Luca Bati, he succeeded his teacher as *maestro di cappella* of Florence Cathedral in 1608. Also *maestro di cappella* to the Medici. Canon of S. Lorenzo (1610) and apostolic prothonotary (1615). Founded the Accademia degli Elevati in 1607, and his close association with Ferdinando Gonzaga led to the performance of his *Dafne* in Mantua in early 1608. Also contributed to the 1608 Mantuan wedding festivities.

Gardano, Angelo (1540–1611), printer and publisher. Inherited the distinguished press established in Venice by his father, Antonio, and printed Monteverdi's *Sacrae cantiunculae* (1582) and the first (1587) and second (1590) books of madrigals. After his death, the firm was directed by his son-in-law, Bartolomeo Magni, who issued Monteverdi's seventh book of madrigals (1619), *Scherzi musicali* (1632) and *Selva morale e spirituale* (1640–1). Bartolomeo or his son Francesco edited an anthology of motets (1645) including one work by Monteverdi.

Gastoldi, Giovanni Giacomo (1554–1609), composer. Employed as a deacon, then singer and music teacher at S. Barbara, Mantua, from 1572, succeeding Wert as *maestro di cappella* in 1592. Published much sacred and secular music: his ballettos were particularly popular in northern Europe.

Gesualdo, Carlo, Prince of Venosa (*c.* 1561–1613), composer. A member of one of the oldest families of the Neapolitan nobility, his second marriage to Leonora d'Este in 1594 brought him into influential contact with Ferrarese musicians. His madrigals are distinguished by their dense chromaticism.

Giacobbi, Girolamo (1567–*c.* 1629), composer. Successively choirboy (1581), assistant to the *maestro di cappella* (1595) and *maestro* (1604) of S. Petronio, Bologna. Associated with Banchieri, he also provided music for *intermedi* and other dramatic entertainments, importing the new Florentine recitative to Bologna.

Gombert, Nicolas (*c.* 1495–*c.* 1560), Flemish composer. A pupil of Josquin Desprez, he was in the service of the Emperor Charles V from 1526 to *c.* 1540 and (by 1534) canon of Notre Dame, Tournai. His polyphony is characterized by its rich textures and technical virtuosity.

Grandi, Alessandro (*c.* 1586–1630), composer. Associated with the Accademia della Morte, Ferrara, over the 1600s, then a singer in St Mark's, Venice, from 1604 to *c.* 1607, returning to Ferrara as *maestro di cappella* of the Accademia dello Spirito Santo from 1610 to 1614. By 1615, *maestro* of Ferrara Cathedral, and then singer (1617) and vice-*maestro di* *cappella* (1620) at St Mark's, Venice. In 1627, he became *maestro* of S. Maria Maggiore, Bergamo, where he died of plague.

Grillo, Angelo (*c.* 1550–1629), abbot and poet. A Benedictine, he travelled widely serving his order. His pious spiritual verse provided ample fodder for contemporary composers (including Monteverdi), and his important letters (various editions, 1603–16) document his views of musicians of the day. Also wrote poetry under the name Livio Celiano.

Guarini, Giovanni Battista (1538–1612), poet and playwright. A brilliant early academic career (at 19 he was Professor of Rhetoric and Poetics at Ferrara) led to service with Duke Alfonso II d'Este as a courtier, diplomat and poet (1567–97). His pastoral play *Il pastor fido*, first published in 1589–90, generated academic controversy but was extremely popular (it was staged in Mantua in 1598); verse from the play and from Guarini's *Rime* was a favourite of contemporary madrigalists.

India, Sigismondo d' (*c.* 1582–*c.* 1629), composer and singer. Of Sicilian birth, he had a peripatetic career in the courts of northern Italy prior to becoming (1611) Director of Chamber Music to Carlo Emanuele I, Duke of Savoy. Left Turin in 1623, settling in Modena, Rome and again Modena. In 1627, he lost to Monteverdi the commission of music for the forthcoming wedding of Duke Odoardo Farnese and Margherita de' Medici. A superb madrigalist and monodist, he vies with Monteverdi as perhaps the most versatile composer of the period.

Ingegneri, Marc'Antonio (*c.* 1547–92), composer and instrumentalist. Born in Verona, he probably studied with Vincenzo Ruffo, and perhaps with Cipriano de Rore in Parma. Had charge of music at Cremona Cathedral from the mid 1570s: Monteverdi was his pupil.

Kauffmann, Paul (1568–1632), German printer. Joined the Gerlach press in Nuremberg in 1589, directing the firm from 1594 to 1617. His reprints and anthologies were important in bringing Italian music (including Monteverdi's) to Germany.

Lappi, Pietro (*c.* 1575–1630), composer. *Maestro di cappella* of S. Maria delle Grazie, Brescia, from *c.* 1593 until his death, he published much church music, including a volume of *Concerti sacri* (1623) with a contrafactum of Monteverdi.

Luzzaschi, Luzzasco (?1545–1607), organist and composer. A pupil of Cipriano de Rore, he was organist to Duke Alfonso II d'Este at Ferrara, also playing a large part in the court music (his madrigals for the Ferrarese *concerto di donne* were published in 1601) and training young Ferrarese musicians, including Girolamo Frescobaldi.

Magni, Bartolomeo. See **Gardano**.

Manelli, Francesco (*c.* 1594–1667), composer, singer, impresario and poet. Trained and first employed in and around Rome, he joined Benedetto Ferrari in inaugurating 'public' opera in Venice with his *Andromeda* (1637). Appointed singer (1638) at St Mark's, Venice, but continued to work for the theatre in Venice and on tour, writing four other operas. In 1645, entered with his family the service of the Duke of Parma.

Marenzio, Luca (1553/4–1599), composer and singer. Led a peripatetic, somewhat free-lance career, although he was associated with the Este family and for a time had the support of Grand Duke Ferdinando I de' Medici and also of several noblemen and prelates (the Orsini and Aldobrandini) in Rome. He died just after a trip to Poland. Perhaps the most gifted and popular madrigalist of his period.

Marino, Giambattista (1569–1625), poet. Despite his licentious career, he enjoyed the patronage of the courts of Turin (1608–15) and Paris (1615–23). The *concettismo* and *meraviglia* of his extravagant poetic style – seen in his *Le rime* (1602, revised as *La lira* in 1608 and 1614) and in his *Adone* (1623) – established important trends in seventeenth-century Italian verse.

Martinelli, Caterina (1589/90–1608), singer. Moved from Rome to Mantua in 1603 and lodged with Monteverdi. She sang in Gagliano's *Dafne* (1608) but died of smallpox before she could take the title-role of Monteverdi's *Arianna*. His *Lagrime d'amante al sepolcro dell'amata* (in the sixth book of madrigals, 1614) was written in her memory.

Martinengo, Giulio Cesare (d. 1613), composer and singer. In the choir of Padua Cathedral, then (1601) *maestro di cappella* of Udine Cathedral. Followed Giovanni Croce as *maestro* of St Mark's, Venice, in 1609; succeeded by Monteverdi.

Merula, Tarquinio (1594/5–1665), composer, organist and violinist. Had a roving, sometimes scandal-ridden career, ranging from his native Cremona to Lodi and Warsaw (as organist to King Sigismund III of Poland, *c.* 1621–6), then alternating between Cremona and Bergamo (*maestro di cappella* of S. Maria Maggiore, 1631–2 and of the Cathedral, *c.* 1638–46). Published a wide range of sacred, secular and instrumental music.

Milanuzzi, Carlo (d. *c.* 1647), composer, organist and poet. An Augustinian monk, he led a peripatetic career in northern Italy, including spells in Perugia and Verona. Organist at S. Stefano, Venice (1623–9), and Finale di Modena (1629–*c.* 1634), then *maestro di cappella* of Camerino Cathedral. Published sacred and secular music: his fourth book of songs (1624) contains four pieces by Monteverdi.

Monteverdi, Giulio Cesare (1573–1630/1), composer and organist, younger brother of Claudio M. In service in Mantua until his dismissal in 1612, then organist at Castelleone (near Cremona) and (1620) *maestro di cappella* of Salò Cathedral. Defended his brother in the *Dichiaratione* to the 1607 *Scherzi musicali* and wrote secular and theatrical music: one collection of motets (1620) also survives.

Morsolino, Antonio (*fl.* 1588–94), composer and editor. Produced the anthology *L'amorosa eco* (1588) and his *Il primo libro delle canzonette* (1594); the latter contains four works by Monteverdi.

Orlandi, Santi (d. 1619), composer. Perhaps a Florentine, he rivalled Gagliano for the protection of Prince Ferdinando Gonzaga and joined Ferdinando in Rome on his elevation to the Cardinalate (1608). Replaced Monteverdi as Duke Francesco (then Duke Ferdinando's) *maestro di cappella* in 1612. On his death, he was succeeded by Francesco Dognazzi.

Pallavicino, Benedetto (1551–1601), composer. First employed as an organist in his native Cremona, he joined the court of Duke Guglielmo

Gonzaga by 1584 and was appointed his *maestro di cappella* on the death of Wert in 1596. Succeeded by Monteverdi.

Peri, Jacopo (1561–1633), composer, singer and instrumentalist. A pupil of Cristofano Malvezzi, he entered the service of the Medici at Florence and became associated with the prominent Florentine patron Jacopo Corsi. Collaborated with Ottavio Rinuccini on the first operas, *Dafne* (1598) and *Euridice* (1600), as well as producing other entertainments and chamber songs.

Pesenti, Martino (*c.* 1600–*c.* 1648), harpsichordist and composer. Blind from birth, he established a prominent position in Venice as a composer of small-scale vocal and instrumental music.

Peverara (Peperara), Laura (*c.* 1545–1601), singer. Virtuoso soprano and leading member of the Ferrarese *concerto di donne*. Tasso dedicated verse to her, and her name was enshrined in two madrigal anthologies printed in Ferrara, *Il lauro secco* (1582) and *Il lauro verde* (1583).

Phalèse, Pierre (*c.* 1550–1629), Flemish printer and publisher. Took over the firm of his father, Pierre (*c.* 1576), and was the leading music printer in Antwerp. His reprints (including Monteverdi's third to fifth books of madrigals in 1615) and anthologies were important in disseminating Italian music north of the Alps. His heirs continued the business, further reprinting Monteverdi.

Porter, Walter (*c.* 1587–1659), English singer and composer. Tenor in the Chapel Royal from 1617, and appointed Master of the Choristers at Westminster Abbey in 1639. Claimed to have studied under Monteverdi.

Profe, Ambrosius (1589–1661), German organist, teacher, publisher, composer and theorist. Career spent mainly in Breslau (Wroclaw); his four-volume *Geistliche Concerten und Harmonien* (1641–6), plus the *Corollarium* (1649), introduced Italian sacred works (some by Monteverdi) to eastern and central Germany.

Raverii, Alessandro, printer, relative of Angelo Gardano. From 1606 to 1609, reprinted music largely from the Gardano catalogue, including (1607) Monteverdi's first and second books of madrigals.

Rinuccini, Ottavio (1562–1621), poet and librettist. Born into a noble Florentine family, he was a member of several academies in the city. Associated with the prominent patron Jacopo Corsi and provided texts for numerous Medici entertainments. Also visited the court of Maria de' Medici, Queen of France. Wrote the texts of *Dafne* (1598) and *Euridice* (1600) for Peri – librettos also set by Gagliano and Caccini respectively – and of *Arianna* and the *Ballo delle ingrate* for Monteverdi. Monteverdi also set other verse by him, including 'Zefiro torna, e di soavi accenti' (1632) and the *Lamento della ninfa* (1638).

Rore, Cipriano de (1515/16–1565), Flemish composer. Associated with Adrian Willaert in Venice in the 1540s, *maestro di cappella* at Ferrara by 1547, and in Farnese service in Parma in 1561. Succeeded Willaert as *maestro* of St Mark's, Venice, in 1563 but returned to Parma in 1564. The most important madrigalist of the mid century; Monteverdi claimed he was the founder of the 'second practice'.

Rossi, Luigi (*c.* 1597–1653), composer, singer and instrumentalist. A pupil of Giovanni de Macque, he was in service at the Neapolitan court. Moved to Rome, forming associations with the Borghese and Barberini families, and was also organist at S. Luigi dei Francesi (from 1633). Important composer of operas (including *Orfeo*, premièred in Paris in 1647) and cantatas. Copied Add. MS 30491 (London, British Library), which includes Monteverdi's *Lamento d'Arianna*.

Rossi, Salamone (1570–*c.* 1630), composer and instrumentalist. As a Jew, he had limited opportunities for employment in Mantua but was closely associated with the Gonzagas, providing vocal, instrumental and theatrical music for court entertainment. His instrumental music is significant, while the connections between his first three books of five-part madrigals (1600, 1602, 1603) and Monteverdi's have yet to be fully explored.

Rovetta, Giovanni (*c.* 1595–1668), singer, instrumentalist and composer. Boy treble, instrumentalist and then (1623) bass at St Mark's, Venice. Appointed vice-*maestro di cappella* in 1627, and *maestro* (succeeding Monteverdi) in 1644. His fine music merits revival.

Rovigo, Francesco (1541/2–1597), organist and composer. A pupil of Claudio Merulo, he was in service at the Mantuan court in 1577. Organist to Archduke Karl II at Graz (1582), and from 1590 organist at S. Barbara, Mantua.

Sabino, Giovanni Maria (d. 1649), composer, organist and teacher. A priest, he held various musical posts in Naples. His *Psalmi de vespere* (1627) contains a setting by Monteverdi.

Sacrati, Francesco (1605–50), composer. Active in opera in Venice and on tour in the 1640s: his *La finta pazza* (1641) was a great success. From 1649, *maestro di cappella* of Modena Cathedral. May have composed some of the music for Monteverdi's *L'incoronazione di Poppea* as it survives in later sources.

Saracini, Claudio (1586–*c.* 1649), composer, singer and lutenist. Born into a noble Sienese family, he travelled widely in Italy and elsewhere. His fine monodies are full of Gesualdo-like chromaticism and rhythmic idiosyncrasies. The first piece of his *Le seconde musiche* (1620) is dedicated to Monteverdi.

Schütz, Heinrich (1585–1672), German composer. Studied law at the University of Marburg but then (1609–13) went to Venice to study with Giovanni Gabrieli. From 1613, organist to Landgrave Moritz, then spent the rest of his career in service to the Elector of Saxony at Dresden (effectively Kapellmeister from 1617, and formally so from at least 1619). A second visit to Italy in 1628–9 brought him into contact with Monteverdi, whose music profoundly influenced him.

Simonetti, Leonardo (d. after 1630), singer. Boy soprano in service at Graz from *c.* 1596–1609, then (1613) castrato at St Mark's, Venice. Editor of three collections of Venetian music, including the *Ghirlanda sacra* (1625) with four motets by Monteverdi.

Soriano, Francesco (1548/9–1621), composer. Trained in Rome, he was *maestro di cappella* of the Gonzaga court from 1581 to 1586, and spent the rest of his career as *maestro* of major churches in Rome (culminating in the Cappella Giulia of St Peter's from 1603). Perhaps the most distinguished of the post-Palestrina generation in Rome.

Striggio, Alessandro (?1573–1630), diplomat, librettist and musician, son of the composer Alessandro (*c.* 1540–92). As a court secretary and councillor to the dukes of Mantua, he rose to high office within the court. Librettist of Monteverdi's *Orfeo* (1607) and author of other entertainment texts sent to the composer in Venice, he remained Monteverdi's main friend and ally in Mantua.

Strozzi, Giulio (1583–1652), poet and librettist, member of a prominent Florentine family, adoptive father of the singer Barbara S. Trained in law, he spent the last three decades of his career in Venice. Member of the libertine Accademia degli Incogniti and founder of the Accademia degli Unisoni in 1637 (for which Monteverdi provided music). Wrote librettos for Cavalli, Manelli, Monteverdi (*La finta pazza Licori*, 1627; *Proserpina rapita*, 1630) and Sacrati, plus smaller-scale occasional verse (e.g. *I cinque fratelli*, set by Monteverdi and performed in Venice before Grand Duke Ferdinando II de' Medici on 8 April 1628).

Tasso, Torquato (1544–95), poet and playwright, son of the poet Bernardo T. (1493–1569). In the service of the Este from 1565, his precocious career was crowned by his pastoral play *Aminta* (1573) and the epic *Gerusalemme liberata* (published 1581). Insanity led to incarceration in Ferrara from 1579 to 1586; he spent the last years of his life in Naples and Rome.

Viadana, Lodovico (Grossi da) (*c.* 1560–1627), composer. A friar, he took his name from his birthplace (near Parma). *Maestro di cappella* of Mantua Cathedral from 1594 to 1597; later held musical posts in Cremona, Concordia and Fano. His *Cento concerti ecclesiastici* (1602) was an important early collection of small-scale motets for voice(s) and basso continuo.

Vincenti, Alessandro (*fl.* 1619–67), printer and publisher. In 1619, he inherited the press founded by his father Giacomo (see **Amadino**) and printed a wide range of music, including Monteverdi's *Madrigali guerrieri, et amorosi* (1638), *Messa... et salmi* (1650) and *Madrigali e canzonette... libro nono* (1651), plus an anthology (1634) with two songs by the composer.

Wert, Giaches de (1535–96), Flemish composer. Came to Italy as a boy singer, serving in Avellino (near Naples), then Novellara and elsewhere in northern Italy. By 1565, *maestro di cappella* of S. Barbara, Mantua. Served the Gonzagas for the rest of his life—but also had personal connections with Ferrara – as a distinguished composer of secular, sacred and theatrical music.

Zarlino, Gioseffo (1517–90), theorist and composer. A Franciscan and a pupil of Adrian Willaert. Appointed *maestro di cappella* of St Mark's, Venice, in 1565. His *Le istitutioni harmoniche* (1558), the major theoretical text of the century, clearly reflects his association with Willaert: Monteverdi owned a copy and acknowledged Zarlino to be the chief theorist of the 'first practice'.

Appendix D

Select Bibliography

EDITIONS, FACSIMILES, ETC.

Giovanni Maria Artusi, *L'Artusi, overo Delle imperfettioni della moderna musica* (Venice, 1600; facs. ed. Bologna, 1968)

——, *Seconda parte dell'Artusi overo Delle imperfettioni della moderna musica* (Venice, 1603; facs. ed. Bologna, 1969)

Giovanni Gabrieli, *Opera omnia*, ed. Denis Arnold and Richard Charteris, 'Corpus Mensurabilis Musicae', xii, in progress (American Institute of Musicology, 1956–)

Marco da Gagliano, *Music for One, Two and Three Voices (1615)*, ed. Putnam Aldrich, 'Series of Early Music', ii, v (Bryn Mawr, 1969, 1972)

Carlo Gesualdo di Venosa, *Sämtliche Madrigale für fünf Stimmen*, ed. Wilhelm Weismann, 6 vols. (Leipzig & Hamburg, 1957–62)

Luzzasco Luzzaschi, *Madrigali per cantare e sonare, a uno due e tre soprani (1601)*, ed. Adriano Cavicchi, 'Monumenti di Musica Italiana', ii/2 (Brescia & Kassel, 1965)

Luca Marenzio, *The Secular Works*, ed. Steven Ledbetter and Patricia Myers, in progress (New York, 1977–)

Claudio Monteverdi, *Tutte le opere*, ed. Gian Francesco Malipiero, 17 vols. (2/Vienna, 1954–68)

——, *Opera omnia*, 'Instituta et Monumenta', i/5, in progress (Cremona, 1970–)

——, *12 composizioni vocali profane e sacre (inedite) con e senza basso continuo*, ed. Wolfgang Osthoff (2/Milan, 1978)

——, *Lettere, dediche e prefazioni*, ed. Domenico de' Paoli (Rome, 1973) *see* Stevens

Claudio Monteverdi, Separate Works (select list):

Beatus vir (I, 1640–1), ed. John Steele (London, 1965)

Christmas Vespers, ed. Denis Stevens (London, 1961)

Dixit Dominus II (1640–1), ed. John Steele (London, 1983)

Gloria concertata (1640–1), ed. John Steele (Philadelphia, 1968)

Il combattimento di Tancredi et Clorinda, ed. Denis Stevens (London, 1962)

Il quinto libro de madrigali (1605), ed. Karin Jacobsen and Jens Peter Jacobsen (Egtved, 1985)

L'incoronazione di Poppea, facsimile of Venice manuscript (Milan, 1938; Bologna, 1969); ed. Raymond Leppard (London, 1966); ed. Clifford Bartlett (Huntingdon, 1989); ed. Alan Curtis (London, 1989); facsimile of Naples manuscript, ed. Thomas Walker, 'Dram-

227

maturgia musicale veneta' (forthcoming)
Laudate Dominum I (1640–1), ed. Denis Arnold (London, 1966)
Laudate pueri Dominum (a 6 voci) (SV 311), ed. Denis Arnold (London, 1982)
L'Orfeo, facsimile of 1609 edition (Augsburg, 1927); ed. Denis Stevens (London, 1967, rev. London, 1968); facsimile of 1615 edition (Farnborough, 1972); ed. Edward H. Tarr (Paris, 1974)
Magnificat a sei voci (1610), ed. Denis Arnold (London, 1968)
Magnificat I (1640–1), ed. Denis Stevens and John Steele (London, 1969)
Messa a 4 voci da cappella (1640–1), ed. Denis Arnold (London, 1962)
Messa a quattro voci da cappella (1650), ed. Hans F. Redlich (London, 1952)
Missa 'In illo tempore' a 6, ed. Hans F. Redlich (London, 1962)
Ten Madrigals, ed. Denis Arnold (London, 1978)
Vespers (1610), ed. Denis Stevens (London, 1961); ed. Jürgen Jürgens (Vienna, 1977); ed. Clifford Bartlett (Huntingdon, 1986)
Giovanni Pierluigi da Palestrina, *'Pope Marcellus Mass': An Authoritative Score, Backgrounds and Sources, History and Analysis, Views and Comments*, ed. Lewis Lockwood (New York, 1975)
Benedetto Pallavicino, *Opera omnia*, ed. Peter Flanders and Kathryn Bosi Monteath, 'Corpus Mensurabilis Musicae', xcix, in progress (American Institute of Musicology, 1982–)
Jacopo Peri, *'Euridice': An Opera in One Act, Five Scenes*, ed. Howard Mayer Brown, 'Recent Researches in the Music of the Baroque Era', xxxvi–xxxvii (Madison, 1981)
Denis Stevens (trans.), *The Letters of Claudio Monteverdi* (London, 1980)
Giaches de Wert, *Opera omnia*, ed. Carol MacClintock and Melvin Bernstein, 'Corpus Mensurabilis Musicae', xxiv, 17 vols. (American Institute of Musicology, 1961–77)

SECONDARY SOURCES

Anna Amalie Abert, *Claudio Monteverdi und das musikalische Drama* (Lippstadt, 1954)
Gerald Abraham (ed.), *The Age of Humanism, 1540–1630*, 'The New Oxford History of Music', iv (London, 1968)
K. Gary Adams and Dyke Kiel, *Claudio Monteverdi: A Guide to Research* (New York & London, 1989)
Alessandro Ademollo, *La bell'Adriana ed altre virtuose del suo tempo alla corte di Mantova* (Città di Castello, 1888)
Putnam Aldrich, *Rhythm in Seventeenth-Century Italian Monody* (New York, 1966; repr. Ann Arbor, 1978)
Willi Apel, 'Anent a Ritornello in Monteverdi's *Orfeo*', *Musica Disciplina*, v (1951), 213–22
Nella Anfuso and Annibale Gianuario, *Preparazione alla interpretazione della Ποίησις monteverdiana* (Florence, 1971)

Denis Arnold, 'Alessandro Grandi, a Disciple of Monteverdi', *The Musical Quarterly*, xliii (1957), 171–86

——, 'Music at the Scuola di San Rocco', *Music & Letters*, xl (1959), 229–41

——, 'The Monteverdian Succession at St. Mark's', *Music & Letters*, xlii (1961), 205–11

——, *Monteverdi Madrigals*, 'BBC Music Guides' (London, 1967; repr. London, 1975)

——, 'Monteverdi's Singers', *The Musical Times*, cxi (1970), 982–5

——, 'Cavalli at St Mark's', *Early Music*, iv (1976), 266–74

——, *Giovanni Gabrieli and the Music of the Venetian High Renaissance* (London, 1979)

——, *Monteverdi Church Music*, 'BBC Music Guides' (London, 1982)

——, 'The Second Venetian Visit of Heinrich Schütz', *The Musical Quarterly*, lxxi (1985), 359–74

Denis Arnold and Nigel Fortune (eds.), *The Monteverdi Companion* (London, 1968); rev. as *The New Monteverdi Companion* (London, 1985)

Karol Berger, *Theories of Chromatic and Enharmonic Music in Late 16th-Century Italy* (Ann Arbor, 1980)

Antonio Bertolotti, *Musici alla corte dei Gonzaga in Mantova dal secolo XV al XVIII* (Milan, 1891; repr. Bologna, 1969)

Lorenzo Bianconi, '*Ah dolente partita*: espressione ed artificio', *Studi Musicali*, iii (1974), 105–30

——, *Il seicento* (Turin, 1982); trans. David Bryant as *Music in the Seventeenth Century* (Cambridge, 1987)

David Blazey, 'A Liturgical Role for Monteverdi's *Sonata sopra Sancta Maria*', *Early Music*, xvii (1989), 175–82

Stephen Bonta, 'Liturgical Problems in Monteverdi's Marian Vespers', *Journal of the American Musicological Society*, xx (1967), 87–106

David Boyden, 'Monteverdi's *violini piccoli alla francese* and *viole da brazzo*', *Annales Musicologiques*, vi (1958–63), 387–401

Murray C. Bradshaw, *The Falsobordone: A Study in Renaissance and Baroque Music*, 'Musicological Studies and Documents', xxxiv (American Institute of Musicology, 1978)

Reginald Smith Brindle, 'Monteverdi's G Minor Mass [1650]: An Experiment in Construction', *The Musical Quarterly*, liv (1968), 352–60

Bruno Brizi, 'Teoria e prassi melodrammatica di G. F. Busenello e "L'incoronazione di Poppea"', in Maria Teresa Muraro (ed.), *Venezia e il melodramma nel Seicento*, 'Studi di Musica Veneta', v (Florence, 1976), pp. 51–74

Howard Mayer Brown, 'How Opera Began: An Introduction to Jacopo Peri's *Euridice* (1600)', in Eric Cochrane (ed.), *The Late Italian Renaissance, 1525–1630* (London, 1970), pp. 401–43

Pietro Canal, *Della musica in Mantova: notizie tratte principalmente dall'archivio Gonzaga* (Venice, 1881; repr. Bologna, 1977)

Tim Carter, *Jacopo Peri (1561–1633): His Life and Works* (PhD diss.,

University of Birmingham, 1980; repr. New York & London, 1989)

——, 'A Florentine Wedding of 1608', *Acta Musicologica*, lv (1983), 89–107

——, *Music in Late Renaissance and Early Baroque Italy* (London, forthcoming)

James Chater, '"Cruda Amarilli": A Cross-Section of the Italian Madrigal', *The Musical Times*, cxvi (1975), 231–4

——, *Luca Marenzio and the Italian Madrigal, 1577–1593*, 2 vols. (Ann Arbor, 1981)

Geoffrey Chew, 'The Perfections of Modern Music: Consecutive Fifths and Tonal Coherence in Monteverdi', *Music Analysis*, viii (1989), 247–73

Alessandra Chiarelli, '*L'incoronazione di Poppea* o *Il Nerone*: problemi di filologia testuale', *Rivista Italiana di Musicologia*, ix (1974), 117–51

Alan Curtis, '*La Poppea Impasticciata*, or Who Wrote the Music to *L'incoronazione*', *Journal of the American Musicological Society*, xlii (1989), 23–54

Marianne Danckwardt, 'Das Lamento d'Olimpia "Voglio voglio morir": Eine Komposition Claudio Monteverdis?', *Archiv für Musikwissenschaft*, xli (1984), 149–75

Stefano Davari, *Notizie biografiche del distinto maestro di musica Claudio Monteverdi, desunte dai documenti dell'Archivio storico Gonzaga* (Mantua, 1885; also pub. in *Atti e memorie della R. Accademia virgiliana di Mantova*, x (1884–5), 79–183)

Christine J. Day, 'The Theater of SS. Giovanni e Paolo and Monteverdi's *L'incoronazione di Poppea*', *Current Musicology*, xxv (1978), 22–38

Domenico de' Paoli, *Monteverdi* (Milan, 1979)

Graham Dixon, 'Monteverdi's Vespers of 1610: "della Beata Vergine"?', *Early Music*, xv (1987), 386–9

Robert Donington, *The Rise of Opera* (London, 1981)

Alfred Einstein, *The Italian Madrigal*, trans. Alexander H. Krappe *et al.*, 3 vols. (Princeton, 1949; rev. Princeton, 1971)

Paolo Fabbri, 'Tasso, Guarini e il «divino Claudio»: componenti manieristiche nella poetica di Monteverdi', *Studi Musicali*, iii (1974), 233–54

——, 'Inediti monteverdiani', *Rivista Italiana di Musicologia*, xv (1980), 71–85

——, 'Concordanze letterarie e divergenze musicali intorno ai «Madrigali a cinque voci . . . Libro primo» di Claudio Monteverdi', in M. di Pasquale (ed.), *Musica e filologia* (Verona, 1983), pp. 53–83

——, *Monteverdi* (Turin, 1985)

Iain Fenlon, 'The Monteverdi Vespers: Suggested Answers to Some Fundamental Questions', *Early Music*, v (1977), 380–7

——, *Music and Patronage in Sixteenth-Century Mantua*, 2 vols. (Cambridge, 1980, 1982)

——, 'Monteverdi's Mantuan *Orfeo*: Some New Documentation', *Early Music*, xii (1984), 163–72

Ludwig Finscher (ed.), *Claudio Monteverdi: Festschrift Reinhold Hammerstein zum 70. Geburtstag* (Laaber, 1986)

Nigel Fortune, 'Italian Secular Monody from 1600 to 1635: An Introductory Survey', *The Musical Quarterly*, xxxix (1953), 171–95

Claudio Gallico, 'Newly Discovered Documents Concerning Monteverdi', *The Musical Quarterly*, xlviii (1962), 68–72

——, 'Monteverdi e i dazi di Viadana', *Rivista Italiana di Musicologia*, i (1966), 242–5

——, 'Emblemi strumentali negli "Scherzi" di Monteverdi', *Rivista Italiana di Musicologia*, ii (1967), 54–73

——, 'I due pianti di Arianna di Claudio Monteverdi', *Chigiana*, xxiv (1967), 29–42

——, *Monteverdi: poesia musicale, teatro e musica sacra* (Turin, 1979)

Carolyn Gianturco, *Claudio Monteverdi: stile e struttura* (Pisa, 1978)

Jane Glover, *Cavalli* (London, 1978)

Hugo Goldschmidt, *Studien zur Geschichte der italienischen Oper im 17. Jahrhundert*, 2 vols. (Leipzig, 1901–4; repr. Hildesheim, 1967)

Donald Jay Grout, *A Short History of Opera* (2/New York, 1965)

James Haar, *Essays on Italian Poetry and Music in the Renaissance, 1350–1600* (Berkeley & Los Angeles), 1986

Barbara Russano Hanning, *Of Poetry and Music's Power: Humanism and the Creation of Opera* (Ann Arbor, 1980)

Helmut Hell, 'Zu Rhythmus und Notierung des "Vi ricorda" in Claudio Monteverdis *Orfeo*', *Analecta Musicologica*, xv (1975), 87–157

Imogene Horsley, 'Monteverdi's Use of Borrowed Material in "Sfogava con le stelle"', *Music & Letters*, lix (1978), 316–28

Robert Mario Isgro, *The First and Second Practices of Monteverdi: Their Relation to Contemporary Theory* (DMA diss., University of Southern California, 1968)

John J. Joyce, *The Monodies of Sigismondo d'India* (Ann Arbor, 1981)

Joseph Kerman, *Opera as Drama* (New York, 1952)

Jeffrey G. Kurtzman, *Essays on the Monteverdi Mass and Vespers of 1610* (Houston, 1979)

Silke Leopold, *Claudio Monteverdi und seine Zeit* (Laaber, 1982)

Susan Kaye McClary, *The Transition from Modal to Tonal Organization in the Works of Monteverdi* (PhD diss., Harvard University, 1976)

Carol MacClintock, *Giaches de Wert (1535–1596): Life and Works*, 'Musicological Studies and Documents', xvii (American Institute of Musicology, 1966)

Timothy J. McGee, '*Orfeo* and *Euridice*, the First Two Operas', in John Warden (ed.), *Orpheus: The Metamorphosis of a Myth* (Toronto, 1982). pp. 163–81

Dean T. Mace, 'Tasso, *La Gerusalemme liberata*, and Monteverdi', *Studies in the History of Music*, i (New York, 1983), pp. 118–56

Maria Rika Maniates, *Mannerism in Italian Music and Culture, 1530–1630* (Manchester, 1979)

Raffaello Monterosso (ed.), *Claudio Monteverdi e il suo tempo* (Verona, 1969)

James H. Moore, *Vespers at St. Mark's: Music of Alessandro Grandi,*

Giovanni Rovetta and Francesco Cavalli, 2 vols. (Ann Arbor, 1981)

——, 'The *Vespero delli Cinque Laudate* and the Role of *Salmi Spezzati* at St. Mark's', *Journal of the American Musicological Society*, xxxiv (1981), 249–78

——, '*Venezia favorita da Maria*: Music for the Madonna Nicopeia and Santa Maria della Salute', *Journal of the American Musicological Society*, xxxvii (1984), 299–355

Margaret Murata, 'The Recitative Soliloquy', *Journal of the American Musicological Society*, xxxii (1979), 45–73

Reinhard Müller, *Der stile recitativo in Claudio Monteverdis 'Orfeo'* (Tutzing, 1984)

Alois Maria Nagler, *Theatre Festivals of the Medici, 1539–1637* (New Haven & London, 1964; repr. New York, 1976)

Anthony Newcomb, *The Madrigal at Ferrara, 1579–1597*, 2 vols. (Princeton, 1980)

Frits Noske, 'An Unknown Work by Monteverdi: The Vespers of St. John the Baptist', *Music & Letters*, lxvi (1985), 118–22

Wolfgang Osthoff, 'Zu den Quellen von Monteverdis "Ritorno di Ulisse in patria"', *Studien zur Musikwissenschaft*, xxiii (1956), 67–78

——, 'Zur Bologneser Aufführung von Monteverdis "Ritorno di Ulisse" im Jahre 1640', *Österreichische Akademie der Wissenschaften: Anzeiger der phil.-hist. Klasse*, xcv (1958), 155–60

——, *Das dramatische Spätwerk Claudio Monteverdis* (Tutzing, 1960)

Claude V. Palisca, *Baroque Music* (2/Englewood Cliffs, N. J., 1981),

——, *The Florentine Camerata: Documentary Studies and Translations* (New Haven & London, 1989)

Andrew Parrott, 'Transposition in Monteverdi's Vespers of 1610: An "Aberration" Defended', *Early Music*, xii (1984), 490–516 (and note *Early Music*, xiii (1985), 73–6)

Hubert Parry, 'The Significance of Monteverde', *Proceedings of the Musical Association*, xiii (1915–16), 51–67

Nino Pirrotta (and Elena Povoledo), *Li due Orfei: da Poliziano a Monteverdi* (2/Turin, 1975); trans. Karen Eales as *Music and Theatre from Poliziano to Monteverdi* (Cambridge, 1982)

Music and Culture in Italy from the Middle Ages to the Baroque: A Collection of Essays (Cambridge, Mass., 1984): including (pp. 217–34) 'Temperaments and Tendencies in the Florentine Camerata'; (pp. 235–53) 'Monteverdi and the Problems of Opera'; (pp. 254–270) 'Theatre, Sets, and Music in Monteverdi's Operas'; (pp. 271–316) 'Monteverdi's Poetic Choices'

Giuseppe Pontiroli, 'Della famiglia di Claudio Monteverdi: parentele e relazioni', *Bollettino Storico Cremonese*, xxv (1970–1), 45–68

Henry Prunières, *Monteverdi, His Life and Work*, trans. Marie D. Mackie (London, 1926; repr. New York, 1972)

Hans F. Redlich, *Claudio Monteverdi: Life and Works*, trans. Kathleen Dale (London, 1952; repr. Westport, 1970)

Stuart Reiner, 'Preparations in Parma – 1618, 1627–28', *The Music Review*, xxv (1964), 273–301

——, 'La vag'Angioletta (and others): i', *Analecta Musicologica*, xiv (1974), 26–88

Rivista Italiana di Musicologia, ii/2 (1967) [Proceedings of the Convegno Internazionale di Studi Monteverdiani, Siena, 28–30 April 1967]

Michael F. Robinson, *Opera before Mozart* (3/London, 1978)

Jerome Roche, 'Monteverdi: An Interesting Example of Second Thoughts', *The Music Review*, xxxii (1971), 193–204

——, *North Italian Church Music in the Age of Monteverdi* (Oxford, 1984)

——, *The Madrigal* (2/Oxford, 1990)

Margaret Ann Rorke, 'Sacred Contrafacta of Monteverdi Madrigals and Cardinal Borromeo's Milan', *Music & Letters*, lxv (1984), 168–75

Ellen Rosand, 'Music in the Myth of Venice', *Renaissance Quarterly*, xxx (1977), 511–37

——, 'Seneca and the Interpretation of *L'Incoronazione di Poppea*', *Journal of the American Musicological Society*, xxxviii (1985), 34–71

——, 'Iro and the Interpretation of *Il ritorno d'Ulisse in patria*', *Journal of Musicology*, vii (1989), 141–64

——, 'Monteverdi's Mimetic Art in *L'Incoronazione di Poppea*', *Cambridge Opera Journal*, i (1989), 19–43

Felix Salzer, 'Heinrich Schenker and Historical Research: Monteverdi's Madrigal *Oimè, se tanto amate*', in David Beach (ed.), *Aspects of Schenkerian Theory* (New Haven & London, 1983), pp. 135–52

Elia Santoro, *La famiglia e la formazione di Claudio Monteverdi: note biografiche con documenti inediti*, 'Annali della Biblioteca governativa e libreria civica di Cremona', xviii (Cremona, 1967)

——, *Iconografia monteverdiana*, 'Annali della Biblioteca governativa e libreria civica di Cremona', xix (Cremona, 1968)

Edward B. Savage, 'Love and Infamy: The Paradox of Monteverdi's *L'incoronazione di Poppea*', *Comparative Drama*, iv (1970), 197–207

Leo Schrade, *Monteverdi: Creator of Modern Music* (New York, 1950; repr. New York, 1979)

Eleanor Selfridge–Field, *Venetian Instrumental Music from Gabrieli to Vivaldi* (Oxford, 1975)

Licia Sirch, '"Violini piccoli alla francese" e "canto alla francese" nell'*Orfeo* (1607) e negli "Scherzi musicali" (1607) di Monteverdi', *Nuova Rivista Musicale Italiana*, xv (1981), 50–65

Angelo Solerti, *Le origini del melodramma: testimonianze dei contemporanei* (Turin, 1903; repr. Hildesheim, 1969)

——, *Gli albori del melodramma*, 3 vols. (Milan, 1904; repr. Hildesheim, 1969)

Manfred H. Stattkus, *Claudio Monteverdi: Verzeichnis der erhaltenen Werke; kleine Ausgabe* (Bergkamen, 1985)

Denis Stevens, 'Where are the Vespers of Yesteryear?', *The Musical Quarterly*, xlvii (1961), 315–30

——, '*Madrigali guerrieri, et amorosi*: A Reappraisal for the Quatercentenary', *The Musical Quarterly*, liii (1967), 161–87

——, 'Monteverdi's Double-Choir Magnificat', *The Musical Times*, 110

(1969), 587–9

——, 'Monteverdi's Necklace', *The Musical Quarterly*, lix (1973), 370–81

——, *Monteverdi: Sacred, Secular, and Occasional Music* (Cranbury, N. J., & London, 1978)

——, 'Monteverdi, Petratti, and the Duke of Bracciano', *The Musical Quarterly*, lxiv (1978), 275–94

——, 'Monteverdi's Other Vespers', *The Musical Times*, cxx (1979), 732–7

——, 'Monteverdi's Earliest Extant Ballet', *Early Music*, xiv (1986), 358–66

Edmond Strainchamps, 'The Life and Death of Caterina Martinelli: New Light on Monteverdi's "Arianna"', *Early Music History*, v (1985), 155–86

Oliver Strunk, *Source Readings in Music History* (London, 1952)

Zygmunt Szweykowski, '"Ah dolente partita": Monteverdi–Scacchi', *Quadrivium*, xii/2 (1971), 59–76

Pierre M. Tagmann, *Archivalische Studien zur Musikpflege am Dom von Mantua (1500–1627)* (Bern, 1967)

——, 'The Palace Church of Santa Barbara in Mantua, and Monteverdi's Relationship to Its Liturgy', in Burton L. Karson (ed.), *Festival Essays for Pauline Alderman* (Salt Lake City, 1976), pp 53–60

Gary A. Tomlinson, 'Madrigal, Monody, and Monteverdi's "via naturale alla immitatione"', *Journal of the American Musicological Society*, xxxiv (1981), 60–108

——, 'Music and the Claims of Text: Monteverdi, Rinuccini, and Marino', *Critical Inquiry*, vii (1982), 565–89

——, 'Twice Bitten, Thrice Shy: Monteverdi's "finta" *Finta pazza*', *Journal of the American Musicological Society*, xxxvi (1983), 303–11

——, *Monteverdi and the End of the Renaissance* (Oxford, 1987)

Emil Vogel, 'Claudio Monteverdi', *Vierteljahrsschrift für Musikwissenschaft*, iii (1887), 315–450

Glenn E. Watkins, *Gesualdo: The Man and His Music* (London, 1973)

Gunner Westerland and Eric Hughes, *Music of Claudio Monteverdi: A Discography* (London, 1972)

Jack A. Westrup, 'Monteverdi's "Lamento d'Arianna"', *The Music Review*, 1 (1940), 144–54

John Whenham, *Duet and Dialogue in the Age of Monteverdi*, 2 vols. (Ann Arbor, 1982)

John Whenham (ed.), *Claudio Monteverdi: 'Orfeo'*, 'Cambridge Opera Handbooks' (Cambridge, 1986)

Wolfgang Witzenmann, 'Die italienische Kirchenmusik des Barocks: ein Bericht über die Literatur aus den Jahren 1945 bis 1974', *Acta Musicologica*, xlvii (1976), 77–103

Simon Towneley Worsthorne, *Venetian Opera in the Seventeenth Century* (Oxford, 1954; repr. New York, 1984)

Index

Accademia degli Animosi (Cremona), 16, 172, 174
Accademia degli Elevati (Florence), 221
Accademia dei Filoleuteri (Venice), 219
Accademia dei Floridi (later, Accademia dei Filomusi, Bologna), 34, 178, 180, 181, 218
Accademia degli Incogniti (Venice), 218, 219, 226
Accademia degli Intrepidi (Ferrara), 13, 53, 156, 194
Accademia degli Invaghiti (Mantua), 16
Accademia degli Unisoni (Venice), 185, 226
Achillini, Claudio, 190, 198, 199, 217
Agazzari, Agostino, 95n.1, 167, 185
Agnelli, Scipione, 28, 35, 190, 197
Ala, Giovanni Battista, 177, 213, 217
Alberti, Filippo, 192, 193
Albrecht V, Duke of Bavaria, 221
Aldegati, Domenico, 185
Allegretti, Antonio, 192
Allegri, Gregorio, 120n.1
Amadino, Ricciardo, 4, 10, 13, 57, 189, 191, 193, 194, 195, 196, 197, 202, 205, 217, 226
Ambrosini, Pietro, 191
Anderson, Emily, 160n.4
Andreini, Giovanni Battista, 176, 179, 190, 217
Andreini, Virginia, 19, 217
Anselmi, Giovanni Battista, 84–5, 180, 202, 203
Antwerp, 11, 145, 170, 193, 194, 195, 197, 207, 213, 224
Arcadelt, Jacques, 182
Archilei, Antonio, 217
Archilei, Vittoria, 217
Argotta, Agnese, Marchese di Grana, 8
Ariosto, Ludovico, 78
Aristotle, 34
Arlotti, Ridolfo, 194
Arnold, Denis, 32n.9, 45n.32, 58n.5, 99n.5, 127n.8, 142n.15, 155, 156, 159, 159n.3, 161, 165, 216n.j, 227, 228, 229
Artusi, Giovanni Maria, 11, 11n.6, 12, 13, 13n.9, 16, 57, 63–4, 64,

144, 144n.2, 151, 153, 156, 158, 159–60, 159n.3, 166, 169–70, 170, 171, 172–3, 175, 217, 227
Atti, Francesco degli, 198

Bach, Johann Sebastian, 151, 153, 154
Badoaro, Giacomo, 110, 110n.10, 190, 218
Banchieri, Adriano, 11, 11n.6, 34, 34n.12, 94, 144, 144n.2, 166, 178, 184, 218, 221
Baranardi, Odoardo, 210
Barblan, Guglielmo, 20n.20
Bardi, Giovanni de', 219
Bargnani, Ottavio, 174
Baroni, Muzio, 218
Basile, Adriana, 9, 69, 174, 218, 228
Basile, Leonora, 218
Basile, Margherita, 38, 218
Basle, 170
Bati, Luca, 221
Bavaria, 1, 221
Becker, Carl Ferdinand, 49n.2
Beethoven, Ludwig van, 76
Belli, Ippolito de, 180
Bembo, Giovanni Matteo, 177
Bembo, Pietro, 193
Benevoli, Orazio, 45, 171, 186, 218
Benintendi, Ottavio, 14, 14n.10, 32
Bentivoglio, Enzo, 182, 183, 183n.5, 193
Bergamo, 19, 24, 40, 182, 222, 223
Berlin, 210
Bernhard, Christoph, 149, 151
Berti, Giovanni Pietro, 33, 84, 87, 135, 180, 218
Bianchi, Giulio Cesare, 137, 177n.2, 178–9, 211, 213, 218
Bianconi, Lorenzo, 165n.12, 229
Blazey, David, 162n.6, 229
Böddecker, Philipp Friedrich, 187, 214, 218
Boethius, 87
Bologna, 34, 151, 165, 177, 178, 180, 181, 185, 202, 216, 217, 218, 221, 232
Bonardo, Giovanni Maria, 192
Bonini, Severo, 20n.20

235

237

241